Empowered by Love
We Are Not Alone

Other Books by Arleen Lorrance:

Facing Cancer Without Fear
The Theatre of Life
The Love Principles
The Two
Images
India Through Eyes of Love
Born of Love
The Love Project Way (with Diane Kennedy Pike)
Why Me? How to Heal What's Hurting You
Musings for Meditation
Buddha From Brooklyn
Channeling Love Energy (with Diane Kennedy Pike)
The Love Project

Other Books by Diane Kennedy Pike
As Mariamne Paulus:

Yin, Yang and You
The House of Self
Awakening to Wisdom
Four Paths to Union

As Diane Kennedy Pike:

Life As A Waking Dream
The Love Project Way (with Arleen Lorrance)
My Journey Into Self: Phase One
Life Is Victorious! How to Grow Through Grief
Cosmic Unfoldment
Channeling Love Energy (with Arleen Lorrance)
The Wilderness Revolt (with R. Scott Kennedy)
Search

As Diane Kennedy:

The Other Side (with James A. Pike)

Empowered by Love
We Are Not Alone

By

Arleen Lorrance
Diane Kennedy Pike

*A Spiritual Memoir
about living consciously and
being the change you want to see happen*

A Teleos Imprint Book
LP Publications • Scottsdale, AZ

A Teleos Imprint Book

Published by LP Publications
7439 E Beryl Avenue
Scottsdale, AZ 85258-1020

Copyright 2017 by Arleen Lorrance and Diane Kennedy Pike
All rights reserved.

The Teleos Institute World Wide Web site address is
http://www.teleosinstitute.com

Library of Congress Cataloguing-in-Publication Data

Names: Lorrance, Arleen, 1939- author.
Title: Empowered by love : we are not alone / by Arleen Lorrance and Diane K. Pike.
Description: First edition. | Scottsdale : LP Publications, 2018. | "A spiritual memoir about living consciously and being the change you want to see happen."
Identifiers: LCCN 2017048358 (print) | LCCN 2017045482 (ebook) | ISBN 9780916192624 () | ISBN 9780916192617 (trade pbk. : alk. paper)
Subjects: LCSH: Spiritual biography. | Lorrance, Arleen, 1939- | Pike, Diane Kennedy. | Spirituality. | Spiritual life. | Consciousness--Miscellanea.
Classification: LCC BL72 (print) | LCC BL72 .L67 2018 (ebook) | DDC 204.092/2
[B] --dc23
LC record available at https://lccn.loc.gov/2017048358

First Edition, 2018

Printed in the United States of America

Dedication:

to all those who are living
The Love Principles
and
Being the Change
right where they are

With deep gratitude to those who have
supported our work over all these years,
and with special heart-felt acknowledgment of
Eleanor Arnau, Lily Jean Haddad, and
Suzanna Neal

Special thanks to **Linda Reisser** *for her careful proofreading and helpful questions and suggestions as we refined our manuscript.*

Contents

Supporting Spiritual Growth 11
Finding Each Other 15
Different Pathways 30
Our Awakenings 42
Our Lives Converge 66
Endings and Beginnings 82
The Challenge of Roots and Differences 95
Shared Values 120
Our Physical Relationship 139
Beginning Our Work:
      The Love Principles in Action 148
Our Work Takes Form 173
Publishing 192
Problems Are Opportunities 215
Love As Unblocked Energy 221
Expanding Our Repertoire 244
Foreign Journeys Into Self 263
Deeper Inner Growth Work 303
Clouds Gather 329

Personal Crises 342
Life Is A Waking Dream 354
Making Changes 371
Inner Guidance & Conscious Choices 385
Doors Open, Doors Close 418
Adapting and Thriving 431
Spiritual Graduate Work 443
Respecting & Loving the Body 451
Why Do Spiritual Work? 475
Celebrating The Love Principles 485
Who Originated 'Be the Change'? 503
The Waking Dream Method 514
A Series of Wisdom Books 523
Other Expressions of Our Work 535
A Transformational Partnership 542
Shifts in Consciousness 565

Photos

Arleen and Diane laughing 125
Arleen and Diane 1972 147
Ms. Buttons Honey Love 161
The Love Principles by Ann Gurley 180-181
Arleen and Diane 2015 573

Empowered by Love
We Are Not Alone

Some people are drawn by love,
        Some by mutual attraction,
Some by loneliness,
        Some by convenience.

Most Companions-on-the-Way
        are drawn by Inner Directive

Drawn to a work of Service,

Devoted to Personal and Spiritual Growth,

United in a commitment to Conscious Living.

Supporting Spiritual Growth

Those of us who feel a deep inner longing for spiritual fulfillment are attracted to others who share that longing. Often, we do not even know how to name what we are looking for and when we see or feel it in another, we may have no words for what draws us.

Religions tend to have all the answers, making them a comfortable place to settle if the beliefs satisfy your longing. However, if the desire for answers and fulfillment causes us to look beyond established doctrine, we are drawn to the unknown, to individuality, and to constant questioning. We open to expansion in the inner self to find the more that is waiting to be revealed to us.

In the late 1960's, the two of us awakened in consciousness. We each began living in a realm of no boundaries, in the energy world that exists beyond form, and in universal love. We experienced our Oneness with all that is. We had shifted beyond belief to knowing.

We were each fortunate to meet first one, then another, and then many others with whom we could share our deep inner spiritual journey. We were not alone. We know how blessed we were and are. Not only were there many others stirring in their psyches to satisfy a spiritual thirst, but increasing numbers of books began to be written that nurtured and guided people on their way.

When the two of us met, we knew we had "a work" to do together. We did not want to start a new organization or institution nor did we want to be "teachers" in the traditional sense. We wanted instead to link people together in unconditional love, to form a Love Family based on inner spiritual connections rather than on external forms or shared beliefs. We wanted to be models of the process of spiritual unfolding when it is done in the midst of everyday life. In the process, we learned a lot about continuous spiritual growth and how to facilitate it in ourselves and in others.

We share that story here because it is an example of how to partner in joint spiritual unfolding, how to celebrate the power of unconditional love, how to be present to others on their individual journeys, and how to create a network of seekers who can be there for each other even if they have never met personally. There are thousands of people in our Love Family who have access to each other simply because they are linked in consciousness through a common commitment to being their highest and best. When we began our work, we could not have known that 45 years later a borderless community of individuals would become a support system for each other because they knew they were One. We know that others have formed similar networks.

The two of us have found that the quickest and easiest way to find other awakened beings is to open to those you meet along the way and speak unabashedly from the core of your knowing. Those to whom you speak will either ignore what you say because they have no frame of reference for it or you will see their faces light up and you will know they are kindred spirits and potential new companions on your journey.

We hope you will benefit from our personal growth journey. We have devoted ourselves to the integration and embodiment of what we have come to know through our spiritual growth process and to encouraging that in everyone whose lives we are privileged to touch along the way.

*From every human being
there rises a light
that reaches straight
to heaven.
And when two souls
that are destined
to be together find each other,
their streams of light
flow together,
and a single brighter light
goes forth from their
united being.*

BAAL SHEM TOV

Finding Each Other

When people ask, "How did the two of you meet?" we always respond, "It's a long story, but the short version is 'Diane's face appeared in a series of Arleen's paintings.'"

Here is the story.

In 1971 Arleen was given a scholarship to participate in a facilitator training program in San Diego. On the first day of the training she was seated on a table (something she used to do on a regular basis in those days) when a woman she did not know came into the room. Arleen immediately leapt off the table and ran over to the woman, saying "I need to show you my spiritual paintings. Will you come with me to see them?"

Arleen did not know why she felt so strongly about taking Patricia Bradley to see her paintings, but she had learned to follow her intuition and it had been very strong this time. Patricia was also used to following *her* intuition, so she did not hesitate to accept Arleen's invitation.

Arleen, then 32 years old, had begun a series of acrylic paintings while finishing her Master of Fine Arts degree at Brooklyn College in New York. In the paintings, which Arleen had allowed to emerge on the canvas without directing the brushes, a face had appeared. At first it was skeletal, but with each subsequent painting the face had become clearer. The costume designer for Arleen's graduate thesis production was psychic. Arleen showed her the paintings and Kendra told her that this was a woman she had not yet met, someone she loved, and someone who would be like a godmother to her. When Arleen completed the last of the series of paintings in San Diego, the face was very identifiable, but Arleen did not know who it was.

As Arleen showed Patricia the paintings she told her the story of the face that had appeared and pointed it out in each painting. Patricia suddenly said, "My friend Diane has to come to see these paintings."

Arleen responded, without a moment's pause, "Do you mean Diane Kennedy Pike?" as if there was only one "Diane" in the country. Patricia said, "How did you know that?" Arleen said, "I didn't."

In fact, sometime prior to that meeting Arleen had read an article in *The Ladies Home Journal* that was a serialized version of Diane's book *Search* that told the story of how the Pikes had lost their way in the Judean in September, 1969. Arleen had never heard of Diane or her famous husband, Bishop James A. Pike, but she had been impressed with the fact that Diane reported talking to the rocks in the desert. Arleen strongly resonated with that detail because she had had a spiritual awakening in September 1969, around the very time the Pikes were lost in the desert. (This synchronicity would later turn out to be one of the many coincidences or life parallels between the two of us.) Since that time, Arleen knew her Oneness with All and experienced the life force, the energy, in everything, including rocks.

Because Diane had talked to the rocks, her name had probably been stored in Arleen's consciousness, but she had no idea why it popped out when Patricia mentioned her friend Diane. Moreover, Patricia did not know why she felt Diane needed to see the paintings. Arleen was glad to have the potential opportunity to show Diane the paintings, not because Diane was well-known but because Patricia had such a strong intuition about it.

Patricia made a phone call to Diane asking her to come to San Diego. Diane knew that Patricia had gone to a facilitator training program there and she was eager to respond to Patricia at what appeared to be a time of need, so she agreed to fly from Santa Barbara, where she lived, to San Diego.

It was not uncommon for Patricia and Diane to spend long hours in deep conversation, and they spent that Saturday afternoon and evening exploring the questions and dilemmas that had come up for Patricia during the training. Over dinner that evening Patricia said, "I want you to meet a woman who is in the training and go to see her spiritual paintings."

All Diane's inner warning lights came on. Ever since the death of her famous husband she had been deluged with letters from psychics from all over the country telling her that they had had communications from her husband from the other side. She read the letters with a mixture of interest and skepticism, seldom finding anything that sounded remotely like what Jim might have wanted to say to her.

The words "spiritual paintings" evoked in Diane a feeling of "Oh, no, here we go again." She scrambled to respond without putting up barriers to Patricia. "How about this?" Diane asked Patricia. "I promise I will meet this woman and see her paintings the next time I am in San Diego." Diane figured this was a safe promise because she had been in San Diego only twice before and had no plans to go there in the future. Patricia acceded and Diane departed the next day feeling she had gotten away with something.

On Monday morning Diane got a phone call from her editor at Doubleday in New York City. He asked if she would be willing to go to San Diego (!) to speak to the West Coast salesmen for Doubleday. Diane laughed out loud, although Alex had no way to know what was funny about his request. He went on, "We will pay your expenses and put you up at the Hotel Del Coronado where the salesmen are meeting."

Diane told Alex she would be happy to go,

while inside she was congratulating whoever in the universe arranges such things because she knew she was really going to San Diego to meet this woman that Patricia spoke about and see her spiritual paintings.

A week later, on Sunday morning, September 29, 1971, Diane was at the Hotel Del Coronado. When she walked into the lobby, a small, sprite-like woman who had been seated on a couch with her back to Diane, leapt to her feet, spinning around as she did, so that she landed facing her. Diane was startled and has no memory of what she said or how she responded. Arleen remembers knowing immediately that she loved this woman. The feeling was very strong, but because she was living only in that present moment, she did not connect the feeling of love with her psychic friend Kendra's prediction of the meeting to come.

Arleen and her husband Dick drove Diane to their apartment near the ocean on Bermuda Avenue in the Ocean Beach area of San Diego.

Arleen was one ongoing burst of enthusiastic energy. She immediately took Diane by the arm and led her into a room to show her the paintings. She talked nonstop, explaining that these paintings had "painted themselves" and that a mysterious face had painted itself into them, starting in a skeletal form and taking on more definition from painting to painting.

As Arleen showed Diane the first painting, she pointed to the lower right corner of it and said,

"See the face?" Diane did not, but she knew intuitively that "she" was that face. Simultaneously Arleen suddenly knew that Diane was in fact the woman in her paintings. She felt a chill and her breath stopped but she didn't say anything because the whole event seemed surreal.

The photo on the right is slightly enhanced in black and white in case the reader, like Diane, has trouble seeing the face in the painting.

From painting to painting Diane continued to feel like a psychic dud because she did not perceive the face, but internally she knew with growing certainty that "she" was the face. In the final painting, Diane could see the face. Diane remembers, "She had my hair, my lips, and my eyes. The identity was undeniable, but I said nothing about my recognition. I did not want to be presumptuous; after all, I had only met this woman a couple of hours before." Arleen also said nothing about recognizing Diane as the face in the paintings.

The photo on the right, in black and white, is slightly enhanced to make the face more evident.

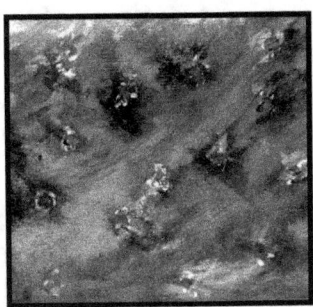 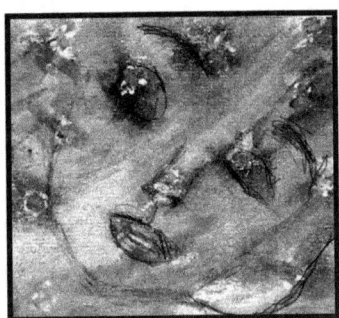

Diane felt as though she had been hit by a large wave of energy. She was overwhelmed and left speechless. She had to catch a plane and Dick said he would drive her to the airport since Arleen had another appointment. As Diane was saying goodbye to Arleen at the door, Arleen said with certainty, "We're not finished. We have a lot more to talk about. When can we get together again?"

Diane was in the process of packing up her home in Santa Barbara to move to Denver, but she said, "Why don't the two of you come for the weekend in a fortnight?" It was agreed.

When Diane left and got on the plane, she sat down in a seat near a window and immediately went into a deep sleep. The next thing she knew the flight attendant was calling to her, saying, "We are about to land. Please fasten your seat belt." Diane felt as though she was climbing out of a deep well. She had no idea who she was or where she was. Today she would say that she had been pulled into a finer frequency where she could reconnect with the significance of meeting Arleen, but on that day, she had no memory of what had transpired while she was asleep. Instead she focused on reorienting herself to her present circumstances.

Arleen was very excited about the encounter and looked forward to further exploration. She could feel the life force rising in her but had little by way of future images to which to attach it. She knew that she would tell Diane when they next met in Santa Barbara that she, Diane, was the face in her paintings.

It was to the credit of both of us that we had each long ago learned the disciplines of not jumping ahead, of not trying to determine on the mental level what all of this might mean, and of not immediately picturing where this might lead in both our lives. Doing any of those things might interfere with what was to unfold, what was germinating in the larger energy field. We each put one foot in front of the other in order to experience what was potentially emerging without imposing upon it our thoughts, hopes, or desires. We had no idea what was happening and that was superb because our thoughts in no way limited the shape of tomorrow. We both proceeded without any expectations but rather with open heart centers and great expectancy. We both felt something greater than the two of us was at work and that we had not been drawn together by accident.

This approach is one of the most important things to learn when developing intuition. On the mental level we often project into the future and we nearly always try to figure out why things happen the way they do. On the intuitive level it is essential to take things one step at a time, trusting that the way will be shown as we move forward. We both know this to be an ideal way to meet spiritual companions, to connect on deep levels, and to open to what might be wanted of us.

Later in the day of our initial meeting, Arleen felt compelled to write a letter to Diane, even though we had just parted. She wrote, "I know we'll be together again (physically) soon, very soon, but soon has never quite been soon enough for me in anything." She continued by sharing what had come to her immediately during our encounter. "I loved you right away. I'd loved you for a long time. It's not so much that I'd known you before in other lifetimes but rather that I'd been waiting for you for some reason, like the woman in my paintings who keeps getting clearer and closer. I don't know why I was waiting for you. I haven't ever even thought about waiting for anyone. I know only that the moment I saw you I knew I no longer had to wait for you. I felt at peace and really beautiful inside."

Arleen hadn't shared this before Diane left her apartment because she didn't want to inundate her. Diane's experience on the airplane showed that that had already occurred and that she had been flooded with powerful energy.

Arleen's letter continued. "Somehow in some way however remote, we are either going to be of service together or we are going to be of help to one another ... Until now I have been riding out in the wilderness, being of service as a lone entity, using Dick as my cloak of love, my shield, my refuge. Today I got a projection of the future and saw the two of us in service. It was as if the debts of the past had been paid and we were ready to move on together."

Arleen had forgotten a momentous event that had occurred in the 12th year of her life. She had had a dreadful encounter with her mother who had been exceedingly cruel. Arleen had gone up to the roof of her apartment building in Brooklyn, N.Y., determined to end her life with a leap over the edge. She had longed for love expression from her mother all of her life and had found only mild fulfillment in her teachers. But life's harshness had become overwhelming.

Arleen lacked the courage to jump. Depressed and dejected she began to descend the stairs. When she reached the foot of the first landing, she looked back and up and "saw" a voice in the open doorway to the roof which revealed the sunlit sky. The voice said, "You will find the woman you are looking for." Then it was gone.

Arleen had been overcome with the message and the feeling of having been visited by something like an angel. She hadn't seen a figure in the doorway; nor had she actually heard a voice. The best she could say at the time was that she saw a change in the intensity of light in the center of the doorway and the energy of that light spoke those words to her. At age 12 Arleen had no knowledge of communication on other levels of consciousness, of communication that is pure energy and cannot be registered as either sight or sound.

She also had no frame of reference for the message itself, so she attached it to a personal desire to have a mother who was gentle and kind and knew how to love. Her quest for a loving mother continued for 26 years, long after meeting Diane who was in no way a mother figure for her, until she came to know that she was not so much seeking to *be* loved as *to* love.

But on this 29th day of September, 1971, Arleen had not put together the two pieces: the angelic message that she would find the woman she was looking for and her telling Diane that from the moment she saw her she knew she no longer had to wait for her. This awareness was to come later.

That's the story of how we met. Now the rest.

The Santa Barbara Weekend

On Friday afternoon, almost two weeks later, Diane, then 33 years old, suddenly realized that it was 4:00 p.m. and she had guests coming. She asked her friend Hal Conklin to welcome Arleen and Dick when they arrived. Then she rushed out to do some shopping for food for the weekend.

When she arrived back, Arleen and Dick were waiting out on the balcony. Diane welcomed them and excused herself to go to the kitchen to prepare dinner. Shortly, Arleen joined her in the kitchen. Diane said, "You know, I didn't say anything when I was with you in San Diego because I didn't want to be presumptuous, but I am the face in your paintings."

Arleen nearly jumped through the ceiling. As she landed she said, "I didn't say anything either because *I* didn't want to be presumptuous, but I knew that you were the face in the paintings."

Although those revelations were baffling, we did not dwell on what it might mean that Diane's face appeared in Arleen's paintings. Instead we got down to the basics of getting to know one another.

In the course of the weekend, Arleen told Diane about **The Love Project** she had initiated at a high school in Brooklyn, New York in November, 1970. As she described each of the six **Love Principles** she had registered and introduced and how they had changed the school environment and the lives of the people who had begun to practice them, Diane shared specific experiences in her own life in which she had learned the same truths, though not in the same words as **The Love Principles**. That was the first instance of a long series of parallels we uncovered over the first couple of months.

(In the course of this book we will print in bold "The Love Project," "Love Principles," and each of the individual principles; they are so fundamental to our work that we refer to them throughout this memoir.)

On Saturday afternoon Diane took Arleen and Dick sightseeing in Santa Barbara. When we visited the beautiful Santa Barbara courthouse, the two of us spontaneously began to play "hide and go seek" in a courtroom. Two children playing together became another theme in our relationship, never planned, always spontaneous.

On Sunday morning Diane took her guest to church with her at the Santa Barbara Mission. When it came time for Communion, the congregation began to file to the front of the church. Arleen turned to Diane and asked, "Is this the intermission?" Differences in their background began to surface: that was Arleen's first experience of attending a church service; her orientation was to theater performances. She had little or no religious background, unlike Diane whose early Protestant life was filled with church going.

After a whirlwind weekend, Arleen and Dick returned to San Diego. Within two weeks Diane had vacated her Santa Barbara home and moved to Littleton, Colorado, just outside of Denver. When Diane arrived at the cabin where she was to take up residence, there was a package waiting for her from Arleen. Diane registered great surprise, but her friend Laurel Keyes, with whom Diane had planned to start a retreat center, told her later that she (Laurel) knew immediately that Diane had, in effect, already "left" to go work with Arleen. Diane remained more or less clueless as she opened the box which contained several small gifts to welcome her to Littleton.

We continued to get to know each other through almost daily letters and long telephone calls. When we had racked up a $300.00 telephone bill (quite substantial in 1971), Diane got a call from the phone company asking her what she planned to do about the phone bill. Diane responded, "Pay for it?" Apparently, the phone company was not used to such a large bill and didn't want to get stuck with it.

Diane flew to San Jose to be with her family for the Thanksgiving weekend. A group of her friends and associates were exploring with her the possibility of creating a TV program. Diane invited Arleen and Dick to join them, feeling that Arleen's theater background would be helpful. The next gathering of that group was in Santa Barbara over the New Year's weekend. During one of the breaks, Arleen pulled Diane aside and said, "We need to talk."

Arleen said, "There is 'a work' for us to do together." Diane asked, "What is it?" Arleen said, "I don't know, but it is important."

Diane did not have a corresponding intuition, but she was open to what Arleen was saying and she trusted that if it were true, the two of them would come to know what "the work" was.

Different Pathways, One Goal

> Teachers of the Wisdom have used a simple metaphor for hundreds of years to illustrate the nature of a spiritual pathway. They speak of a mountain that represents ultimate Truth, or what most people refer to as "God." There are many ways to ascend that mountain. At the base of the mountain the various Pathways seem very far apart. Aspirants give different reasons for climbing and their longings seem quite different one from the other. However, as they climb they discover that their Paths merge, for there is only one Truth.
>
> When Union is realized at the summit, aspirants find they are one with each other as well as with the ultimate Truth. That Union is experienced as the fulfillment of the meaning of human existence. The term "spiritual Pathway" takes its meaning from this metaphor. (Pike as Paulus, *Four Paths to Union*, page 19)

The four pathways, based on Swami Vivekananda's writings and translated into English, are Devotion, Action, Contemplation, and Self-Mastery.

A Shared Life of Purpose

A lot of groundwork had been laid prior to our

meeting each other. A short summary is that the two of us had agreed to meet in this lifetime after we had both awakened in consciousness. Once again mystery enters the picture and our rational minds would demand to know, "What do you mean you agreed to meet in this lifetime? What lifetime were you in when you agreed to meet in this lifetime? What *are* you talking about?"

Neither of us has any memory of having known each other in a previous life. But Arleen had had dreams, or sleep experiences, in which she had intimations of what might be coming. In one of Arleen's sleep experiences she saw herself sitting in space on the edge of a planet beside another woman. The two of them were dangling their feet into the universe and seemingly peering into the future.

We are quite sure our rational minds would not accept this as the time and place, or should we say, time-out-of-time and non-place, when we agreed to meet once we awakened in this lifetime. But it doesn't matter. What is important is that both of us had that sense, that we listened to it, and that we followed it. That is how one lives a conscious life while being guided by intuition and how one might find one's way into a spiritual union.

In the early months of becoming acquainted we each recognized that we had come together for a purpose. True to our individual spiritual pathways, we each stated the purpose differently.

Arleen, focused on action, intuitively knew we had "a work" to do together. Diane, devoted to self-mastery, intuitively knew we had come together to speed up our personal and spiritual growth and unfoldment.

When we register something that we know through intuition, we bring it into form on the mental level in order to talk about it. Of necessity, the words and concepts we use are those familiar to the personality that is expressing the intuition. It takes time to live out the intuition in order to discover its full implications and to test the validity of the original expression of it.

We merged those two intuitive perceptions of our reason for coming together and throughout our long years of association we have "done a work" and we have "speeded up our personal and spiritual growth."

One might expect that two in a spiritual union would share similar spiritual practices. In our case that was not so, and our differences made for strength in our partnership. In fact, the two of us have continued to walk different Pathways even while living in a spiritual union.

When people come together and merge their very different backgrounds and approaches to living and to spiritual growth, they cannot help but benefit from each other, even as and if they continue to choose what is harmonious for themselves. People in a union don't have to be the same; they need only to be true to themselves and to honor the other person's personal choices for self. Would that people around the world functioned that way in relation to each other.

Arleen and the Pathway of Action:

I walk the Pathway of Action. The Yogic philosophy would call me a Karma Yogi. I think of myself as one who "does," one who embodies what she knows, because unless I am doing that, the knowing has little validity for me. My favorite motto is, "When I see it, I be it."

I brought the doer into the work Diane and I created together. Most of our sessions are experiential so that people can take the wisdom they receive in the teaching and make it immediately practical. This is of great benefit to everyone who works with us. Their minds, feelings and bodies are all brought into play together so they can become what they have learned.

My meditative practice consists of being fully present in each moment of living and bringing the whole of self and what I know to that moment. This opens me to finer frequencies, to insights, to the flow of the More.

For example, one day I was in my car waiting at a long red light. My hands were tightly gripping the wheel creating unnecessary tension. I was monitoring my personality/character-self who was growing impatient. Because I was present, I saw that it was I who created the impatience and disharmony through the personality.

I immediately made a new choice. I took a deep breath and on the exhale, it came to me that I was stopped "for the Light." What a blessing! I moved into joy approaching ecstasy. I reflected, "Imagine that! Numerous times a day those of us who drive are stopped 'for the Light' and given time to drink it in, to be graced by it." I have shared this insight with others and encouraged them to "stop for the light" both physically and metaphorically whenever possible. My living-every-minute-meditation brought this wonderful seeing into my awareness.

Before I was five-years-old, I would "disappear" into my coloring as I applied my crayons to the picture in front of me. I had a way of closing out everything around me and fully entering the point of focus I held. I didn't know that I was practicing concentration and active meditation, but in fact I was!

As a pre-teen, I assigned myself daily regimens to promote excellence. Every afternoon I would stand at the curb and throw a rubber ball at my apartment building wall. The objective was to make the ball arch from the ridge of the building, across the distance and into my hands. The arch had to be perfect. Once I achieved my goal, I added other stipulations to the practice, setting a number of perfect arch throws in a row (usually an impossible number) before I could say I had mastered the challenge. I devised many such regimens, as if I was establishing criteria for initiations into some unknown next level of functioning. Again, I was learning to concentrate and to actively focus on a chosen objective, something that teachers of meditation encourage.

I never did anything unless it was with an almost unrelenting fierceness of purpose. I seemed tuned in to an inner taskmaster to whom I never minded yielding.

To this day, it remains foreign to me to sit in silence, eyes closed, stilling the mind in meditation. My mind is most silent when I am "in the zone" of commitment to an activity, to a creative project, to immersion in writing a poem, etc.

I was brought up in a household devoid of religion. I always considered that a great blessing and an advantage that I had in life because I did not need to extricate myself from belief systems or rituals. I never prayed, not for anything, not to anything. And, I had serious doubts about something everyone referred to as God, an amorphous Being to whom people prayed. It was a long time before I came to any clarity on the subject. A deity outside of self that ruled over everything never rang true for me.

Long into my exploration of the subject, I came to see, to know, that God is a shorthand word for the Power of Creation. God is all that is, is in everything, is of everything and everyone, but is not separate from anything or anyone because that would be spiritual schizophrenia. God is all that is good and all that is horrible, all that is.

When I witness a terrible occurrence and I say, "Oh my God," what I am really saying is, "There, that is an expression of the Power of Creation. That horror *is* God." Just as when I see a magnificent sunset and say, "Oh my God," I am really saying, "There, in front of me, is God, the Power of Creation in all its glory, right before my eyes."

When someone is diagnosed with cancer and I say, "Oh God," meaning how terrible, I need to realize that cancer is God, an expression of life and creation. There is nothing that is not God. If I were to create a false view and separate life into good and bad, I would be separating myself from the All that is. I would bring imbalance to my life and to the Whole if I sought to retain what is pleasing and to eliminate the distasteful. It can't be done.

It is more in keeping with reality to acknowledge my oneness with All that is when I utter the words, "Oh God." About everything I see and experience, I need, in truth, to be saying, "That's God" and "That's God" and "That's God."

Once I saw this clearly, I could use the word God easily. The entire universe became the mirror into which I looked and saw the Power of Creation and myself as a fully participating part of that whole.

Diane and the Pathway of Self-Mastery

I aspired to self-mastery from the time I was very young, without calling it that. Perhaps it was because I was raised in a fundamentalist Methodist Church. I was taught that I was born in sin and needed to be saved in order to avoid going to hell where I would suffer forever in hell-fire. I took that very seriously and literally. I definitely did not want to go to hell and suffer forever! Therefore I sought to live a good, Christian life according to the teachings of the church.

In addition, from early on I had what I would now call mystical experiences. My trouble was that, believing I had been born in sin, I didn't feel worthy of those mystical experiences. When I spoke of them to ministers, they did not affirm or confirm their validity. Experiences of salvation were strictly defined with images of Jesus reaching down to lift you up into heaven and heavenly choirs singing in recognition of your salvation. Our Sunday school books had color illustrations of such events, and people gave testimonies to their own experiences of the same.

I spent my early years praying nightly to Jesus to save me. I attended as many evangelistic crusades as I could, and I always went forward for the altar call, praying that I would hear heavenly choirs as I knelt and waited. I did not experience the prescribed salvation as a child or teenager, but I continued to pray and ask.

In my late teens and early twenties I turned to psychology to try to understand myself. When the humanistic psychology movement came along, I read and worked with many self-help books to try to heal the inner split between the expectation of salvation taught in the church and my own shortcomings.

After my experiences of awakening at age 27 (described in chapter three), I was introduced for the first time to the philosophy of Yoga, the oldest and most well-developed system for understanding and developing the psyche that there is. Through Yogananda's *Autobiography of a Yogi* and his lessons from the Self-Realization Society, I found my spiritual pathway. In Yoga, it is called Raja Yoga, the King of Yogas. In English, it is Self-Mastery. I finally felt at home with a spiritual approach.

The key to this Pathway is to use the self as a laboratory in which to test and prove the various spiritual teachings and practices. Nothing is taken on faith alone. Every principle or approach is to be proven through personal experience or discarded as irrelevant. This is why Yoga is called a science. Every tenet is to be proven in the laboratory of self. Nothing is taken on faith based on the experience of someone else.

In the Christian church the Pathway of Devotion is predominant and disciples are expected not only to take things on faith but to trust implicitly the testimony of others. I found it a great relief to step onto a more scientifically-oriented Pathway.

I immediately began to work with Hatha Yoga (for the physical body), with Pranayama (for breath control), with directing energies through the chakras (spiritual wheels of energy corresponding to points on the human body), with concentration and meditation. I wanted to be able to understand the mystical experiences I had had and I wanted to know God directly through my own experience.

I found my way to a teacher named Vitvan who integrated his own Methodist upbringing with Western science and with Eastern teachings. I used his teachings to achieve the integration I had longed for.

When Arleen and I began to work together, I brought philosophical understanding to her strongly intuitive approach. I taught methodology (the how) while she urged action (the what). Our two approaches made our work more all-encompassing and made it easier for many people to feel at home with us. Our focus on the heart center and learning to live in unconditional love compensated for the fact that neither of us was walking the Pathway of Devotion so familiar in our predominantly Christian culture.

Arleen:

I admired Diane's fine mind and her ability to translate formal Wisdom Teachings into modern language that could be more easily understood by today's students. She was also able to communicate the ways and means of getting to a next step in spiritual unfolding. She could articulate the process of moving forward, whereas I tended to see the end result and to go there in one leap. My mode was fast and sure, but it was not so easy for me to fill others in on how I got there.

Putting together the leap and the process was a gift we had as joint facilitators.

Using Diane's example over the years I learned to elaborate on my insights and to use my mental skills to communicate to others the steps taken. I developed greater skill in translating my images, intuitions, and insights into words so that others could benefit from what I saw and intuitively knew.

Diane:

I was inspired by Arleen's strong intuition and her creativity. I recognized my intuition in relation to major decisions but not so much in my day-to-day living, and I had never thought of myself as creative. Over the years of working and living with Arleen, I learned to listen to my intuition more consistently and to recognize my creativity. I learned from Arleen that I didn't need to process everything endlessly. Once I had an insight I could move more quickly to embody the new awareness.

I also benefited enormously from Arleen's urge to action. Although I was consistent in my daily practice of Yoga stretches, I had never engaged regularly in physical activities. With Arleen, I took daily hour-long walks, played tennis daily, or swam daily. These were disciplines that have helped me to keep my body in good shape through the years.

My preferred approach to illness of any kind was self-healing. This meant that I observed what was going on in my body, researched in self-help books how to promote well-being, and drew on alternative healing methods whenever possible. Only as a last resort did I turn to Western medicine.

Arleen on the other hand went immediately from symptoms to a doctor, and she encouraged me to do the same. Over the years, I learned to find the balance between our two approaches and I am grateful for that integration of her approach with mine.

Our Awakenings

Diane had long known that she wanted to find a partner who shared her spiritual life fully. She had thought that partner would be a man, but now it seemed something else was emerging. We were open to whatever was ready to come into being. We knew that mental concepts such as "each of us would find a male spiritual life partner" were simply that, concepts. They were based on the notion of standard relationships that both of us were individually raised on. Remaining open to unexpected relational configurations represented an upheaval of the norm.

When something unknown is emerging, it is best if the participants stay out of the way and do not seek to impose limits. If we *had* imposed limits we might not have considered there was "a work" for us to do and a unique union for us to have. By staying open and being willing, a force larger than our limited vision could take hold of our lives and bring the new into being without restraints.

We shared extensively with each other about how we had each come to cosmic awareness.

Arleen's Process of Awakening

In 1967, my husband Dick and I appeared in a low budget film together in which I had the lead role. It was shot in New York City and was supposed to be sold to television. Because the producer had difficulty with the sale, he decided, without asking permission from the actors involved, to add salacious scenes to the film so that it could be sold to porno houses. Dick and I had no idea this change was in process but the finished product would result in a major shift in my life.

We traveled to see the movie in New Jersey, at a porno house, in the spring of 1968. We were horrified by the changes to the film. It did not help that our names had been changed in the credits. I was so stricken that on May 13 of that year I awoke in the night with all the symptoms of a heart attack. Dick rushed me to the hospital where he worked. I was stabilized. The next morning, I went to the office of the hospital cardiologist who informed me that I was suffering from pericarditis, an inflammation of the lining of the heart, which he attributed to a virus. In those days, the treatment was complete rest, six weeks out of commission.

From the moment of the diagnosis, I felt the strange sensation of all my energy being withdrawn. It was as if I internalized the diagnosis and merged with the symptoms of the illness. I was so limp and incapacitated that I could not even lift my hand to comb my hair. I had no appetite and went down to a weight of about 98 pounds.

What I didn't know at the time was that the jolt to my heart at age 29, because of the film disaster and the inflammation that seeing it caused to my heart lining, was the beginning of the opening of my heart center. I had never heard of chakras and would not have had a way to understand that the heart chakra was opening, but I learned later that that was in fact what was occurring.

There is a term many associate with spiritual awakenings. It is "going to bed." The initiate is physically affected to the point of having to retreat to bed for as long as it takes for the opening to a new level of consciousness to occur. I went to bed for six weeks and then was on limited activity for six months. I had to relearn how to do the simplest things and had great difficulty climbing even one step at a time.

Having no idea still that this was a heart-chakra-opening experience, I slowly recovered and returned to teaching high school in Manhattan near to where we lived.

A Spiritual Mother and Teacher

In the summer of 1969, Dick and I embarked on a six-week driving trip across the United States. It was a wonderful, rich experience for both of us. As we approached the Northwestern States, I began to feel a magnetic pull to California. I didn't know why but I stayed present to what I was feeling. The sensation intensified when, in the late afternoon, we approached the mountains of East Glacier Park, Montana. The sun hovered above the peaks and I had my first taste of what could be called a mystical experience. It was otherworldly, magnificently strange. I began to hear what I would later call "the Music of the Spheres." The sounds were high-pitched, ethereal, and mesmerizing. To this day, with a simple shift of consciousness, I can hear that music as my head center opens just as it did during that first experience.

By the time we reached the Canadian Rockies, the magnetic pull to California was even stronger and the Music of the Spheres, louder. During our drive, I had a beyond-the-body experience. I, my consciousness, was suddenly above the mountain tops looking down on our car traveling on the road between the peaks. I clearly saw myself and Dick in the vehicle as I looked down from my lofty vantage point.

Such a shift might have caused the average person to "freak out." I did not, but neither did I know the meaning of the event. To my credit as a burgeoning spiritual initiate, I did not conjecture or rush to make sense of what was transpiring. Had I done that I would have tried to fit the experience into my narrow knowledge at that time of the reality of life. I might have called it a hallucination or a flight of fancy. Instead of trying to label it from my limited perspective I chose a phrase that has continued to serve me every day since: *This is what happened.* Period. No explanation. No speculations. No trying to make sense of it. *It simply was/is.*

When we arrived in Carmel Valley, California, I came to learn something about the magnetic pull. We had gone to visit Evelyn Nolt and Philippa Hastings. I had met Ev ten years earlier, in 1958, when I went to register for acting classes at the Herbert Berghof Studio in Greenwich Village. I had been one of the early graduates of the High School of Performing Arts Drama Department in 1956 and was ready to resume my career in theater. At least I thought that was the reason for going to the studio. In fact, I would now say that I was there to meet Ev who would turn out to be my spiritual mother/teacher/guide.

When I approached the registration desk back then, Ev barely lifted her head in greeting, but for a brief moment our eyes connected and I immediately sensed this person represented something important I needed to know. I had never felt this depth of connection with anyone before. I didn't know what to say or ask, so I remained silent, but the intuitive knowing was firmly imprinted on my consciousness.

I developed a small friendship with Ev and Pip but within a very short time they picked up stakes and headed for a new life in Carmel Valley, California. In the summer of 1960, when I was

21, my first love, Michael, died, also at the age of 21. It was a profound setback that led to a back injury and three days in the hospital. I wrote to Ev to try to make sense of Michael's early and tragic demise. Ev wrote back a long letter in which she talked about Michael's life journey and described it as packing up his life belongings and traveling through the veil to the other side. I had no frame of reference for this description or for life in-or-after death and filed it away as a beautiful poetic expression.

Now, nine years later, I stood before Ev and, looking once again into her eyes, connected with her soul to soul. We could barely break the bond. Finally, Ev said, "Perhaps I was your mother in some other lifetime." It was as if thousands of bells starting ringing, even though I had no concept of past lives at that point. This was the beginning of my stepping beyond ordinary functioning and opening to finer frequency realms.

As Dick and I proceeded down the coast of California after the visit in Carmel Valley, I had my awakening in consciousness. Standing near the ocean in Big Sur, I looked down into a flower and began to merge with it. The form of the flower disappeared and its vast energy field was revealed. I entered that energy field, became one with it, and became one with everything there was. Separation of any kind vanished and my perspective on life was completely and eternally altered. The event was as simple as it was extraordinarily profound.

Nothing was the same for me after that early September 1969 breakthrough. I had awakened.

When we awaken we realize that we had been sleep-walking through life, living on automatic. To awaken is to become conscious of that fact and to see oneself and the natural world in an entirely new way. The results of such an event are life-changing, as we will share throughout this book.

I wrote to Ev and told her of the experience. Ev knew precisely what had occurred. I didn't know then how rare it was to have someone be able to fully receive the description of a spiritual experience.

Ev sent me books to read about expanded consciousness and the Ancient Wisdom. The two of us exchanged extensive letters over the next several months about the texts and the whole new world that was opening to me. In fact, it was Ev who sent me *The Ladies Home Journal* story about Diane Kennedy Pike and her experience of being lost in the desert in 1969.

It is so clear that when we feel something stirring in us and we don't exactly know what it is, we will be rewarded if we open ourselves to the more, to the unknown, to the unexpected. As we go forward, putting up no limits or protective barriers, we send forth an invitation to as-yet-unmet potential spiritual companions with whom to unite in the quest for greater awakening. Diane and I did this (still do this!) repeatedly in our lives, and were wonderfully surprised by who was waiting around the next corner.

Touching into Past Lives

During that period of being educated spiritually by Ev, I had many meaningful adventures such as exploring past life recalls with Joan Grant and Denys Kelsey.

Joan Grant had the capacity to tune in at will to other people's past lives as well as her own and many meticulous transcripts of sessions exist in which she recounted the previous lifetime of one of the people in the room. Working with her husband, Denys, a psychiatrist who regressed the individual through hypnosis, the two were able to serve as guides into the recall, should it occur, and to enable the material to be used for healing in this lifetime where traumas existed that might have had previous roots.

In one of my initial sessions I experienced chills and body tremors as I experienced being born. I discovered myself in a bubble-like container that was inside a larger container. Outside my own enclosure, I could hear sounds that I might now compare to nature: a flowing brook/the blood rushing through my mother's veins, and thunder/when she coughed. The most prominent sound was the continuous lull of her breathing.

I will offer comparisons from now to seek to capture what I experienced as the "being" in the recall. I felt as if I was living in cellophane at the bottom of the sea. Life moved around me. I was perceiving sensory elements while *being* them, rather than sensing them as separate from me.

After a while I began to experience "my place" getting smaller. The bubble seemed to be closing in on me, encroaching on the space I had. I didn't sense that I was growing larger but that my environment was becoming smaller.

The birth experience was very painful, as if I were being ripped from my own flesh. I was being pushed and pulled simultaneously into an unfamiliar life form. I was thoroughly exhausted and drained. I discovered that I had been transported. It was as if I had been stuffed into a physical frame that was entirely too small to house all of me. My awareness was of being cramped, subdued. I could see light reflections and shadows from behind my closed eyelids. These were moving around me as if separate entities. My sensing was now from me, through a body, to what was outside myself. I felt trapped, enclosed, and unable to be free. Within a short time, my connection with knowing who I was began to diminish.

The Fear of Death

In a later session, I began to have recalls that connected with areas I had worked with in this lifetime. I had always had a fear of death and though I had worked with it on many levels and in therapy sessions, I could not move past the fear.

Working with Joan and Denys I put the fear to rest by experiencing the dying process. To my surprise, it was the opposite of the limiting moment of birthing.

I touched my life as a soldier who was driven to suicide because of the breakup of a love relationship. He jumped into a canal and drowned. In the recall, I experienced the death fully, feeling the weight of tons of water upon my chest and my inability to breathe as my lungs filled. Then, I "died." Suddenly, there was nothing, no more struggle. Joan asked repeatedly, "Where are you?" I realized *I* was there! I wasn't "dead." I looked down and saw my physical body floating face down in the water. It was exactly as I had left it, uniformed and lifeless.

Then I became aware of *me*. I could not see or feel me but I knew I *was*, "breathing" in a different way. There was no inhalation, exhalation process; rather there was a flow of air/clarity as if an infinite ripple on an endless, still lake.

I did not even notice "passing over;" that is how easy the actual transition had been. The death was a complete release from the body and I felt myself merging with boundless light and endless space. I came to know an unfathomable freedom and expansion. Death was a continuation of soul life into a next dimension, a finer frequency. It was an ecstatic experience to realize I was not dead! Rather than alive, I would say I was alight; merged with all that is.

Unconditional Love

One of those recalls clearly laid the groundwork for my devotion to a life of unconditional love. I touched into the short life of John Selby who lived in the 1700's in the village of Danbury, in England. John's severe cleft palate disenabled him from speaking and he was put into the care of a nursemaid, Mrs. Burns. He was so disfigured that people turned away and other children made fun of him, shunned him. John felt only compassion for the limitations they exhibited. But he made fast friends with birds who flocked to him and small animals who connected with his kindness and did not turn from his distorted face. John had been born to learn to live in perfect harmony in a seemingly imperfect body. His deformity was for the purpose of the "re-formity" of his soul. John died when he was very young but in his short life he made a tremendous contribution through his expressions of love to everything and everyone.

In that recall, I had a clear picture of the village of Danbury. In the 1970's, Diane and I visited there and on the wall in the 15th century church there was a drawing of how the village looked centuries ago. It was exactly as I had described it in my recall session.

Past life recalls, when facilitated by responsible and ethical persons, can be very helpful in clarifying certain aspects of our lives. In my case, I had a foretaste of my awakening when I experienced both birthing and dying, and I saw the power of unconditional love as I witnessed John Selby's life experience. These experiences not only opened my eyes a little wider but they helped prepare me for what was to unfold in my life.

For those who doubt there is life after death or that there is such a thing as past life recalls, here is another perspective that might make the above easier to digest. The perspective is this: all lives are really one life being lived in the now. That "now" is comprised of all that ever was and all that ever will be. Hence, I, Arleen, living right now, may have touched into the life of John Selby and drawn on his life experience so that I might incorporate what he learned into my daily life in order to fulfill my purpose of being unconditionally loving. Whether tapping into a past life recall or tapping into continuous life expressions, each of us can embody universal learning and evolve to greater heights in the life with which we are currently identified.

Sleep Travel

The most amazing events that happened during the time Ev was "educating" me occurred during sleep-travel.

These sleep experiences were not dreams but journeys in the energy world. I went to "classes" where I was given important "instruction." There were no physical classrooms or identifiable teachers but there was a kind of tutoring from unseen energy sources. Each night I would go "deeper" into the void of learning. When I would wake from these sleep journeys I would see myself coming through realms of consciousness until I was awake. But upon awakening, I could not remember anything of what I had been taught. The one thing I did know was that when I was ready to embody what I had learned (to *become* the wisdom) I would remember.

In November 1970 I remembered. I was teaching at Thomas Jefferson High School in Brooklyn, New York. There was fight in the auditorium; two boys were threatening to kill one another and their fellow students were clamoring for blood. I was the only teacher to respond to the potentially catastrophic event. I didn't even think about what to do. I jumped up and rushed into the center of the maelstrom. I opened my heart center, put out my hands toward the hearts of the two boys, and the chaos fell away. The screaming ceased and the combatants turned and left. I stood trembling as if lightning had shot through me.

Following the incident, I stood before my class and we all wept together over the fight and the horrendous conditions of violence in the school. We vowed we would do something about it, together. The bell rang. I went to my office and sat down to calm myself. Then came the moment of remembering. A ray of light burst into the room and on that ray of light came the six **Love Principles**. I knew I was to bring them to the school. They were not to be talked about; they were to be lived. I knew that this was what I had learned in my sleep travel and that I was now ready to embody that wisdom. I started **The Love Project** and it completely changed the school and my life. (Lorrance, *The Love Project*, LP Publications, 1972.)

The Love Project

During the seven months I conducted **The Love Project**, I was literally functioning in a higher and finer than normal energy frequency. My head centers were open to Light and the Music of the Spheres was present. I describe the time period as one in which my feet seemed not to touch the ground. I had expanded stamina and my ability to achieve and produce exceeded any other period in my life. Most of the time, I sang wherever I went.

From November 1970 to June 1971, three months prior to meeting Diane, I taught classes at the high school, served as Human Relations Coordinator and wrote and directed shows and events, and was an assistant Dean of Girls and Chairperson of the Speech and Theatre Department. Simultaneously, I was responsible for all **Love Project** activities which I developed and ran in the after-school hours. I wrote and distributed "The Seeker Newsletter" to keep the faculty apprised of **Love Project** activities and was interviewed often by representatives from *Look* magazine and daily newspapers.

I traveled twice to California during that time, once to share **The Love Project** at the National Center for the Exploration of Human Potential, and once to explore possible employment in the school systems in the state.

In addition to all this, I was in the process of completing my Master of Fine Arts in Theatre Directing. I attended classes at night, completing the necessary assignments, and I researched and wrote an extensive thesis. To top it all off, I directed a full-scale thesis production which was required for my degree.

As if this was not enough, I fully maintained my marriage relationship and Dick and I took on the task of packing up our apartment and moving/driving across the country at the end of June to resettle in the West.

Looking back on all this, it hardly seems possible that one human being could accomplish all that, but when one is functioning in an altered state, anything is possible.

Diane's Process of Awakening

I was on a spiritual journey from the time I was a child. At age three I had my first experience of what I would now call a Divine Presence.

I was enveloped by a warm and powerful energy and knew that I would never need to be afraid because I would never be alone. That was an intuitive knowing at a very young age which has never left me.

At age twelve I felt and saw a stream of white light pour out of my heart center toward a group of elderly people and knew that I would live a life of service. That intuitive knowing also never wavered.

When I was nineteen, I heard my inner voice for the first time. It told me, "God wants you to be a teacher in a mission school." Based on that inner message, I chose my college major and signed up to go as a short-term missionary immediately upon graduation. The program established by the protestant churches was a predecessor to the Peace Corps and provided an opportunity for college graduates to serve overseas for two or three years with only a few weeks of training followed by language study.

I was assigned to teach in a bilingual school in Montevideo, Uruguay. After a month of training in the challenge of cultural differences, I went to San Jose, Costa Rica for four months of Spanish language study, following which I flew to Montevideo for three years of teaching in Crandon Institute, a Methodist school.

Until I left for Central and South America, I had been totally immersed in church life and it never occurred to me that I would "serve" outside the institutional church. However, in both Costa Rica and in Montevideo I had an opportunity to experience for the first time how divisive belief systems could be. Missionaries actually competed with one another and those who were more fundamentalist held prayer meetings for the Methodists (and others.) The fundamentalists did not believe that we "others" had been saved, and therefore, they believed we were not worthy to be representatives of Christ. That was my first experience of being disillusioned with the faith of my upbringing.

Upon my return to the States at the end of 1962 I suffered culture shock in reverse. The entire country was in upheaval over race relations and the cities were burning. John Kennedy was the new president and before I really got to experience him, he had been assassinated. I felt like a stranger in my own country.

I was in New York City attending Teachers College at Columbia University to attain a Master's Degree in English as a Foreign Language with the intention of returning to Uruguay as a full-time missionary. However, the intensity of the culture shock on top of my experience in Uruguay precipitated an inner crisis. As I experienced it, my mind was functioning on three tracks at once: it was attending to the daily course of events in my life, it was studying and writing papers for graduate school, and it was trying to sort out what was "wrong" with me internally. The rapidity with which my mind was functioning terrified me; I thought I was going crazy.

I went to the library to research signs of losing one's mind (this was before the days of Google!). I found a reputable book that said, among many other things, if you thought you were going crazy you probably weren't. That was somewhat reassuring, but I was still terrified.

Fortunately, a pastor from my student days at Stanford University, a good friend, happened to come to New York at that time and called to invite me to dinner. I cried my way through our dinner as I poured out my fears to him. He told me he would contact the Board of Missions for me to cancel the speaking tour they had scheduled for me and he also contacted friends of his who lived in Scarsdale, just north of NYC, to see if I could live with them for a time. All of that was a godsend.

I completed my Master's Degree, passing the exam with honors; this contributed to my feeling that something was very wrong with me that I could do so well mentally when I was so full of anxiety. I went to my representative on the Board of Missions and asked to be referred for counseling. She sent me to a psychiatrist. I wanted to talk with him about my fears about not being normal, but from the first day he was convinced he knew what was wrong with me: that I had low self-esteem and that was why I had taken a job as a missionary with very low pay.

This was a blatant example of someone who knew nothing about the spiritual life and was therefore unable to be of help to me. I had experienced a similar lack of understanding all through my four years of college when I had tried to talk with ministers about my spiritual experiences and none of them understood what I was talking about. Eventually I quit the therapy and returned to California, still afraid that I was either going crazy or having a nervous breakdown.

In California, I saw a counselor at San Jose State and began by telling him what I was afraid of. In one short hour, he assured me I was not crazy and that I could trust my inner feelings to guide me. By now the Board of Missions had told me they would not send me back to Uruguay unless I had two years of psychotherapy because I had quit seeing the psychiatrist they had recommended. I took that as a sign and decided I was not going to submit to two years of psychotherapy and therefore would not return as a missionary.

Instead, I taught English for a year at my old high school in San Jose and was then hired as the Director of Youth and Children's Work at the Palo Alto United Methodist Church.

It was before going as a counselor to a summer youth camp sponsored by the Palo Alto church that I heard my inner voice for a second time. It said, simply, "You will meet someone." I thought that was not very helpful, but on the day I was boarding the bus for the camp, the voice spoke again: "She's the one you are to meet." Clearly, inner voices speak succinctly, giving only as much information as is needed in the moment.

Seated in the front seat was a woman with her head purposely buried in a book. I said, "May I sit here?" That was the beginning of a friendship with Patricia Bradley. I knew immediately that Patricia had something I needed, I just didn't know what. In the year that followed it was as if I kept my ears attuned for the next inner message. One evening more than a year later, Patricia said, "I want to share something with you." I knew immediately, "This is it."

Being guided by intuition is like following lighted stones in a dark night. The guidance is totally trustworthy, but there is no way to predict how long the intervals between "stones" will be. My meeting of Patricia and knowing that she had something I needed was a direct parallel with Arleen's meeting of Ev and intuiting there was something for her in Ev. In both cases, we were drawn by the inner spiritual connection, not by anything external.

Patricia described her experience of awakening and then offered to loan me a book by Maurice Bucke called *Cosmic Consciousness*. Thus began an exploration into a new domain. Until then my orientation to spirituality was confined to my traditional Methodist upbringing. I thought of my various experiences as "spiritual," never mystical, even though no one in the church had ever validated them for me. Now, under Patricia's guidance, I began to read about consciousness and the potential for expanded realms of perception. Thus, Patricia served me in the same way as Ev served Arleen, offering guidance and suggesting books to read about other realms of consciousness. This is the blessing of not being alone, of having spiritual companionship and guidance. Both Arleen and I had that kind of support.

About a year later I was going to a convention in Columbus, Ohio, for professionals in Christian Education. Before I left I had a powerful dream in which I fell off a roller coaster. When my body hit the ground, it was broken and bloodied. I was watching from above the body and saw a guard running toward it. In the dream I thought, "There's no need to hurry. The body is dead." Then I woke up. I was not shaken by the dream, but rather strangely comforted because I realized that I had not died with the body.

When I told the dream to Patricia, she asked, "What are you afraid of?" I did not know anything of which I was afraid. Off I went to Ohio with a question, rather like a Zen koan, "What am I afraid of?" For a week, I asked the question internally without stopping. At the end of the week the breakthroughs began. The answer to the question was, "It is myself I fear." And then, "What if I am nothing?" And finally, "I am nothing, absolutely nothing."

That was the moment of liberation as I let go of my need to "be" something, let go of my identification with my personality, and descended into the void before me. After a time, I emerged from the blackness of the void and soared into a new realization: that I was completely free, just to be. I burst into laughter that was so profound it lifted me into pure energy.

I saw that everything was energy and that I was one with all that is, absolutely essential to the Whole but no more important than anyone else. I knew that death had no power over my consciousness, that my body was perfect, that power was available to me to do whatever I needed or wanted to do, and that all relationships were practice sessions for learning how to merge with the divine. I was filled with a joy I had never known before.

In the days that followed I realized that I had been made whole; I no longer experienced inner conflict or anxiety. I was completely at peace within. I also realized that none of my prior beliefs could account for the vastness of what I came to know in those five or six days of awakening. I was able to read scriptures and *know* what the author meant to communicate. I could not think of God or Jesus as I had thought of them before. I knew I needed to completely rebuild my world view to make it large enough to embrace what I had seen. I had truly been born anew, but not in the way I had been taught to expect in my upbringing in the church. It was as if for the first time my eyes were open to see the world as it really is: pure energy.

I had awakened. It was 1965 and I was 27 years old.

The Meaning of Awakening

Most humans live in what we would call an objective state of consciousness. That is, they look at the world around them as separate from them, as objects of their perception. In all Wisdom Traditions, this objective state of consciousness is talked about as a dream state because it is not the "reality" of the energy world. If we are dreaming though seemingly awake, then to wake up is to discover the energy world.

More than that. To wake up is to discover that we are not the seemingly separate bodies and personalities that we thought we were. It is to come to know ourselves as the one who "dreams" and therefore the one who creates the reality of the dreams, believing them to be real. It is a radical shift of perception of both the outer world and the inner world of "self." It is for that reason that Carl Jung once said, "To look outward is to dream; to look inward is to awaken."

When we awaken, we function more consistently through intuition, which is responsive to the energy world, and we are no longer bound by time and space. It was for that reason that the two of us had agreed, or so it seemed to us, to find each other *after* we had awakened. Only through intuition could we have found each other when our waking dream lives had been so very different and so separated by both time and space. Once we had each awakened, we could be drawn to each other intuitively and remember our intention, formed before we incarnated, to do a work together.

Arleen had said, "There is a work for us to do together." Diane was open. The two of us proceeded by being present to what was unfolding.

Our Lives Converge

It is quite an experience to function on parallel tracks, so to speak: the intuitional track and the rational mind track. When intuition is strong, as it has been for both of us, there is no question that it can be trusted. The intuition presents as a knowing, not a thought. But the limitation of intuition is that it is not accompanied by any explanation or justification of any kind. There is no elaboration. It is just a simple knowing which you either follow or you don't. Also, intuition reveals only one step forward at a time, so to follow it is like walking in the dark. This is the primary difference between walking a spiritual path and following a prescribed religious faith.

The rational mind, on the other hand, can hardly stand not to have explanation, justification or elaboration. It simply rebels, asserting through thoughts: "What are you thinking? What are you talking about? How can this be? What do you mean, Diane's face appeared in the paintings?" The mind almost shouts out its protests, and it has a lot of support from the people closest to you who want some way to fathom your decisions even when you have no explanation for them except that it "feels right."

Both of our minds were in agreement that there was no rational explanation for what was occurring in our lives, but it was abundantly clear that we had come together for a purpose that was not yet known to us and that we both trusted. So we proceeded, letting the intuitional track guide the way even though we did not know where it would lead us.

By June 1972 our lives had completely changed; we were buying a house in San Diego and starting our life and work together even though we still did not know what form that work would take. From the time we met at the end of September 1971 until June 1972, a nine-month birthing process, we were each thrust into a powerful vortex of energy that served with magnetic force to careen us toward the creation of a new form we could never have imagined. Here is how it all unfolded.

Diane's Preparation

I had been dating a lawyer in New York City while I was earning my Master's Degree and, later, working for the Methodist Office at the United Nations. We were considering marriage. I kept feeling that to marry him would be a compromise for me because he did not share my depth of spiritual commitment though he was respectful of mine.

Following my experiences of awakening in November of 1965, I decided to take some summer school classes at the Pacific School of Religion at Berkeley, California. An intriguing man referenced as a cutting-edge theologian in a *Time* magazine article was to teach two courses, one in "The New Theology" and the other in "The New Morality." I thought both courses would be stimulating for me since I was trying to rebuild my world view following my awakening. However, my principal motivation was to see if I would meet a minister who shared my commitment to a spiritual life.

On the first day of classes the teacher, who was James A. Pike, Bishop of the Episcopal Diocese of California, asked if anyone was driving to San Francisco after class. I raised my hand, as did others, and he pointed to me and said, "I need a ride to Grace Cathedral." I was happy to provide the transportation, and I was delighted to discover a natural flow of energy between us as we traveled from Berkeley across the Bay Bridge and to Grace Cathedral in San Francisco.

The next day of classes Bishop Pike came up to me during a morning break and invited me to have lunch with him; he said he wanted to thank me for the ride. Several other students joined us, so it was not a very personal event, but at the end of the day as I headed in my car toward San Francisco, Bishop Pike passed me in his car and honked at me. I registered immediately, "He likes me!" Sure enough, the next week he arranged to be driven to class so he would need a return ride to the Cathedral and he asked me to drive him. As we traveled across the Bay Bridge on that day I had the strange experience of "knowing" that we were already married.

I did not believe in reincarnation, nor had I ever really thought about it. But when I tried to figure out what it could possibly mean that we were already married, I thought, "Perhaps we were married in a past life." That was my first experience of many of meeting people in this lifetime and sensing that I had known them in a past life.

I continued to drive him back to San Francisco on the remaining days of our classes, and in the months that followed I saw Bishop Pike each time he was in the Bay Area. We discovered that neither of us felt we had to get to know each other; rather it was as if whenever we shared about our pasts, we felt we already knew all of that. It was as if we were in a long-term relationship even though we had known each other only a short time.

As it turned out, my relationship with Bishop Pike in this lifetime was brief: only three years. We merged our professional and personal lives, wrote a book together about his experiences of communicating with his son after his son's suicide (Pike and Kennedy, *The Other Side, 1968),* and dove into a deep study of the historical Jesus. When we were ready to begin writing a book about the historical Jesus, we wanted to complete our research by going in person to the places in Israel that had been central to Jesus' experience.

For that reason, we traveled to Israel at the end of August, 1969, and on September first, we drove in our rented car out into the Judean Wilderness where it is reported, in the New Testament, that Jesus went to fast and pray for 40 days and 40 nights. We wanted to get a direct feeling for what had drawn Jesus and so many others into the Wilderness for that kind of spiritual quest.

The two of us got lost and had to abandon our car when it got stuck and we were not able to free it from the rut it was in. We decided to walk toward the Dead Sea, hoping to reach Qumran where we knew there was water. I tell the whole story in my book *Search* (Pike, 1970), but what I want to relate here is my experience after I left Jim to find help.

We had ended up in a deep canyon. The weather was extremely hot (over 130 degrees) and we had no water, so after walking for about two hours, we were dehydrated and exhausted. We came to a flat rock and decided to lie down and rest. When we did, I realized just how exhausted I was and how desperate our circumstances were, so I tried to climb up out of the canyon. I did not have enough strength to lift myself and I fell down again alongside Jim. I said, "Sweetheart, if we're going to die in the desert, I want to die here beside you." "OK" was his only reply.

After a silence, I remembered several lengthy conversations Jim and I had had just a few weeks before about our inability to comprehend why a person with any degree of rational control in a crisis situation would not do everything possible to save the life of another. I realized that if I stayed there to die beside Jim it would be for a purely selfish reason. If I were to get up and go, there was a slight possibility that I could get help. I realized I had to go on.

When the decision to go was made and I told Jim, a great sense of calm and peace came over me. All fear was gone, all anxiety relieved. I had no fear of dying and no fear of going off by myself. I had to go in order not to distort the meaning of the life Jim and I had shared together. I told him, "If I die in the desert, you'll know that I went because I love you and I was trying to get help for you." He responded, "I know that, I love you too, and if I die here I am at peace and I have no regrets."

I left Jim at 6:10 in the afternoon and I did not find help until 4:10 the next morning. For six of those hours I climbed on the canyon walls, and the last four hours I stumbled along the top of the canyon. At one point I slipped and fell tumbling head over heels toward the bottom of the canyon. I knew that when my body hit the bottom it would be killed and I felt no fear whatsoever. When I hit my right elbow on a sharp rock and stopped the fall, I had a surge of joy inside as I remembered Paul's words in his first letter to the Corinthians: "Oh death, where is thy sting?" I knew that death had no power over me.

That experience was a confirmation of what I had intuited in the dream in which I had fallen from the roller coaster and then later had come to know in my experiences of awakening. I was thrilled that the lack of fear of death held firm when it was tested in a real-life circumstance, such as tumbling through the air in the canyon.

I functioned during those ten hours and in the six days following in a completely altered state of consciousness in which I felt that everything was unfolding in perfect order, just as it was supposed to. Some people told me I was in a state of shock. If so, I know that I was shocked into higher consciousness because it totally sustained me for seven weeks after Jim died.

The short time I shared with Jim Pike was totally fulfilling for me. In my book *Life Is Victorious! How to Grow through Grief* (Simon & Schuster, 1972), I wrote of my awareness during meditation over a year later that I had completed three karmic tasks with Jim.

The first was to realize a deeper understanding of the vow of chastity I had taken for many lifetimes. I came to see that it has to do with purity of heart more than with abstinence from sexual engaging. I saw that if God is *by choice* at the center of our lives, then we cannot, do not, and will not adulterate our own divine beings. This has freed me to live in loving appreciation of and gratitude for my physical body and without fear of the power of sexual energy.

The second karmic task was to learn that God is not the same as the church. Though I had been raised to believe that the church is God's body on earth, I came to see that God is alive in all beings everywhere, in nonbelievers as well as believers. This is a perception that Jim Pike shared with me and together we were breaking free of the limitations of our earlier belief. After Jim died, I left the church. After a year or so I had an experience of coming out of a kind of "fog" in which I had been living, a kind of hypnotic trance induced by my total immersion in the church and her teachings.

I was surprised to discover that there are many spiritual people who are not associated with any church. That was new to me. And I am glad to be free of the group psyche that pulls me down into private world, automatic functioning where I felt separate from those who were not church-going Christians. I could not have done the work of teaching the Ancient Wisdom if I was still held in that hypnotic cloud.

The third karmic task had been to learn to love perfectly. In my relationship with Jim, I didn't even have to set aside preferences, they were just gone. On only one occasion was I tempted to report that he had hurt my feelings. As I was walking toward him, my inner voice said, "No you don't. Not in this relationship." I was learning about unconditional love; it was a preparation for the work I would do with Arleen.

Arleen's Preparation

During that first weekend in Santa Barbara in October, 1971, I shared extensively with Diane about **The Love Project**. I presented a scrapbook of photos detailing how I had led my high school students through a series of events that changed the school during a seven-month period from a place of negativity, non-attendance, and frequent violence into a learning hub and a loving environment. The shift was so radical that parents came to ask why their teenagers suddenly wanted to go school; they had never experienced that before. The program was so successful that it was written up in newspaper articles and in *Education Today*. *Look* magazine sent a journalist and the well-known photo-journalist Charlotte Brooks to cover the project for three months with the intention of doing a feature story on it.

Those participating in the program practiced the following six **Love Principles** that I brought into being in November, 1970:

Be the Change
  You Want to See Happen
Create Your Own Reality Consciously
Have No Expectations
Problems Are Opportunities
Receive All People as Beautiful
  Exactly as They Are

Provide Others with Opportunities to Give.

My growing exposure in the media led to an invitation from the National Center for the Exploration of Human Potential to participate in their facilitator training in San Diego, in June, 1971, which resulted in my meeting participant Patricia who brought Diane to see my unusual paintings.

This sounds like a clear-cut path where one thing leads to another. In fact, following one's intuition requires the individual to make choices along the way. These choices play a big role in determining what will actually come into being. There is no magic in it; there is the willingness to listen within, the ability to weigh what is in harmony with the whole that seems to be emerging, and the commitment to embody what you see and know.

A leader at the training in San Diego laid temptation in my path. He wanted to get me on television, have me lead a campaign, and emblazon **The Love Principles** on t-shirts. This did not fit with my knowing that **The Love Principles** came as a pure gift and that the only way they worked was for individuals to practice them and live them. I rejected the offer, focusing instead on the spiritual nature of the principles and how I had received **The Love Project** and the six **Principles** on a ray of Light.

Prior to my spiritual awakening, I had been in show business and had been focused on becoming a star. Now, I was finally offered that opportunity but chose instead to retain the simplicity and power of the principles and to follow my inner guidance.

I had a similar experience with *Look* magazine. Those doing the story were focused on me as a super-teacher. I insisted **The Love Project** was not about me but rather about shifting consciousness, practicing the principles, and creating positive change. The journalist told me the spotlight had to be on a person and I was it. Oddly, or appropriately, *Look* magazine scheduled the publication date and the entire magazine folded just before the story was to appear in print. I never viewed that as a mere coincidence. (Charlotte Brooks' photos of **The Love Project** are in the *Look* collection in the Library of Congress. Many of them are also featured in my subsequent book, *The Love Project*.)

I was offered a high-paying job in the New York City school system to launch **The Love Project** city-wide. I turned down the job because I knew that change had to come from the bottom up, not from the top down. Besides, I had an inner pull to live in California and to leave the concrete city of New York behind.

During this same time period, before Diane and I ever met, Diane was on a nationwide speaker circuit, first fulfilling engagements her husband had contracted for before his death and then preparing for the publication of her book

Search chronicling her experience of survival in the Judean Desert and her husband's death there. Diane had co-written the best-selling book *The Other Side* with Bishop James A. Pike and she appeared on all the major talk shows promoting her new book, *Search*.

After the two of us began our fledgling work together, Diane realized that being famous as Jim Pike's widow was not in harmony with her own mission in life. She began to turn down invitations to speak and appear on television as "Mrs. Pike" so she could follow her own path.

We each, independently, made choices not to pursue personal fame. Those choices made it possible for our work together to come into being.

Change Starts to Take Place

In November 1971 Diane sold the house she had shared with Jim Pike in Santa Barbara and, to the consternation of friends and family, moved to Littleton, Colorado to work with Laurel Keyes and her group known as the Fransisters. Laurel had become a mentor to Diane after Jim Pike's death, introducing her to the long tradition of Wisdom Teachings.

Diane was looking for direction, and she had a series of dreams of establishing a mountain retreat site. Her dreams resonated with a long-standing vision Laurel had had of such a center for the study of ancient Wisdom Teachings. Diane decided to make the move to discover whether she and Laurel could manifest this dream/vision.

Arleen continued her travels around California, sharing the story of **The Love Project** and looking for a school district in which to continue her work. She received fabulous feedback wherever she went but no job offers. She took an interim job with the City of San Diego as Coordinator of Cultural Activities.

As 1971 ended, Arleen stood on the beach in San Diego gazing at the full moon. It was completely surrounded by a circle of light, a full halo serving as a round reflection of itself. While not superstitious, Arleen allowed herself to take this as a sign of a wonderful year ahead, perhaps even an encircling of her possible work with Diane.

In January, 1972, Diane suggested that Arleen come to Denver to look for employment in a school system there or to see how she might join in the work with Laurel Keyes. Although nothing came of that exploration, we got to know each other even better, played a lot in the out-of-doors, and promised to continue to remain open to what might be waiting to emerge.

Within a couple of weeks, all that Diane thought she was building with Laurel began to crumble. There was a grave misunderstanding of what each of them was bringing to the project and it threw Diane into a dilemma. She reached out to the few people who might bring her a clear perspective concerning the next steps she was to take. Of the people to whom she reached out, only Arleen responded immediately and Diane flew her to Denver to talk her dilemma through. Diane came to clarity, seeing that she needed to leave Colorado and return to California.

During that crucial meeting in January of 1972, we had what we call a "circle of light" experience in which every part our beings merged in a unified, lighted, unending energy flow. It was so profound an experience there were no words to put on it, and there was certainly no reasonable explanation. It seemed to fit in perfectly with the New Year's circle of light around the moon and also with a rose Arleen brought to Diane when she arrived. As the rose opened it revealed a double heart, merged at the center.

While we marveled at these occurrences, we both refrained from saying things like "This must mean that ..." Both of us preferred to have the More unfold for us rather than trying to tell the Universe what we thought it intended.

Diane sold nearly all her furniture, packed up her office equipment, files and books, and headed back to Santa Barbara. She took up temporary residence in the home of Gertrude Platt, who had been her secretary in Santa Barbara. This may have been a fulfillment of Laurel's intuition on that first night in Littleton that Diane had already left to work with Arleen. For Diane, the move to

Littleton was perhaps the means of breaking from her life with Bishop Pike in order to move forward with Arleen.

A Deep Recognition

After returning to California, Diane visited Arleen and Dick at their ocean front apartment in San Diego. She went to help celebrate Arleen's February birthday. The event was actually quite funny because Arleen had one glass of wine and promptly slept through the rest of the festivities while Dick and Diane enjoyed her birthday cake! Arleen was not much of a drinker.

During that February visit, Diane intuited that both Arleen and Dick were Jewish. This came as a surprise to Diane because Arleen had never mentioned it. The revelation led to many discussions and a flood of sharing about Jewish history by Diane, who had been steeped in that history through her preparation to write *The Wilderness Revolt*. The book was the project that occasioned Jim's death in the Judean desert in Israel. Diane and her brother Scott Kennedy had completed the book in 1971. It was published by Doubleday in 1972. Arleen had never really wanted to be identified as Jewish but was fascinated that Diane had so much to bring to the subject. Arleen had much to learn about her roots in Judaism.

And there, in that afternoon, came the fitting in of Kendra's prediction that Diane would be like a godmother to Arleen!

The next day we took a long walk by the ocean. As we stood on a pier looking down into the very lively waves, Diane said, "Look. The ocean is doing it." Arleen replied, "I know." With those few words Diane had confirmation that Arleen had already awakened. One of the results of awakening is the ability to register the meaning behind words as they are spoken or written. We call this frequency registration. In this case it was a recognition that the ocean, like all things in nature, manifests the perfection of the pattern set for it by the Source. An ocean "waves." That is what it does. This little exchange paved the way for us to open further to the rapidly moving energy currents that were whirling toward a new reality.

We shared with Dick the excitement of what was emerging in terms of the possibility of working together and how it all seemed much bigger than anything the two of us could be dreaming up.

The three of us looked at the practical side of the situation and wondered about finding a large apartment in San Diego that the three of us could share. We were all willing, but very soon it became clear that a much greater change was in process.

Endings and Beginnings

Dick Lorrance, Arleen's husband of eight years, was supportive of us as we explored a possible work. Initially the three of us thought we might share an apartment together. However, that was not to be. Arleen's marriage to Dick had begun with his creating a cocoon of love in which Arleen could grow into the self she was to become. The butterfly was about to leave the cocoon and fly free.

Following the heart disease in 1968 and Arleen's breakthrough to cosmic awareness in 1969, she moved away from sexual love-making. Her breakthrough had enveloped her in a constant high, a state much more exalted than what could arise from a physical orgasm. Dick still wanted sexual engaging; in fact, he wanted their old relationship the way it had been. The new that emerged for Arleen was unsatisfying and unfair to him.

In March 1972, Arleen went to Redding, California to do a presentation of the story of **The Love Project**. Diane picked her up there and we drove together toward San Diego. During that trip, Dick communicated to Arleen that he had begun a sexual relationship with another woman. While this was a surprise to Arleen, it seemed to fall into place as part of a new pattern that was taking form. Arleen told Diane she felt her marriage was ending.

As the marriage frayed, the burgeoning union with Diane was on the rise. On the way from Redding to San Diego we stopped in the Redwoods of Northern California where we had another of our numerous experiences of merging in light. Diane wanted to share an experience with Arleen of a "redwood cathedral" like she had experienced during her teen years of camping out. The circle of redwoods that remains after the mother tree falls away is majestic. The branches of the tall trees arch upward like a vaulted gothic tower and are as inspiring as a cathedral.

Diane led Arleen into such a redwood circle and we lay down on our backs, looking up into the arching branches. We began to sing together the Lord's Prayer. As we finished, Diane suddenly sat up, sensing at her right shoulder the presence or essence of Jesus. For Diane's entire childhood she had prayed every night that Jesus would come to "save" her. He had never appeared. When she had her breakthroughs to Cosmic Consciousness she felt she had received everything that had been promised to her in those early years, and more, even though Jesus did not appear in the experiences.

On that day in the redwood forest, Diane

sensed Jesus's presence/essence. She could sense him as a tender child and as a rugged young adult carpenter. Though Diane heard no inner voice, she registered a communication that it was time for her to go forth "two by two" with Arleen in order to live and express what she had come to know. Implicit in that was the awareness that she would not be associated directly with Jesus in this lifetime.

This represented a great shift for Diane who had been a devoted Christian and active church member all her life. The two of us received the experience as a kind of blessing on our work, and as it turned out, the fact that there were two of us was one of the unique aspects of our work together.

In April of 1972 we went to New York City where Diane had a number of speaking engagements. Arleen was along to watch her in action and to provide feedback. While in the city we continued our exploration of our history and how destiny seemed to be leading us to a work together. We had a synchronistic experience that was quite extraordinary.

Arleen told Diane that she wanted to take her to a church in the city that had been a meaningful "quiet space" for her when she made her theatrical rounds as a hopeful young actor. She had been introduced to the church through an assignment at the High School of Performing Arts in which she had been told to go someplace she had never been. Arleen had never been in a church of any kind and there was one right across the street on West 46th Street. She was amazed upon entering the building that all the sounds of the city disappeared and she was embraced by silence and a special kind of grandeur. Later, after Michael's untimely death, Arleen would light a candle for him whenever she went for quiet time between auditions.

Diane said she would be delighted to visit Arleen's church and that she wanted to take Arleen to the favorite church she and Jim had shared in the city. They loved the Church of St. Mary the Virgin because of its high Episcopal mass, its use of incense, and the choir that sang Bach's music. The church was a New York City landmark, built in 1894 of inspiring Gothic design.

Diane asked Arleen about the denomination of "her" church but Arleen had no idea. Having no religious background at all, it was just a church. We were excited to discover each other's meaningful site.

The morning of the excursion, Diane had an intuitive "hit" while showering that the church she and Jim loved was the very same church Arleen had taken as a sanctuary. You can only imagine how startling the coincidence would be, given the thousands of churches in New York City, if it turned out to be the very same one! We headed out and Diane's "hit" was confirmed when Arleen led them to West 46th Street and Saint Mary the Virgin Episcopal Church.

This was one of the long list of converging

points in our journey to find each other and begin a work together. Such synchronicities are impossible to explain but also impossible to dismiss.

When Diane was 12 years old, she felt and saw a stream of white light pour out of her heart center and knew that she would *live a life of service.*

When Arleen was 12 years old, she experienced the light for the first time in the pure energy of the angel that appeared in the doorway announcing that Arleen would find who she was looking for.

Years later, when Arleen first connected with Evelyn Nolt (who taught Arleen to *live a life of service*) she immediately sensed that this person represented something important she needed to know. When Diane boarded a bus and sat down beside Patricia Bradley, she knew immediately that Patricia had something she needed. A year later, when Patricia told Diane she wanted to share something with her, Diane knew immediately that this was what she had been waiting for.

Diane appeared in Arleen's paintings while we lived on separate coasts. Arleen had her spiritual breakthrough in September 1969 during the time Diane and Jim were lost in the Judean Desert. Arleen merged with a flower in nature in California while Diane communed with the life in the rocks she was climbing on in Israel.

When we started our spiritual studies we both had the experience of confronting esoteric material that was difficult to put into action because it was written in such obtuse language. For Diane, it was the writings of Vitvan and for Arleen, the books of Alice Bailey. Yet, we both knew equally and intuitively that great wisdom was being presented, wisdom that resonated as truth in each of our beings. Both of us went on to bring those esoteric teachings into practical form that could be fully embodied in the lives we were living.

We also both knew that the same teaching and spiritual principles have been brought in by seers throughout the ages and the language they use needs to be restated and updated in each generation so that it can be understood and applied in the current times. We each had been imprinted in energy by what we studied and we each knew that we would play a role in the updating and restating.

It was even clearer by the end of the week together in New York that the two of us had been drawn together energetically and it had just been a matter of time until we would meet.

Synchronicities, coincidences, and parallel occurrences all contributed to our meeting and beginning a work together. It is as if there is an energy web from which threads of connection extend and beckon. Sometimes there is follow-through on a thread and a linkup occurs. We feel that to be true in our case. One or the other of us might have broken the outreach of the threads. Then both of us might have gone in different directions and our lives would likely have unfolded in alternative ways. But, in our case, we each walked an unseen pathway in the web toward each other and our lives converged in a powerful way. The keys to the convergence are openness, listening, following inner guidance, staying true to self at every step, and being willing to upheaval the status quo of our current lives (**having no expectations but rather abundant expectancy**).

On the flight to Santa Barbara where we were to meet Dick and attend the wedding of our mutual friend Hal Conklin, Diane asked Arleen if she would share responsibility for the funds she had inherited upon Jim's death, sums that came to her from insurance policies. Arleen was not sure what that responsibility would be nor how much the funds amounted to, but she agreed to be co-steward as an act of trust between us.

When we arrived at the Santa Barbara wedding, as if swept by a gust of force over which she had no control, Arleen stood with Dick outside the home where the wedding was taking place and gave him back her wedding ring. They had both moved on from their union together and it was time to end it symbolically and actually.

Both of us were in the grips of an energy wave that was moving faster than either one of us could comprehend. But we were both willing to take the journey and commit to being of service.

We drove to San Diego to close the apartment Dick and Arleen had shared.

The Pain Caused by Endings

Arleen: While this time period was exciting and filled with promise, it was also very difficult for me, and for Dick as well. The love the two of us had shared had been so great that parting, even though the new was pounding on the door, was filled with grief.

I had met Dick just after Michael's death. I went to work at his agency for young adults to conduct their drama program. I was 21; Dick was 44. He was in his second marriage. It was a good marriage but, even with children, something had been missing for Dick. When I walked into his office he knew immediately that I was the love of his life; I was that certain someone he was connected with over past lifetimes. He didn't tell me, not for another four years. During those years, Dick served as a listening ear for me as I poured out my struggles and dreams. Once a week after work we would go for coffee and apple pie with melted cheese. He didn't share about his life much; he was serving more as a counselor-friend.

A few months before my 25th birthday several major changes were set in motion. I endured a dark time in my life. I wrote Part One of a long poem entitled "Just a moment, Just a taste." (The entire poem was published in my book *Buddha from Brooklyn*, LP Publications, 1975.) In it, I described being in an undercurrent of emotional pain. I wouldn't let others see the rawness inside. I desperately sought to be loved, to be held, but, ironically, I wouldn't let others in. This kept me from receiving the love that was coming toward me. I wrote the poem so that I could fully enter the agony I was creating for myself, to get the beneath the rubble of my life, and to drag myself through the "emotional muck."

On New Year's Eve, 1963, I stayed with an older woman actor friend whom I viewed as a mother figure. During our time together, I risked. I opened myself and revealed the inner scream that had tormented me for so many years of my life when I felt unbeautiful and unloved. I had never asked anyone to love me, to hold me. This night, I did. I was fully met by my friend, cradled and embraced, rocked by a mamma who sang "baby, baby" to me as she held my head close while I sobbed.

Moments such as this are life-changing. They enable the release of years of inner torture. When I left in the very early morning I experienced a long-sought freedom. I was a block from the United Nations building, which I took as a symbol of peace in my own life. On the way home to Brooklyn in a taxi, I saw my surroundings in a whole new way. I merged with the rising sunlight. I saw outer beauty because I had touched my inner beauty. I was at one with myself and with the world. I began writing Part Two of my long poem as the newly emerging being I had become. My life was filled with new promise. My cab driver

Endings and Beginnings

began to speak to me of his love affair with dawn. He was a beautiful soul. The two of us merged in that sharing in a celestial bond. When I left the cab, I noticed his first name on his license. It was Prophet.

I felt I had been given a sign. It was time for me to live in a new way. Change was occurring directly in front of me. It was time for new dimensions of consciousness. I had broken with patterns of misery and was ready to live in joy,

I called Dick and told him I needed to talk about what had happened. The next day he took me on a long drive to visit friends in Pleasantville, New York: artist Burne Hogarth and his wife Connie, a well-known peace activist. We talked the whole way up and the whole way back. The news that I related became the impetus for Dick to reveal the profound love he felt for me. I had always loved him but knew he was married and much older and I had never entertained the thought of our having a love relationship.

Everything changed after our talk that day and on April 13, 1964 we consummated our bond with eight hours of love-making. The rest of our relationship fell into place with the same rapidity as our marriage ended eight years later. Dick announced to his wife of 20 years that he was quitting his job and returning to his lifelong dream of being an actor. He left their home at the end of June for two months of summer stock in Michigan. He didn't tell her that I was going with him.

Dick and I always considered April 13 as our wedding date, even though it wasn't official for another two years. Our marriage was filled with love and I grew in leaps and bounds during that time. There were ups and downs, of course, but neither of us could have anticipated what was to happen after eight years when my life completely shifted as the new came charging in during the spring of 1972.

As I worked, with Diane's help, at closing up the apartment Dick and I had shared, I dealt with waves of grief and sadness over the ending of my marriage. Diane remarked that for a few months my complexion lost its vibrancy and was replaced by grey. It was not easy for me to engage in conversation with new people during that period. I needed time to experience loss and to withdraw into myself.

Finding Our Way to the New

After closing the apartment in San Diego, we drove north, first to Santa Barbara, spending time at the home of Diane's former secretary Gertrude Platt, and then on to San Jose to live at Diane's parents' house for a time while we continued our exploration and looked for a place in the Bay Area where we might share a residence.

While in San Jose, Diane suggested that Arleen write the story of **The Love Project** and a book by that name was eventually published (*The*

Love Project, LP Publications, 1972). The writing of the book helped Arleen to lift up out of grief because she was able to reconnect with the high frequencies in which she had lived during those seven months of **The Love Project** in Brooklyn. It was during our time in San Jose that Diane suggested that perhaps we should call our work **The Love Project**. That felt good to both of us.

Arleen suggested that San Diego might be a good place for us to live since it had a big airport and beautiful weather. At the beginning of August 1972, we drove south to look for an apartment that would suit our needs. As we left Los Angeles, Diane registered intuitively that a house was waiting for us in San Diego. She didn't want a house, but just as you can't "fight city hall," you can't argue with intuition.

When we arrived in San Diego, we checked into a hotel and began looking in the newspaper listings to see what was available to us. We each made selections that drew us and discovered we had both chosen the exact same realtor. By now we were not surprised by this. The thread of synchronicities was continuing. We made an appointment with the realtor who gathered from both of us detailed information about what we wanted in a home. The realtor took us to three locations in the morning, collected more data about preferences from us, and said she would pick us up after lunch and take us to three more sites.

At the last site in the afternoon of that first day of looking, the realtor took us to Point Loma Heights and drove to a street at the top of a hill. Below us, as we made our way down the hill on Orchard Avenue, was a grand vista of the Pacific Ocean. We immediately perked up. Three quarters of a block down the hill we stopped at a small house that had been built the year Arleen was born, 1939. The rooms were small, the living room had dark drapes and old dark carpeting, there were two bedrooms, one bath, and a small family room that been added on and could serve us as an office. Intuitively Diane knew immediately this was the house that was waiting for us. It had been on the market for two years. Once Arleen stepped out onto the back patio which overlooked the ocean, she was sold. The asking price was $39,500 but our offer of $37,500 was accepted. We bought the house on day one of looking.

Diane took out a small mortgage and the deal was done. To add to the perfection of the way things were unfolding, it turned out that the monthly payments on the mortgage were the exact amount of the widow's pension Diane was receiving from the Episcopal Church Pension Fund, $197. Diane laughed, saying, "Well, we may not have anything to eat, but at least we will have a roof over our heads."

We moved in at the beginning of September and left almost immediately for a trip to the Middle East led by Diane and her brother Scott. .

The Challenge of Roots and Differences

Because we were both awake in consciousness, we welcomed the opportunity that our spiritual union provided to refine our personality expressions so that we could be clearer channels for the higher frequencies of consciousness of which we had had substantial tastes. We had both experienced the oneness in which there are no separations, and we recognized that all personal and group values and preferences are limited and arbitrary and can be very divisive. We wanted to be able to express the unconditional love we knew to be fundamental to the universe, the basis for our oneness, the one binding force that held us all together and that we wanted to share with others.

We knew that our different backgrounds provided us with rich material for uncovering personality patterns that limited our expression of awakened consciousness. During our first year of living together we took advantage of many different experiences to explore our differences.

Our first opportunity was on a trip to Egypt, Jordan and Israel in September of 1972. Diane and her brother Scott Kennedy had organized this trip before the two of us met. Arleen had never traveled overseas and Diane suggested she go on this trip as a way to get to know Diane better and also as a way to experience her own Jewish roots.

Diane and Scott had worked with Bishop James A. Pike on a study of the historical Jesus for a couple of years before the Bishop's death in the Judean desert. They had made two trips to Israel as part of their research. On the first trip, they spent time with Israeli scholars and made visits to sites associated with the Biblical story of Jesus' life. On their way back to the United Sates, the three stopped in England to meet with scholars there who had researched the historical Jesus.

After Pike's death, Diane and Scott returned to Israel in 1970 and spent four months finishing the book Jim Pike had planned to write; it was published in 1972 under the title *The Wilderness Revolt*. During those four months Diane and Scott not only read extensively and traveled all over Israel, but they studied Hebrew briefly at the Hebrew University in Jerusalem and Scott spent a month on a kibbutz in the Negev.

The result was that Diane and Scott offered trips to Israel during which they shared their own understanding of Jesus' role in the history of Israel and took people touring to important historical sites. This led to something the two of us later incorporated into our work, called "Journeys Into Self." These were travel experiences to foreign cultures that included group meetings led by the two of us offering opportunities for personal growth.

Diane's mother and father also went on the September 1972 trip, so Diane had an opportunity to observe how they responded to Arleen while also experiencing her own reactions. Because Arleen was newly transplanted from New York, and because she grew up in a Brooklyn Jewish "ghetto" even though her family was not religious, Arleen's style of expression was very foreign to Diane's Midwestern protestant family patterns.

First of all, Arleen was "loud." It wasn't until later that Diane learned that nearly everyone who lived in New York City was "loud" because the city itself was so noisy you could hear each other only if you raised your voices. Diane on the other hand had grown up being encouraged to "tone it down" when she raised her voice in enthusiasm or laughter. The contrast in those two styles alone was startling.

In addition, Arleen was outspoken, saying whatever came into her mind no matter when or where or to whom. For example, the travel group was having lunch in the Valley of the Kings in Egypt. There were many other tourists in the restaurant as well as Egyptian guides and servers. Suddenly Arleen jumped up, flinging her arms in the air, and shouted, "Next week in Jerusalem!" Silence rang out in the large room. Scott and Diane wished they could disappear in the aftermath of what they felt was a provocative and probably offensive shout-out because relations between Jews and Arabs, or in this case Jews and Egyptians, were tense. Arleen, meanwhile, was not aware that she had committed what many considered a social and/or political affront.

Later Diane tried to explain to Arleen why she and others were upset by her outburst. Arleen thought her new WASP (White Anglo Saxon Protestant) friends were overly sensitive. She found it hard to relate to people who rarely if ever expressed their feelings or shared spontaneously. They were more foreign to her than the foreigners she encountered in the Middle East. It seemed to Arleen that Diane's people and church friends were contained, unreal, robotically polite, and too purposely soft-spoken. If she had been in Brooklyn she would have described them as terribly constipated on many levels. Arleen never thought of her loud pronouncements or expressions of feelings as outbursts. "Her people" were "out there" all the time.

In another incident on the trip Arleen announced she was going to give a gift to our tour guide, a 1967 Palestinian refugee. It was the night before the group was to cross the Allenby Bridge into Israel, a land where for the first time in Arleen's life she would experience what it was like to be in a religious majority. She told the group of eight having dinner together that she was going to tell Jacques that she loved him, saw him as beautiful, and wished him a speedy return to his home. As a Jew by birth (even though not practicing) it made it all the more important to her to let him know that it was possible for a Jew to love an Arab. The reactions at the table to this news included fear of being killed or detained in Jordan for traveling with a Jew, to annoyance that she was showing off her Jewishness, to accusations that she was not caring about others in the group. It was deemed inappropriate for Arleen to tell Jacques that the two of them were "one" and Arleen was criticized for not conforming to the style of behavior of the group.

Arleen chose to disregard those reactions. Instead of allowing those reactions to affect her she looked at what was important to her. She saw that to react out of fear was to function from an immobilized place which produced irrational thoughts. She did not accept that there was a group style of behavior that was the acceptable way. Arleen was also told she was being too sensitive about being a Jew. It was *telling* for Arleen that a member of a majority group, a white Anglo-Saxon Protestant, was informing a member of a minority group, a Jew, that she was being too sensitive.

Arleen saw that she had an opportunity to build a bridge between Jew and Palestinian. She was **being the change she wanted to see happen** and it was important for her to follow through. The next morning she delivered her gift to Jacques. It was received by him with joyful tears and a warm grasping of hands. It was an exchange of international understanding, and of love energy. Arleen was glad she had not passed up the opportunity, and those who had been frightened by the possibility of the exchange were relieved. For Arleen, it represented the meaning of visiting the "holy" land.

There were other elements that the group found disturbing. Arleen had little regard for religion of any kind, so when the group visited Bethlehem and the Christian shrines there, Arleen made fun of the whole scene. She didn't mean to be rude but rather she saw herself as pointing out fanciful beliefs. Many Christians in the group were offended by her remarks, including Diane's parents, and Diane herself found she was hurt by Arleen's disrespect for believers and for Jesus for whom Diane still felt a deep love that went all the way back to her childhood.

Arleen had not had exposure to religious systems and thought the idea of a savior made little sense, whether Christians had one or Jews were still waiting for one. She saw religion as inventing things to sustain their institutions. She had no patience for the rules and regulations of Judaism, for religious rituals, and for the wishful practice of prayer. She thought the Jewish custom of seeking forgiveness on Yom Kippur by fasting was ridiculous because those same Jews would go forth the next day and begin committing sinful acts all over again. She saw religions as hypocritical. Believers used passages from the Bible to justify their positions, but they simultaneously left out huge sections that were outdated in today's world. Arleen actually had an aversion to religion, viewing it as the most divisive force in human interaction. She didn't have to let her views be known during the trip but they tumbled loudly from her anyway because she didn't have much experience in restraining herself, nor did she view restraint as a value. She saw restraint as a suppression of self and of expression.

These and other incidents during the two week trip were occasions for us to explore our feelings, beliefs, reactions, and patterns of behavior. It was not until late in the trip that Arleen had a chance to experience how "loud" New York Jews were. A group from New York was staying in the same hotel as our group in Beer Sheba and in the evening after our group was ready to go to bed, members of the New York group were out in the hallway "talking" at the volume level they were accustomed to in New York. Arleen heard them (you couldn't help but hear them) and said to Diane, "I see what you mean." This was one of the first times in her life she had heard how others might be hearing her.

On another trip to New York City, Arleen took Diane to meet her family in Brooklyn. By then Arleen had told Diane about her upbringing and had described her parents, Rose and Irving Udoff. However, Diane still experienced a kind of culture shock. For example, we sat down to have lunch in her parents' apartment. Because Diane was the guest, the plates were passed to her first. She took bread and then put a slice of each kind of meat on her bread. (Diane had not announced that she was a vegetarian out of her pattern of being a "gracious guest.") However, Irving stood up and said in a loud voice, "You call that a sandwich???? I'll show you a sandwich!" He then stabbed his fork into the meat and piled it high on Diane's bread. Then with great satisfaction he sat down and said, "I don't want my neighbors to think we didn't feed you!" Diane dutifully ate her enormous meat sandwich without a comment, and later we had an opportunity to explore this difference in family patterns and styles.

One time we were invited to do a workshop in the home of a Jewish woman in Los Angeles. She invited many of her friends for the daylong workshop, and at the lunch break she took Arleen aside and told her that her friends were very uncomfortable with Diane. She said they felt they couldn't trust her because she was so soft-spoken and unexpressive. We laughed about it together later because it was the opposite and balancing response to the people from Diane's culture who found Arleen's style offensively loud.

We once went to see a play on Broadway about the relational life of an Italian family. The family members were loud, noisy, bossy, and blaming. It was funny to watch them interact and we immediately agreed that the New York Italians could easily have been Jewish New Yorkers. The play was a comedy and everyone in the audience laughed at the abusive family antics. However, when this behavior occurs at your own family table, it is a very different story. Diane said she found the play believable only because she had sat at table with Arleen's family.

These are only a few examples of many, many experiences that stretched the two of us out of our comfort zones and caused us to look at engrained personality patterns that "lived us" rather than our consciously choosing to live through them. We responded to all these occasions as **problems that were opportunities** for our own growth into greater consciousness and greater responsibility for **creating our own realities consciously.**

Diane's rather large extended family found Arleen difficult to integrate into their patterns, and they did not always make her feel welcome. Diane had to struggle with wanting to remain a part of the family but not wanting to perpetuate the unconscious patterns. She urged Arleen to continue to be herself in their presence and she hoped that her family would manage to **receive Arleen as beautiful exactly as she was.** In fact that did occur, but it took about twenty years and many difficult encounters for Arleen to be fully integrated into the family. Late in this process Diane's sister finally confessed that she had been deeply offended the first time we visited in her home because Arleen sat on her coffee table, something she had forbidden her young girls to do. Of course, in keeping with the Kennedy style, she did not ask Arleen to get off the table nor did she express her feelings until years later.

In addition to personality and upbringing differences, there were great discrepancies in our early lives and in the opportunities that were afforded us.

Arleen's youth was spent playing games on city concrete. There was nothing soft in her environment. In spite of the book about the tree that grew in Brooklyn, it hadn't grown on Arleen's street. There was nothing green. There were no birds. In fact, there was very little sky. Only a thin patch of it was visible over the apartment houses across the street. Her only personal outdoors was her fire escape.

Arleen would often sit at the window of her parents' bedroom and look up at the small bit of sky. She hoped that one day she would get to travel to other places in the world. Little did she know that her work with Diane would take her to over 88 countries. Millions of people lived in Arleen's home city and the noise and bustle was endless. Arleen saw her dad only on Sunday because he worked six days a week, during the day as a cutter in the garment industry and in the evenings and on Saturday as a shoe salesman. Her mother stayed at home and literally ruled the family. She berated Irving, saying she had to be mother/father/nurse, etc. In truth, she loved being in a dominant position. Rose's two older sisters also dominated their husbands. When the relatives would gather in Rose and Irving's apartment there were unending arguments, sometimes even hair-pulling matches. This was no happy family.

Arleen's family lived in a small walk-up apartment with a kitchen, living room, two bedrooms, one of which was very small, and one bath for the family of five. She and her older sister and younger brother shared the very small bedroom. Arleen's desk was a board on the back of the closet door that could be raised and lowered. Arleen was very creative but her expressions needed to be miniature because there was simply no space into which to expand.

Diane grew up in a farming community, Newman Grove, Nebraska, in a large home surrounded by trees, grass, and flowers. Diane's father was a well-known and successful businessman and her mother was very active in church and organizations around town. The population was 1,000 and most everyone knew everyone. It was perfectly safe for children to go outside to play and not to return until meal time. Diane and her best friend Jody walked a country mile to Jody's farm and rode Jody's horse. Diane's grandfather also had a farm and Diane went with him to milk the cows and feed the pigs. One of Diane's uncles had a farm so Diane got to play with her cousins in a totally rural environment.

In town, Diane could walk two blocks to the

community pool in the summer and go sledding down hills in the winter. Diane's family sat down together for three meals each day, though sometimes her dad would be called away from the table for an emergency at his filling station. Family time was very important. In addition, both of Diane's parents came from families of six children and large extended family gatherings were frequent. Diane enjoyed relationships with grandparents, aunts and uncles, and cousins. It was an idyllic childhood that Diane wouldn't trade for anything. Her childhood was happy and carefree.

On one of our explorations of our roots, Diane took Arleen to the town in which she spent her childhood. Arleen could hardly believe what she saw. Diane had grown up in "the country." That's what city kids called these wide-open spaces that were so lush and green. The corn was as high as that elephant's eye, actually growing in the ground. Arleen had always thought that food had its origin in the grocery store on the corner.

Diane told Arleen she would take her on a tour of Newman Grove. Arleen was puzzled when she saw that they were going to walk. Her image of a downtown required a bus or subway journey. They arrived downtown in about five minutes. Arleen discovered that the supposed downtown area was two blocks long with a few essential public places. Two blocks long and five minutes from anyone's home! This was mind blowing to Arleen.

The two of us went to visit Jody on her farm

near Lincoln, Nebraska. It was one of our most amusing experiences. We walked around the barnyard and Arleen kept stepping on mushy things that oozed up around the soles of her shoes. Diane had not bothered to warn her that there were all kinds of animal droppings everywhere. They looked like rocks or pebbles to Arleen. It was messy.

Soon we came to a pen with little pink piglets. They were adorable. Arleen wanted to hold one. She put its bottom in the palm of one hand and patted its head with the other. Before very long, the hand holding the pig's bottom was filled with something warm, moist, and squishy. Arleen shouted, "Oh no, look what it did!" Diane said simply, "Well you were petting its head. It was obviously very moved!"

Diane's Nebraska relatives were earthy, good people. Arleen found them very easy to relate to. They seemed to like her as well. Arleen enjoyed the big spread at their patio table until the sky began to darken and thunder and lightning struck. Arleen almost jumped out of her skin and fled into the house. The family had a good laugh about the frightened city kid. They simply remained at the table and went on eating.

We planned a special treat for Arleen's New York parents for their 50th wedding anniversary. We flew them out to San Francisco and picked them up there to give them a tour of a lifetime. When we took them to have dinner at Diane's parents' home in San Jose, Rose could not get over how large their home was. She walked down the halls counting the doors (to rooms and closets).

Then began the theme of the trip as far as Diane was concerned. Whenever Rose saw something she admired she would ask, "How much did that cost?" That went on for days until Diane thought she couldn't stand it. Diane had never paid much attention to how much things cost. She began to recognize that pattern in her as a sign that she had never had to count her pennies and had been blessed to live in abundance.

Arleen, on the other hand, grew up knowing that she had to bargain for everything to get the lowest possible price. Both her parents were champions at the art of bargaining. The pattern was so strong that Arleen used to agonize if she felt she had paid too much for something. That kind of suffering went on for many years.

Traveling in foreign countries was always a learning experience and a young man in Srinagar (in Northern India) taught Arleen something about bargaining that helped to make a dent in her pattern. He brought his case of lacquered goods to our hotel and laid out his wares. We made numerous selections. Diane knew from her many trips that salesmen enjoyed the ritual of negotiating on price and she settled for a cost that made both of them happy.

Alas, Arleen's hard bargaining style kicked in. She kept demanding that the young man take his price down. He accommodated as long as he could. Finally, Arleen got up and demanded her final offer be accepted or she was leaving. In a soft and pained voice, the salesman looked directly into her eyes and said poignantly, "Madame, you have to give me *something*." It was immediately clear that the price Arleen had suggested would leave him with no profit whatsoever. She looked into his face and saw how poor he was compared to her Western wealth. If she could have melted into a puddle she would have. Instead, she sat back down and asked him what he would consider fair. She met his price and the two of them had tears in their eyes as they closed the deal. She has never forgotten him or the lesson she learned.

Bargaining was a skill that was highly valued in Arleen's family because it was also rooted in the family's financial status. Every dollar her father brought home was hard earned and it was important to be able to pay less rather than more for goods and services. Both her parents had been severely affected by the Great Depression and it left a deep imprint. It wasn't that Arleen lived in "poverty consciousness" but she certainly did not have Diane's orientation of living in abundance.

Diane's approach to money was so alien to Arleen that Arleen felt she was visiting a foreign country whenever the two of them discussed finances. Diane served as a great teacher to Arleen in this area. Diane lived in "the Universal Flow." She had a sincere knowing that whatever was needed by way of dollars would "appear" if it was in harmony to proceed with an endeavor. Arleen tended to worry instead. Time and again over our decades together, what was needed did in fact appear. It was as if Diane had one of those mythical oil lamps that you rub and the genie appears to inquire of your wishes. The money that was needed usually appeared precisely when it was required, not weeks in advance as Arleen might have preferred as a cushion against disaster. (Arleen tended to be dramatic about finances.)

A fine example of this occurred when we ordered a fancy new IBM Selectric typewriter to help with publishing in our office. On the very day it was to arrive, a check came in the mail from a friend to whom Diane had lent money years before. Diane had forgotten all about it because it was and is her practice when she lends money to think of it as a gift and to let go of it. Another foreign concept to Arleen. The check arrived in the morning. It just happened to be the exact amount needed to cover the IBM which was delivered that afternoon and for which we wrote a check knowing it would clear when we deposited the check that had come that morning. It would seem like a fluke if this had happened only that one time, but it happened many times during our years together.

Arleen has learned to trust, to give charitable gifts, to ease up on financial concerns, and to know that all will be well, not necessarily because needed money will be there but because each of us has the inner strength to meet any circumstance.

Arleen still takes a few steps back into concern when the stock market falls, but Diane views it as part of the ups and downs of life. She reminds Arleen that a big loss is only a loss on paper because we didn't have that cash in hand. Since we don't need to spend it now, it is likely that there will be a paper gain soon, and what is needed will be there when the time comes.

Arleen is a lot better than she used to be about finances, but she still retains the observation that Diane lives in some kind of magical realm of abundance. One of the practices Diane taught Arleen that was completely foreign to her was tithing. Diane had learned from the time she was a child to make donations to the church. Then as a teenager she was taught the concept of tithing 10% of her earnings. From her small earnings from babysitting she would give away 10% as an expression of her gratitude and her confidence that she would always have enough for her own needs.

Diane explained the practice to Arleen and urged her to try it. She told Arleen that to give away 10%, no matter how little you have, makes you feel you live in abundance. Arleen began to tentatively practice tithing to nonprofit organizations and found that it did indeed change her feeling about her state of well-being.

Because Arleen was so insecure about finances, Diane suggested that she manage the investment of our mutual funds. Arleen accepted the challenge and responsibility and invited a friend who had inherited money and who had studied how to manage it to teach her what he had learned. He passed on suggestions to her. Over the last four decades Arleen has done very well investing our resources and it has been good practice for her.

When we got together, Diane gave Arleen's "Little Self" a gift of $2,500 in case she wanted to finish her doctoral degree if our work together didn't materialize as we hoped it would. Arleen invested the money and was very proud over the years to multiply it 100 times. This was a definite confidence builder.

Another difference in family patterns was that Diane's extended family maintained strong ties; communication was important among cousins as well as siblings, and frequent family reunions were a given. In Arleen's family, the pattern was the reverse. Siblings had disagreements and severed relationships; cousins communicated only when it was convenient. As a consequence, family did not get together except on the rare occasion of a special event like Arleen's mother's 99th birthday or a funeral.

Diane not only brought Arleen to her family gatherings and reunions but she encouraged her to stay in close contact with her own family. The two of us visited Arleen's parents at least twice a year while they were still in New York and when they moved to Florida we went once a year.

These visits to family uncovered another difference in family patterns. The first time the two of us stayed with Arleen's parents in their Brooklyn apartment, we slept on the fold-out sofa bed in the living room since there was no guest room. There was only one bathroom and there was no privacy at all. Diane was beginning to undress when Rose burst into the living room talking at the top of her voice. (Diane would have called it shouting.) Diane quickly pulled a robe around her, startled at the intrusion, but Arleen and Rose didn't seem to notice.

A few days later Diane asked if there was a near-by Laundromat where she could do some laundry. Irving quickly volunteered to walk the block and a half with her, which Diane insisted was not necessary. However, she graciously accepted his offer to carry her laundry. Then Rose urged forcefully, "*Diane,* put on your jacket so you don't catch cold!" It was August in New York City, hot and humid, so Diane said, "I don't need it." Rose insisted. Finally, in order to get out the door, Diane grabbed her jacket and left.

When Irving and Diane exited the apartment building on the ground floor, a voice rang out from above them: *"DIANE! Put on your jacket!"* Diane looked up and there was Rose, hanging out the window, shouting to her.

Diane was not used to this kind of overbearing control and told Arleen if she had grown up in that household she would have run away at an early age! Diane was used to parents who respected her privacy and trusted her decisions.

One time the two of us joined Diane's family at a cabin at Lake Tahoe for one of their frequent family reunions. It was an A-frame cabin, a completely open space, and the entire family was going to sleep in the same cabin. Arleen said, "What if I want to be alone?" Diane responded, "No one will bother you." Arleen could not conceive of such a thing.

On the second day, Arleen decided to take a nap. Several members of the family were gathered together playing table games, others were in the kitchen preparing the evening meal, children were running in and out, shouting and laughing, and one of Diane's brothers was sitting in the overstuffed chair reading a book to his small child. Arleen stretched out on the couch which was in the midst of everything and went fast asleep. She never got over the fact that not one person interrupted her rest, not even once.

As a result of this difference in upbringings, Arleen had learned to protect her space and her privacy at all costs and Diane was willing to share her space openly with all comers. This led to a conflict on one of the first weekends of our shared life together. A close friend of Diane's arrived unannounced with three others who were traveling with her from Florida to California. Because Pat knew Diane well, she did not hesitate to say, "Can we roll out our sleeping bags in your living room for the night?" And Diane said, "Of course."

Arleen hardly knew what to do with such an intrusion on "her" personal space. That she was upset was immediately apparent to everyone since she was not used to "hiding" her feelings. Pat and her friends left early the next morning, aware that Arleen was very uncomfortable with their presence.

The two of us had an opportunity after they left to talk at length about hospitality and the entertaining of friends and family. It was an issue that never got completely resolved no matter how many times we readdressed it over the years. Early experiences of the lack of privacy had left a deep imprint on Arleen's psyche and though she was able to modify her pattern of self-protection, she never came to enjoy entertaining guests the way Diane did. At least Arleen learned to tolerate it for short periods of time.

Arleen's pattern did not apply only to people Diane wanted to invite. When Arleen's parents came out to San Diego, Arleen found a way to have them stay with friends of ours rather than in our home which was, admittedly, very small. Arleen had a deeply imbedded memory of what it was like to have her mother, especially, invade and take over. Her parents fought a lot of the time. Arleen didn't want their interactions reintroduced into her life.

When we visited Arleen's parents in their condo in Florida, we were often inundated by shouting and arguments between Rose and Irving. One year, toward the end of Irving's life, the fighting got so bad it could be heard all around the complex. We calmly told her parents that we would stay in a hotel if the brouhaha continued.

Years later when Rose came to visit us in Scottsdale, Arleen made a point of telling her that our home is a place of quiet, happiness, and harmony. She said that if Rose wanted to stay with us she was not to bring any negativity along with her. To our amazement, Rose came and was all sweetness and light during her stay! She fit right into the reality that we had created in our home.

The result of uncovering these and many other differences in our roots and family patterns was that we both grew in consciousness and made major changes in our personality expressions. Some of those changes did not please others. Diane's older brother once told her he liked her better when she was "nice," which she knew meant when she conformed to family patterns rather than "making waves" with changes. Arleen on the other hand developed a loving and supportive relationship with her older sister, staying in close communication by telephone and through yearly visits. This broke her family patterns in a way that was valued by her sister and brother-in-law as well as by us.

All of these experiences and many, many more have made us aware of how deep the patterns of early childhood are in all of us and how much conscious jurisdiction is needed to change those patterns. Our work over the years involved sharing with others the techniques we have learned for staying conscious and making choices about how to interact with others. One of our Practice Sessions, The Joy of Roots and Differences, grew out of our own work with our early-upbringing differences. We guided others to new perspectives and to better relations with others in their lives with whom they were sometimes irritated.

The Love Principles have been our constant companions over these years. Each of us has felt committed to the embodiment of the principles as a way of refining our personalities so that we could be more perfect vehicles for the expression of unconditional love. Each of us has worked within to find ways to **create new realities** with regard to old patterned responses, to welcome every **problem as an opportunity** for personal growth by **being the change we want to see happen** rather than trying to change the other. We have learned to **provide each other with opportunities to give** by opening to different perceptions, different modes of behavior, different preferences and different interpersonal skills. We have chosen to live together, and individually, in **abundant expectancy, rather than having specific expectations** of each other. And above all, we have **received each other as beautiful** in all our differences.

Looking at the difficulties involved in two persons from very different backgrounds adjusting to one another, it is easy to see how difficult it is for nations with serious differences of history and ways of being to negotiate peaceful co-existence with one another. There must be equal willingness to expand beyond the customary way of functioning in order to arrive at a blend or a middle way, not just between adversaries but between those who seek to maintain their cherished individuality and, at the same, open of a door of welcome to values and behavior that is foreign, and therefore potentially threatening.

Conflicts and wars on the international level are continuous and often very destructive. It is a wonder the human race hasn't wiped itself out. Nations, family members, couples, and friends would all benefit from living **The Love Principles**: viewing their differences and ***problems as opportunities***, ***receiving each other as beautiful exactly as they are*** and thus being served by their uniqueness, and ***being the change they want to see happen*** rather than demanding that the opposition convert to their way of being. Too often humans forget to provide those different from themselves with the ***opportunity to give*** from those differences. This would enable something larger than each of the participants to emerge. If humans had ***no expectations*** about the results of interactive explorations, they could more easily ***create new reali-***

ties that would serve and benefit the whole.

We did all of this with each other, and continue to do so; it has made all the positive difference possible in stretching the two of us to become more flexible and inclusive than we ever previously knew ourselves to be. It has also enabled us to welcome people from all kinds of backgrounds into our Love Family and to **receive them as beautiful exactly as they are.** Spiritual support is based on recognizing the Real Self (essence or spirit) in each other without getting hung up on or reacting to differences in personality styles. None of us is alone if we relate as spiritual beings.

Shared Values

There were values we shared in common that made it easier for us to live together in harmony. We both chose to live lives of unconditional love, i.e. to function in and the through the heart center with unblocked, free-flowing life force and love energy. We knew this to be a way to say yes to life and to everything it brought. It opened the door to never-ending growth and to uniting in spiritual oneness.

Saying yes, even to unwanted circumstances, enables us to stretch to handle more than we thought we could. Saying yes moves us beyond our preferences and our fixed (often stuck) ways of living. Saying yes is to receive all of life as a blessing as we discover what more is opening to us, what more is wanted of us. It far easier to say yes than to say no, to shut down, to fight what is coming, and to create distress. To respond in these ways creates problems which then have to be worked through. That takes much more energy and it takes much longer than saying yes at the outset and drawing on inner resources to open to and become the more.

The six **Love Principles** that Arleen originated at the high school in Brooklyn in 1970, and that Diane affirmed when Arleen first shared them with her, formed the primary values and the foundation of our relationship and our work together. **The Love Principles** were a way of life, a path of unfoldment, a vehicle for getting to know oneself as spirit, and a means of making love work in everyday life.

The Love Principle *Receive All People as Beautiful Exactly as They Are* was fundamental to how we conducted ourselves. It is what facilitated our practice of unconditional love.

The principle took us beyond the limits of our own private worlds of opinions and preferences. It enabled us to embrace all people for who they are and the contributions they are making through their uniqueness, and to welcome everything because it is an equal part of the whole.

It encouraged us to always move beyond feelings (likes and dislikes, emotional responses, wants and needs) and thoughts (judgments and opinions) about others and how they "should be" and what they "must do."

We knew that the only way to live this principle was to *want* to live it. There could be no "buts" because those emerged from private world feelings and judgments. We valued receiving people into our unrestricted energy fields and into our consciousness, acknowledging who they are and the gifts they have to bring us, even as they may differ greatly in their expression and ways of being.

We valued living as if we were countries with no borders and no immigration laws, but rather an open and easy flow of all aspects of humanity that would merge into one being.

We knew that by **receiving all people as beautiful exactly as they are** we would expand our selves and become more alive than if we lived in our own comfortable shells.

We also valued **receiving ourselves as beautiful exactly as we are**, loving ourselves so that we might more easily love others. Living this way evokes ongoing joy.

The Love Principle *Problems Are Opportunities* was always in the forefront of our consciousness. No matter what confronted us, we both received it as a gift, even if we couldn't immediately see what that gift was. What we knew was that every problem *is* an opportunity. A problem stops us or interferes with our lives in some way. It bothers us, or annoys, or is irritating. When this occurs, the opportunity is that we are being stimulated out of complacency and nudged into the awareness that something more is calling. Problems cause us to regroup, to reassess. Once the energy begins to move, the problem can be seen as the opportunity it really is.

Early in our work together, we were contacted by a friend about something called the "Circle of Gold." It was a way for people to "receive" a lot of money by first giving to others. It was highly organized and seemed like a good idea. We not only participated but we encouraged several of our friends and volunteers to join in. Many of them made a nice profit on the money they invested by giving, but those who made money were the ones who got in on the Circle early. Those who came later, lost money.

It turned out to be a pyramid scheme, but we had not known that. We had never even heard the term before. We were not happy that we had participated and led others into the endeavor even though our intentions were good.

We talked about the experience at length and, knowing that ***problems are opportunities***, looked to see how we could avoid such an error in the future. We realized that we had been too quick to enter into the Circle of Gold; we didn't ask enough questions. We agreed that in the future we would be more circumspect.

That experience led to the adoption of another new value, namely, that if one of us thought something was a good idea but the other had a *serious* question about it, we would both yield to the one who had the question. It didn't even matter if it seemed like a great thing. If it was not equally in harmony for both of us, we would let it go. We have lived by that agreement ever since.

There were two of us, not one, and we recognized there was great benefit in honoring the feelings, the intuition, the knowing, of both. A dual perspective is greater than one person's determination. By living this way, we have eliminated question marks from our choices. It isn't that we became the same but rather that we used our differences as a guide.

We had been sent forth two-by-two and this was an important aspect of that union. The value has served us in our work over four decades in terms of what and how we would teach, whether we would continue with a given approach or focus, where we would live, when we would make new choices, etc.

We both sought to live meaningful lives and to imprint our world in positive ways. That was the work we wanted to do together. We could each see problems around us everywhere and since we knew they were opportunities, we each fully embodied **The Love Principle** *Be the Change You Want to See Happen, Instead of Trying to Change Anyone Else.*

This principle had been a major force during **The Love Project** at Thomas Jefferson H.S. in 1970. The school had been at a crossroads as anger raged in all directions. It was the harnessing of the energy of that anger that helped to enable great change to occur. It seemed such a simple way to function: if you see something you would like to have as a reality, bring it into being *yourself* rather than looking for others to do it or complaining that they are not doing it.

When the two of us joined forces, Arleen knew she and Diane had a work to do together. She wanted to see that happen even though she didn't yet know what it was. Diane was open and willing. Arleen might have waited until she had a clear vision and could come to Diane and say, "Here, this is what we are to do." She could have waited a long time because it couldn't come only from her. She chose to **be the change she wanted to see happen** and did it by saying out loud, simply and clearly, "We have a work to do together." That opened the door, set energy in motion, invited Diane's participation, and told the universe that the two of us were ready.

A big value we shared from the very beginning, a value that continues through every single day, is the expression of laughter. We both laugh heartily, with gusto, at the smallest provocation. Once we get started, we add a repartee that perpetuates the laugh and expands it in all directions. Sometimes the subject can go on for quite a while, evoking more and more laughter.

When this happens, it becomes part of a life-laugh-file-cabinet that can be referred to at any time to set that same laughter in motion all over again.

Diane (left) and **Arleen** at home, laughing in 2011.

One day while living in San Diego, the newly married neighbors in the house above us on the hill knocked at our door. They wanted to know if we told each other jokes all day because they couldn't believe how much and how robustly we laughed all the time. We responded, "No, we don't tell each other jokes, but we do find humor in just about everything."

Alas, those neighbors didn't laugh nearly enough, fought often, and divorced after a few years.

Laughter and the awakening of humor grow out of living life **having no expectations** but opening to every moment with **abundant expectancy**. We didn't ever want to be limited by any expectation we held because we knew that expectations could lock us into restricted views of what was to come. If we clung to expectations we couldn't be open to the unthought of, the surprises that life had to offer.

We knew that living in **abundant expectancy** was like sitting on the edge of our seats, ready to leap up into the new that would stretch us, usually intrigue us, and take us into possibilities beyond our mental conceptions.

Having no expectations makes life like attending a comedy in the theatre. You know something is coming but you don't know what. The more unexpected it is, the funnier it is.

Having no expectations is a great way to be jolted out of the ordinary in which we are comfortable and into the extraordinary. Of course, when the unexpected comes we need to be ready to meet it, to align with it, to be lifted by it, just as when we attend a comedy we need to be ready to laugh and roll with the humor so that we can be amused and entertained.

We love going to the theatre, especially to see comedies where we can express our delight at the unexpected. We began to notice that when there were other seats available, people sitting in front of us would sometimes get up and move because they were annoyed by our laughter. We were befuddled by this. If the play is a comedy, it is meant to evoke more than partial smiles.

The same thing would sometimes happen in the movies. People would turn around and stare at us rather than laughing themselves at the antics on the screen.

We valued laughter too much to diminish our responses. We truly delighted in the times when we were with audiences filled with people with senses of humor. At a San Diego showing of *Victor/Victoria* the whole audience went absolutely wild--together. It was such a great experience that the memory that lingered was not about what happened on the screen but about the rollicking camaraderie of those gathered together.

A similar experience occurred in a London

theatre when the curtain descended momentarily for a scene change in *Round and Round the Garden*. We and many others laughed loudly at the unexpected events at the end of the scene. The laughter subsided, but within seconds, as everyone revisited the moment in their minds, it picked up again, moving through the audience like a rollicking wave. This happened several times until the entire audience was roaring with contagious laughter. The stage manager tried several times to bring up the curtain for the next scene but had to drop it down again because the audience was hysterical. Finally, the laughter died down and seemed to be holding. At that moment, both of us convulsed again and the audience took off like a runaway horse. After a long time, the company was able to go on with the show, but those of us in the audience will never forget the delightful experience.

Diane recalls having a like experience in New York long before she met Arleen. She and a date were watching *The Two Gentlemen of Verona*. At the end of a very funny bit by the two "men," the audience went wild with laughter. The laughter went on so long that finally the cast on the stage broke out of character to applaud the audience who in turn rose to give a standing ovation to the cast. Then, the play went on. Such moments are unforgettable and are tributes to laughter as a way of experiencing oneness with a group of strangers.

Over the years, we have had many opportunities to laugh at ourselves. In 2008 Diane had hip surgery. Arleen brought her home from the hospital in Diane's Toyota Camry. After getting Diane settled at home, Arleen went out in her Toyota Solara to fill a script at the pharmacy and pick up a pizza for dinner.

Arleen remembers the unusual experience. "With hot pizza in hand, I discovered the key would not turn in the ignition. I tried everything, but no luck. A man in a large SUV pulled up and asked if I needed help. He volunteered to try the key. No luck.

"I called home with my tale of woe. Diane asked if I had the right keys; a strange question because I had already made two stops with the Solara before this. I looked at the keys at her suggestion and discovered they were her keys to the Camry, not mine for the Solara. I was perplexed.

"Mr. SUV returned to his vehicle at this point. I asked him if he could drive me the three blocks to my home to get the right set of keys. He agreed and I called to Diane to say I was now getting into an SUV with a strange man but not to worry.

"On the way, I puzzled over how I could have used those wrong keys twice before. Can Toyota keys work in different cars sometimes? I knew that couldn't be right. But then, why did they work twice and not the third time? I simply couldn't figure it out.

"I shifted in my seat and felt something poking my left hip. It was another set of keys (!), mine, for the Solara. I had had Diane's keys in my right pocket from the Camry trip from the hospital!

"I told my driver, with much chagrin. He asked if I was sure those were the keys to my Solara. I shook them and showed him the various medals of Saints, saying, 'Yes, these are mine.'

"He said, 'And now, you also have St. Stephen sitting beside you!' Stephen then drove me back to my car chuckling, "You know this could be the onset of Alzheimer's.' We both laughed. But he added kindly, 'You have a lot on your mind today.'"

While this was a very humorous event, it was also poignant because it spoke of being able to trust a stranger and of the caring and concern of someone willing to go out of his way to help another.

It was an example of another value that we shared through **The Love Principle *Provide Others with Opportunities to Give.***

Arleen needed help and by fully receiving this stranger Stephen as someone with whom she was one, she could move past her mind which might have told her that you don't, under any circumstances, get into a vehicle with someone you don't know because anything could happen and it probably wouldn't be good. Instead, Arleen reached out and provided Stephen with the opportunity to help; and help he did.

It has been our experience that people everywhere want to serve, want to give, want to help, want to participate. They need only to be asked and when they are, they themselves feel they been given *to* because someone thought enough of them to ask. Human beings want and need to be needed. The two of us knew this very well. Our sense of self-worth comes from the feeling that we have something to give, that we can give it, and that it is received, recognized, and appreciated by others.

Our workshops, classes, and travel experiences have always been full of laughter. Many people tell us that our laughs are infectious, and we know from reading many studies that laughter is very good for our physical, emotional and mental health. Laughter also helps enormously to keep things in proper perspective and to keep us from taking ourselves too seriously. We have found it is difficult to laugh when we are too identified with our personalities in a given moment or when we are clinging to an opinion or belief about something. Laughter helps us to not take things personally and to keep energy flowing and moving.

The front door of our home in San Diego was often the site of encounters that evoked laughter. A survey-taker rapped on the door and asked Arleen about her occupation. She told him she was a spreader of love and joy. He recorded this as "N.O.," for "no occupation." It would appear that persons who are out of sync with established categories simply do not exist in the eyes of bureaucracy. He came, he talked with N.O. (no one) and he left.

Or, people fit what they see into their own life experience, or into what they know or don't know. Case in point: the salesman at the front door who read the hand-crafted wooden sign we brought from Israel and greeted Arleen with "Good morning, Mrs. Shalom."

One of the best examples of laughter at our front door was on the day we were expecting David to bring a friend to meet us. At the appointed hour, we opened the door and found two women standing there. David was at the curb with his car. Ahh, we thought, David had brought two friends instead of one.

As is our custom, we threw open our arms in warm greeting, asking "Do you hug?" The women seemed flustered; it was not a usual conversation starter and often people aren't sure they heard what we said. One fellow once responded with, "Oh yes, I *did* have the flu bug last week, but it is gone now." The women before us were so discombobulated by the question that they simply fell into our open arms, as if for protection from the question. Then, looking deeply into their eyes we introduced ourselves and asked their names. We were surprised that Wendy and Barbara had come up to the porch with books and papers when they could have left them in David's car.

By now, David, his blond hair caught like a sail in the high noon sun, was bounding up the stairs to meet us in a midair hug like trapeze artists in a moment of perfect union. A third woman followed behind him. David then introduced himself to the two women we thought had come with him, telling them his name and hugging each of them as they clung to their books and papers lest they be sacrificed altogether to love.

It was getting crowded on the porch but none of us thought to go inside the house because all of us hadn't hugged yet. In the middle of the moderate melee, David, in a cheery, booming voice, announced, "Arleen, Diane, everybody, this is Rachel." Up she came, in she dove, into the hubbub of arms, bottoms, shoulders, heads, and shuffling feet, as we all moved about, jostling for positions that would ensure our hugging everyone. By now we were almost tangled in the ivy and we suggested that we all go in.

We asked David, "If Rachel is the woman *you* brought, who are these two?" Wendy and Barbara flushed as David indicated he thought they were friends of ours and that everyone had arrived at the same time.

In a small, shy voice, Wendy whispered that they were Jehovah's Witnesses, and Barbara, adjusting her pamphlets, quietly proposed that they come by again at a more convenient time.

As they edged toward the door, in an unsuccessful attempt to appear invisible, we all assured them in our inimitable energetic style that we were glad they had come, and that no time was inconvenient for an exchange of warmth and love. We spared them goodbye hugs.

They had come to talk of God and what better way to speak of Divinity than by *being* it *in self*.

Our front door, more than an entrance to laughter, was an entrance to love, a place where it can truly be said, knock and it shall be opened unto you.

Our spontaneity with laughter goes hand in hand with something else we shared from the beginning: an ability to move into our "little selves" or "child within" and to play together. We mentioned earlier the experience of playing in a courtroom in Santa Barbara but the examples are so numerous there's no way to name them all. To this day, we entertain ourselves by playing with words, surprising each other with harmless tricks, telling each other funny stories about incidents that occur during the day, and so forth.

Sometimes this playful side of us even comes out during sessions we are leading. One time we were giving a talk on the **Love Principles** at a Church of Religious Science in California. Diane accidentally knocked over the glass of water from which she was going to drink, spilling water all over the floor. Arleen quickly stepped forward and said, "I'll bet you have never seen anyone walk on water. Watch this!" as she stepped on the puddle of water. The audience roared and applauded. It was a classic moment of playfulness.

Shared Values

We both valued/value being what we call "public/private persons." We easily respond to questions about ourselves and it doesn't matter who is asking. We give the same answer, the truth, to everyone. We don't tell one person one thing and another something else. This is a great way to live because we never have to remember what we said to whom. It is a way of living a consistent life. There are no secrets, no "different strokes for different folks."

In addition, we are communicating that what you see is what you get. We don't have a storehouse of pretenses or affectations that belong to differing circumstances. And we don't teach what we are not ourselves living. We teach by example, embodying what we know to be true for us in any given moment. If what we know changes, we change with it and don't seek to defend the old in any way.

We actually listen to what we are saying, and to what each other is saying. We know this is profoundly important for spiritual teachers. There are so many religious leaders or prominent public figures who not only say one thing and do another, but who make contradictory statements. For example, someone might advocate "love thy neighbor as thy self" while simultaneously condemning that neighbor for a practice or lifestyle that is different from theirs, or that they label as a "sin."

We truly live by the **Love Principle *Receive***

All People as Beautiful Exactly as They Are. *To receive* is to function in unconditional love. *To receive* does not occur in the mind where people are *accepted* or not, but rather in the heart center. *As Beautiful* means to acknowledge that all people have unique roles to play in the whole. Through their very uniqueness, they contribute to that whole that is made up of polarities. The "good" and the "bad" live side by side just the way creation and destruction live side by side. *Exactly as They Are* tells us that people do not need fixing. They especially do not need to be made over into an image of what we think they should be.

We practice this principle every day, not only in relation to others but in relation to each other. And, we practice receiving ourselves as beautiful exactly as we are, even as we change and grow and become something more or different. We do not hesitate to share our shortcomings, mistakes and challenges, because we know that we are all human, growing through approaching **Problems as Opportunities.**

What a different world we would have if people stopped telling others how to live, ceased demanding it by killing them in conflicts and holy (?) wars. Instead, we could ask those who appear different to tell us about how they live, who they are, and why they hold the values they hold. We would all be expanded by such a practice and we would realize that the creative force that brought us into being (with all our differences) knew what it was doing. Only when every one of the millions of expressions of the creative force are seen as essential parts of the whole do we comprehend the nature of that force.

The two of us have been surprised for years that, having come from such different backgrounds, we could live together so harmoniously. We know that it is due to our commitment to **be the change we want to see happen,** rather than trying to change each other.

We came together for a purpose: to do a work together. And, also, to continue our individualizing and our growth as spiritual beings living in the world in unconditional love. There was no mutual attraction on the personality level as one might expect. Instead, there was something larger than each of us and both of us that was drawing us to each other. Our focus on purpose as the point of our uniting gave meaning to our relationship.

We focused on promoting purposeful living and helping to ignite the Divine Spark in those with whom we came in contact. We knew that to live with a guiding focus would allow us to grow individually and together. We were guided by a desire to discover what *is* rather than to dictate what should be, to listen and learn rather than to tell or reiterate, to cooperate more than control, and to worship life in all its forms, not war against it.

These were some of the core values we shared

and lived on a daily basis. They were always open to expansion, addition, or re-evaluation. They served as guide posts and reminders of how to live consciously and how to grow in the process.

Our Physical Relationship

We were drawn together in 1971 by a powerful energy connection in spirit that created a strong bond almost immediately. We were enveloped and moving in a high energy that felt almost euphoric. The tie was so powerful that neither of us questioned it even though, objectively, we might have found reasons to do so.

Both of us had been in loving and fulfilling marriages before meeting. Both of us had been virgins before having intercourse with the men who became our husbands. Neither of us had ever been sexually attracted to women. And neither of us wanted in any way to deny the body and its importance in our lives.

Arleen had moved "beyond the sexual" after her heart disease and the opening of her heart center. Arleen had always enjoyed sexual activity but when her heart center opened and she subsequently broke through to cosmic consciousness, she lived in a state of joy and could easily touch ecstasy by shifting her consciousness. That state was so much more thrilling than what began to feel like mechanical manipulation to achieve orgasm that sexual activity was relegated to a much lesser place in her life. Sexual orgasm could never again equal the ecstasy available to Arleen in the energy world.

This moving on didn't mean the shutdown of the generative chakra for Arleen. That chakra remained open and active to serve its purpose for creativity and for bringing the new into manifestation. It also held surprises for her. On one occasion, Arleen was describing the profound events that occurred during the initial **Love Project**. She reached a high point and discovered that she had just had an orgasm, not just in the genital area, but throughout her entire being. Every cell was buzzing with light.

The fact that Arleen no longer felt a desire for sexual engaging was one of the strongest reasons her marriage ended in 1972 because her husband Dick wanted to continue their sexual relationship.

Although Diane's husband had died, she continued to be sexually active into the first year of our work together. Then she discovered that it was difficult for men to hold the focus on unconditional and universal love when they registered active sexual energy in Diane. When she realized that men in workshops were often sexually attracted to her and sought to enter into relationships with her, she decided that for the sake of our primary purpose, which was to awaken heart center energy, she needed to refrain from sexual liaisons and lift that magnetic sexual energy up from the generative chakra into her heart center. She had learned how to lift energies in her studies of Yogic practices. It took her over a year to complete the process but she managed to clear her field of magnetic sexual energies so that men did not register mixed energetic messages when in her presence.

It remained our intention to stay fully alive and active in our bodies without sexual engaging. Learning how to express affection without involving sexual energies has been an important part of mastering life in the energy world when lived through a body. We have taught this kind of discrimination of energy registry in our classes and workshops and we continue to feel it to be important. To live consciously in a group psyche like ours where sexual energies, attractions, and innuendos are a part of almost every TV show, movie, and advertisement is a daily challenge.

All the great wisdom traditions have taught that sexual energy is only one form of expression of the creative force in the Generative Chakra. Sexual energy is particularly powerful as an electromagnetic force. It almost demands to be expressed through sexual intercourse and it represents a universal urge programmed into the subconscious to guarantee the perpetuation of humanity on the planet. As we humans evolve into higher states of consciousness, however, we learn to direct that primal creative urge into other endeavors, so that reproduction on the physical level ceases to be a primary focus. This does not mean that sexual expression is denigrated, but rather that it is brought into the realm of conscious choice-making rather than being something automatic.

We chose to be very free in expressing our affection for one another and for other people as well. Hugging was our primary mode of expression. We also chose from the beginning to share a bed at night. In our early years, we would often fall asleep in the spoon position, but as we grew older our bodies protested, creating stiff muscles, and we learned to be satisfied with a good-night hug and a snuggle upon awakening in the morning.

We were aware from the beginning that most people probably assumed that we were lesbians since we were living together and were intimately connected with each other. In 1972 when we began our work together, very few lesbians were "out" and when people asked us if we were lesbians it usually felt like an accusation. We, however, were not offended by that suggestion; we responded simply that we were not, and we knew that most people probably went on assuming that we were. We did not feel there was anything wrong with homosexual relationships; that was simply not the nature of our spiritual union.

As the LGBT movement grew over the years, the question about whether or not we were lesbians fell away. We have assumed that for many people it became an accepted perception and that increasingly nobody cared.

We never had any interest in being married. It was not our intention to form a family unit in the ordinary societal sense. We set out, from the beginning, to form a "Love Family." We told people that once we had met them we considered them to be part of our Love Family and that we would always be there for them. Over the years that has been one of our greatest joys.

After the LGBT community won the right, through a Supreme Court ruling in 2015, to marry and to enjoy the same rights as other married couples, we decided to take advantage, especially financial advantage, of the new rights afforded everyone by the Supreme Court approval of "same-sex" marriage.

For over four decades the two of us, although we were partners in the same household with joint funds, paid out a lot more than "legal" couples. We each had to carry our own health care insurance and file our own taxes. We had to have an attorney prepare separate trusts and establish each other as power of attorney for health care.

Over those many years, we sympathetically observed, with great interest, the struggle of gays and lesbians to achieve equal rights. We always cheered them on because they deserved justice and equality. Then, the great transition occurred and the LBGT community became first class citizens in the United States of America. As a bonus, the two of us in a same-sex union also became first class citizens.

As two heterosexuals in a long term spiritual union we looked to see if anything would be lost if we were to legally marry. The answer was no. In fact, there was much to gain. Thus, with gratitude to the gays and lesbians who struggled long and hard for these rights, we decided to marry. After all, we two, as same-sex partners, also struggled with the former inequities, championed equal rights, and communicated with our representatives over the years to obtain those rights because the way our society was structured was not fair.

It all seemed a little strange to us because the nature and meaning of marriage is in a profound transition, but in our union and our work together nothing else changed. We kept our own names and continued as we always had in a relationship of ongoing spiritual growth and unconditional love.

The choice to marry made it possible for us to partake in the wonderful new rights that the Supreme Court had granted to everyone. We rejoiced in the fact that partnerships of every stripe can be blessed and made whole, that gay couples can adopt children without undue hassle, that hospitals can no longer tell partners they can't see the patient because they are not "family," that partners can adopt the social security benefits of the partner who dies, that partners can receive retirement accounts at the same rate and level as the one who died first, and that unions of all kinds can have the same dignity and respect that was once afforded only to a man and woman.

We are grateful that the conservative State of Arizona made it easy for us to obtain a marriage license, dispensed with a smile and an expression of congratulations. And we are grateful that so many people received and respected the partnership the two of us created in 1972 even though it was "unusual" and have extended that acceptance to our new married state. Life has to be lived in society even when we do not conform to the norm. When greater freedom is opened up by changes in attitude and perception that is a gift to be received and celebrated. We are glad to be able to do both in our spiritual union and we certainly embrace and support others who seek to enter into a legal union.

Ours is an unusual partnership: two woman sharing life, work, home, and finances in a union of love. Before legal marriage was possible, we were "as if married" given the above description. Neither of us had ever had any intention of sharing life with a woman. In our early years we were like other females; we dated men and we married. We did not have children but that is true of many heterosexual couples. We could not have predicted that our lives would take this particular relational form. Just as with the rest of our work, in which we created our own reality, we did the same in our partnership.

We see our union as important because it is different from standard pairing. By virtue of that, we offer a model for others who don't want to live alone but can't seem to find a "mate" willing to share similar values and lifestyle. Our union exemplifies an additional way of joining lives that meets the needs of two who seek supportive, encouraging, and loving partnership. It never mattered to us that we were of the same gender. What mattered was that we had the same focus, the same commitment to spiritual growth, the same degree of life-affirmation, and that we were compatible in our work, in our play, in our caring, and in our laughter.

Beginning our Work

Arleen Lorrance *(on the left), age 33, and **Diane Kennedy Pike**, age 34, at home in San Diego in 1972, the year we began our work together.*

Beginning Our Work: The Love Principles in Action

When we returned from Israel in September of 1972 it was time to focus on what form our work would take. The most important thing we did was to listen within to guidance each of us might receive for how our work was to unfold. We have continued this practice for over four decades. We much prefer it to trying to "think" about what might be successful. We knew we had a work to do but we didn't know the shape it would take. We waited and listened and prepared ourselves in every way so that we could meet the new when it became clear to us. Also, because we had been sent forth two-by-two, we moved forward only toward those possibilities that were in harmony for both of us. This too is a practice that has served us well in all our years together.

Over the years we have had the privilege of supporting others as they followed their inner guidance without having a clear vision for how their life and work might proceed. Most people know little about inner guidance so if you tell them you are following yours, or waiting to receive it, they are likely to try to pin you down to a course of action familiar to them. Fortunately, there are more and more of us who trust the inner guidance and therefore others need not be alone.

We were blessed that we both felt the same way about how to live in the world and that we had **The Love Principles** to guide us. We were both well aware that life did not "live us" but that we had choices to make every step of the way. We were indeed creating the life we were living and the work we were developing. **The Love Principle *Create Your Own Reality Consciously*** was in the forefront our awareness at all times.

That principle is based on an inner knowing that all persons bring their own realities into being, but most are not conscious that the creational powers are theirs. "Reality" is whatever is real to each individual. No external or objective reality can be known except from a particular point of view. The observer participates in bringing the reality into being. We perceive visual realities and emotional realities and these can be very different from the person standing beside us in the same moment. We create and attribute meaning and values to life. If we don't realize we are doing this, we tend to believe that everyone else shares our values and what we say is the meaning of life and events. Whole groups grow out of mutually held convictions and they are often in conflict with other groups who are creating different realities.

Creating our own reality consciously made our work very creative and fresh. We designed all of our programs together and allowed new exercises to evolve to give participants a rich experience. For the most part, we participated with those in attendance in the growth activities. In this way, we learned and grew alongside those we were guiding. If an exercise grew stale for one or both of us, we would chuck it and replace it even if it was still helpful to others. As a result, we have developed hundreds of practices over the last 45 years and each has served us personally as well as those who came to our sessions. In addition, we always listen within for when it is time to allow a whole new method to emerge. This is a way of **creating a reality through action and through choice.**

Sometimes, ***creating a reality*** comes as a result of being exposed to a new way of functioning, being drawn to it, and bringing it into being through totally new behavior. Arleen had no experience with "giving money away." No one she had known before did it, or if they did they never told her. One year, long into their life and work together, Arleen received a brochure from The Heifer Project. She had given them $50 the year before. The project gives animals and other help to poor farm families around the world so that they can sustain themselves. Often the family that receives a cow, for example, provides milk for their entire small community, so the gift multiplies itself many times. Arleen had never forgotten the small boy she saw in Egypt who was out in a field with his family buffalo holding a reed and rope. His face was filled with pride that he had been given the responsibility to tend the animal.

Arleen saw that she could make the gift of a water buffalo for $250.00. She was thrilled to think a family somewhere could own their own water buffalo. When she looked further in the brochure Arleen saw that if she increased her gift to $500 she could give a family a heifer. She was torn between the two. She had been so changed by Diane's example of giving, and so ingrained with the value of it, that she suddenly felt herself lifted into a blessed state in which she decided to do both! She wrote a check for $750.00 to the Heifer Project. It was an exalting moment and a confirmation that a value of Diane's was now her own.

When we practice **creating realities consciously** we begin to create our own thoughts and feelings. If those realities are a response to listening to inner directives, to the Will as we identify it, to what we come to know as what is wanted of us, we have the opportunity to align with the Larger Will and to become an active part of the Whole as it emerges.

Fostering Communication

As we set forth on our work together, we established an office in our home in which we could prepare materials for publication: flyers, announcements of upcoming events, and newsletters. Then we sent out an announcement to our two mailing lists introducing our work as "**The Love Project**," suggesting that we would welcome invitations to make presentations of the six principles.

We began publishing what we called *The Seeker* newsletter which would announce sessions we would be conducting and give us the opportunity to write articles to share with what we hoped would develop into a meaningful community. The newsletter was much later transformed into *Emerging,* a magazine which we have continued to publish at least twice a year into this year of 2017. In writing this book we have drawn upon over 45 years of experiences and articles that have been recorded and shared in our biannual publications.

Our magazines over the years have served as a teaching tool, as an inspiration, as a stimulant to readers, and as a consistent energy connection with Love Family members. One woman expressed it this way: "*Emerging* has helped that feeling of still being with you, as well as stimulating my thinking and increasing my understanding and awareness through your excellent writing." Over the years, letters poured in praising the nourishing magazines, often saying they were devoured in one sitting. The most important feedback to us was when individuals read the articles we wrote and shared with us how they applied the teaching and/or wisdom to which they had been exposed. In our articles, we always applied the learning upon which we expounded to our own lives and gave full examples of how we had grown as a result. We are still doing that to this day.

The Love Principle *Have No Expectations* served us very well as we began designing our work.

We both placed great value on listening within for what was wanted of us and what unique contributions we might make together to the spiritual growth of those who joined us in our work. While we always had good ideas and followed through on them, we knew that functioning with ***no expectations*** of what would actually emerge opened limitless possibilities to us. Rather than expectations, we embodied ***abundant expectancy***.

An ***expectation*** is a fixed view based on the past and applied to the future. Anticipating what will happen, how it will happen, and how we will make it happen, can, and often does, lead to disappointment. We knew that if we had ***no expectations*** we would never be disappointed.

We were committed to living in the present moment and bringing our creativity to what emerged as it emerged. We knew that ***expectations*** were limitations because we would be setting restrictions on what might occur in a given situation rather than opening ourselves to unseen, unknown ways of being. We also knew that if we held **expectations** and they actually materialized we might still be missing out on the more we might have seen because we settled for the lesser, for the familiar.

We chose instead to live in **abundant expectancy**, in eagerness and excitement about whatever might emerge. We knew something was always on the horizon, we simply didn't know what or when it would appear. We were always surprised and delighted, and when we didn't predetermine results, there was always learning and new levels that were exposed.

Watching for Open Doors

Since we both had teaching backgrounds we contacted schools and community colleges in the San Diego area. We also reached out to several institutions such as the military and psychiatric hospitals telling them what we had to offer. Everyone responded warmly but insisted that our programs were not right for their constituency.

From the beginning, person-to-person contacts were key to the development of our work. A San Diego resident named Jerry O'Brien contacted us after receiving our initial mailing. He wanted to help us to meet people in the city. He organized a reception for us at a local hotel, in a ballroom called Top of the Arc, and invited about thirty friends of his to attend and a reporter from the *San Diego Union*. That reporter wrote an article that led to a TV interview and to invitations to give talks at adult education classes and local churches.

We had been delighted that Jerry had set our San Diego work in motion; it was clear he was a man of love who saw an opportunity and created the reality. He helped us to experience that we are not ever alone, and he felt affirmed and supported by our receptivity and presence.

Jerry attended his first Practice Session with us in Northridge, CA months later. It was an important weekend for him. He said that "love was born again" in him and that he would never be the same. Sharing with others had always been a big part of his life but during the session he began to see that sharing "helps love last." He wrote, "**The Love Project** taught me how to share. I share now in my joys, in my grief, in my offenses, and in my happiness. I even share my wealth. Friends don't really understand this sharing. Each one thinks when I give I want something in return. All I want is for them to let me be where I am. **The Love Project** helped me learn that love is all encompassing, sees all, knows all, seeks all."

Those early San Diego talks and appearances brought people into our lives who became lifelong friends and part of a support team, working in our office as volunteers until we moved to Scottsdale, AZ 21 years later. In the early years, on the days we were home, a crew of volunteers would meet at our small San Diego home to help us process mail, keep up with our mailing list, send out requested information, process books that were ordered, and prepare flyers and announcements. We could never have kept up with our schedule without the dedication of these faithful helpers: Millie Boucher, Amy Savelli, Ann Dunagan, Lyn Helppie, Carol Adams, Carl Downing, Alice Niderost, Lisa Warneke, Adele Olsen, Dallas Sweig, Elizabeth Tarpley, and others who pitched in a couple of times of year to send out big mailings to our entire list. Joe Savelli became our personal handyman doing necessary small repairs around the house. We were definitely never alone in San Diego, and we reciprocated by being a spiritual support team for others.

A Perfect Dog Named Buttons

Jerry O'Brien did more than introduce us to San Diego. He learned that Arleen wanted very much to have a dog; she had never had one as a child and Diane thought everyone should have at least one dog in a lifetime. Arleen described the dog she wanted: small, white, friendly, frisky, and smart.

Jerry called one day to say that he thought Arleen's dog had been born in the home of some friends of his. We drove out to the east valley to see the crop of puppies that were awaiting adoption. A small, white, friendly, frisky, and smart cockapoo marched right over to Arleen, sniffed her feet and then looked directly into her being with its big black eyes while twitching its black button nose. There was no doubt that this was the dog she had "ordered."

When the puppy was six weeks old and could be weaned from her mother, we went to take her home. The puppy was so small that Arleen was afraid to hold her for fear she would hurt her in some way. Hence, Arleen drove and Diane held the puppy.

It did not take long for us to name her Ms. Buttons Honey Love. We later awarded her a degree, A.P.D. (this stood for "A Perfect Dog.") She turned out to be just that.

When Buttons first came to live at Gentle Haven (the name we had given to our home) she had to be taught many things, all of which she learned very quickly. Her instinct was to catch birds and bring their bodies to the front door. Arleen taught her reverence for life, all life, and Buttons let go of this natural urge. Arleen taught her not to bark when people came to the door, but rather to welcome them.

One day Jerry brought his friend Peter Tucker over to meet us. While we were talking about Peter's approaching tour of duty in Sicily and his hope to join us on a Tour of the Inner Holy Land, Buttons attacked Peter's sneaker, tugging and pulling until she managed to completely pull the lace out of the shoe. Then she proceeded to chew on the lace. We were apologetic but Peter clearly understood and three days later a package appeared on our front porch addressed to Ms. Buttons Honey Love. In it was one sneaker, laced and ready to be chewed.

Buttons loved it, and from that day forward she always had a sneaker around the house to chew on. When she would completely decimate one shoe, we would give her another.

Buttons learned too well the lesson about welcoming people without barking. On one occasion while Arleen was sunbathing in the nude on our back patio, Buttons welcomed in a meter reader and brought him to the back garden so that he could converse with Arleen if he needed to. She didn't bark. She simply stood there with the man, wagging her tail as if to say, "Look who I brought." The man didn't announce himself either. He just stood with Buttons enjoying the "view."

The main thing Buttons was taught was how to behave when we were doing sessions in our home. Just a week or two after Buttons came to live with us, Arleen held her head in her hands, looked directly into her eyes, and fully explained that she was to remain in her bed on the enclosed back porch and not bark or make any noise while the work was going on. When we would take a break, she would be allowed to join everyone.

Buttons never had to be told this again. She understood fully and complied as if she had gone to a training school. The only time she broke the rule was if someone in the session was shedding tears. Then Buttons would quietly enter the room while trying to remain invisible and she would sit down beside the person who was expressing feelings. When the person was able to move on, Buttons would quietly get up and go back to her bed. No one taught her that maneuver; she did it on her own volition out of concern for the welfare of those who seemed to be in pain.

We also taught Buttons not to enter the room where we were eating. We didn't want her to beg for food at the table. She never argued about that rule. One time we were visiting friends in Lake Tahoe. We were going to have dinner out on their balcony with a magnificent view of the Lake. The dinner table was at one end of the balcony, so Buttons sniffed around and determined which part of the balcony was not in the dining area. She then lay down with her nose on the line she had established and stayed there until we finished eating. She was a smart dog!

She instinctively knew about "love-ins" which were breaks in the day when the two of us would lie down on the living room floor for a respite. Buttons would immediately come over, wagging her tail, and stick her face, and wet nose, in between our two heads. She never missed out on a love-in!

Buttons also created her version of the game "hide and seek," disappearing behind a chair, forcing the two of us to call her name, saying "Where's Buttons?" She would peek her head out from behind the chair to see if we were looking and getting "warm;" when she saw us she immediately pulled back in. She would play hide and seek for as long as we were willing.

Often when we traveled by air for our work, Buttons would stay with Love Family members. We explained to her that she could not get too attached to us because we were going to be gone a lot. In the beginning, when she was still a puppy and not yet fully house-broken, Jerry O'Brien would keep her. Eventually Amy and Joe Savelli, who were great dog-lovers, became her regular keepers. The Savellis would come to pick Buttons up and take us to the airport. Then they would pick us up at the airport upon our return and bring us home. So much was the Savellis' house her home away from home, Buttons was sometimes reluctant to return home with us. She enjoyed many privileges with the Savellis, such as sleeping on their bed, which she did not enjoy at Gentle Haven.

Buttons traveled with us when we went by car, including spending several summers with us in Pennsylvania while we were conducting sessions there. She was a great traveler, never getting restless during long trips and adjusting quickly to new accommodations on the road and where we stayed at Allegheny College. Toward the end of her life we left her with friends when she did not see well enough to travel and Lyn Helppie and Carol Adams had her when she had to be put to sleep. We had enjoyed her company for 15 years.

Buttons is featured on this Summer, 1975 issue of the Seeker newsletter to illustrate the **Love Principle** **Have No Expectations.** *She was a master of that principle.*

We considered Buttons a teacher on many levels. She taught us about forgiveness, since even if we accidently stepped on her tail and she yelped in pain, she would turn around and give us a kiss in the next moment. She taught us about ***no expectations***, since she was always eager for whatever new experience awaited her. In fact, she was on the cover of our magazine once, illustrating what ***abundant expectancy*** looks like!

Buttons also taught us about unconditional love. She was eager to offer her love to everyone.

Only twice, when we were out on walks with her, did she raise a question about a stranger by emitting a low growl, something we almost never heard from her. We often wondered what she sensed in those people that we were not aware of.

New Friends

Jerry O'Brien gave us still another unexpected gift. He was friends with Bettye Ackerman and Sam Jaffe, well-known actors who lived in Beverly Hills, CA. Sam Jaffe gave a performance in San Diego in our first years there and Jerry invited the two of them after an evening performance to come with him to Ocean Beach to meet the two of us. They agreed. When the Jaffes entered our living room and Jerry introduced us, the four of us knew immediately that we would be fast friends, and so we were.

On a couple of occasions the Jaffes celebrated Thanksgiving at Gentle Haven with us and other friends. In those days we sat on the floor around a low table. The first time Sam, who was in his 80's, came to eat with us we asked him if he could sit on the floor. He said he would be happy to as long as we promised to help him get up!

Our San Diego Love Family was able to enjoy an evening watching the film "Lost Horizon," followed by a talk and question-and-answer period with Sam. Arleen had a long time special connection with the role Sam played in that film: the

High Lama. When she saw the movie early in her life she knew instantly that "Shangri-La" was not a "place" out there in the Himalayas but rather was an Eden of consciousness that existed in each of us that would be awakened when we were ready.

We enjoyed our friendship with the Jaffes for several years before Sam's death, and for more years with Bettye afterwards. After Sam Jaffe's death, Bettye consented to Arleen's writing a book about his life. It was a lengthy project that brought her incredible joy. It is called *Sam Jaffe, An Actor of Character* (available through Amazon.com).

Forming a Love Family

It was important to us that we not form a new institution, even a small one, so we asked people to serve on the Board of Directors of our nonprofit educational corporation who understood that they were there to support us in our work, not to govern. From the beginning, we instructed the Board of Directors that if the two of us suddenly died, we would want them to disband the corporation. We did not want the work continued as a tribute to us. If we were gone, we would want others to establish their own work.

Rather than have members of an organization, we invited people to become sponsors of our work. We were deeply affected in one of our first years by a letter requesting donations that said to recipients, in effect, "If you don't contribute money to help support me I will not be able to continue my work." We both looked at each other and said, "If money does not come in response our work, we will find something else to do, recognizing that if what we offer does not serve people they will not contribute money to support us." We follow that policy to this day.

We were especially delighted that we never had to advertise. Our work has continued uninterrupted with no need to force anything. That has served as a confirmation that our work is meaningful to people and they want us to continue it. Because we have never advertised, we have worked primarily with small groups of 10 to 25 people in the majority of our sessions. We have enjoyed that because we really get to know people. We have called those we meet our "Love Family."

We did not establish a formal organization or structure. We did not gather in a single location. We recognized all participants in the Love Family as making unique contributions where they were. We did not set up branches of **The Love Project**. Nor was there any official membership. We were an example of how a world community could be built overnight. Without a location, an organization, an agreement on how the community will express itself, without headquarters or formal branches, or even staff, individuals could acknowledge themselves to be active members creating their unique expressions. It was easy for those who "belonged" to say "When I am with

Love Project people I feel I am with my family," or "I have never felt freer to be who I am than I feel in this gathering."

We loved the letter that came from someone who exercised his right to keep himself at distance from the flood of love that came from **The Love Project**: "The winds of anger have blown themselves out. I feel a deep and profound respect for you. In spite of differences of opinion, we never lost our mutual awareness that we have a right to differ...You published my viewpoint *en toto* and ran a companion piece that further demonstrates your inner beautiful selves coupled with undeniable evidence that you practice what you preach."

Many times over the years, we have heard from people we have not seen for a very long time. They will begin by saying, "You probably won't remember me. . ." and are then surprised to find that we do indeed remember them. It has been important to us to maintain those energetic connections because we know that we are all part of one large family of individuals who are awakening and contributing to the Whole. Love Family members are all those who love and who express their love in their own individualized and thus unique ways.

Lily Jean Haddad met us in 1987 after receiving a brochure on the Theatre of Life in the mail. Following that, she did all six Acts of the Theatre of Life and subsequently took training as a teacher of Life as A Waking Dream (LAWD). Fran, who attended her class in Life as A Waking Dream in the early 90's, found Lily Jean's name on our website as a teacher of LAWD and contacted her to thank her for the gift of a simple sentence which had changed her life. Here's what Fran said in a personal e-mail:

> I was, as I often did back then, complaining about a co-worker who was a major thorn in my side. You simply said, 'Fran, this woman isn't your problem, she's your teacher.' From that day forward I've looked at the problems in my life as learning experiences, which has made a shift in the way I think and act. Thank you for being the catalyst that gave me a different perspective on the world around me. The question often comes up—What was the turning point in your spiritual journey? I can always share that event from many years ago. Thank you, Lily Jean for being that pivotal point for me.

In recalling this exchange Lily Jean went on to say, in her e-mail to us:

> Nothing is wasted! Everything is important. We are all messengers. Be mindful of what you say and speak only Truth as you know it. When there are ears to hear, the message will be delivered clearly. Through desire and preparation, we draw to ourselves what we need.
>
> I drew the **Love Project** and Fran. Fran drew me and the LAWD work. LAWD work went out into the greater world of Work. Once again Fran drew LAWD into her life to retouch the source of it. What a web we weave! Is it any wonder they call those places on the internet websites? It is essential that we all do our Consciousness Work for ourselves and for each other.

Not only do people stay connected with us in that great Web, but they stay connected with each other, and so the circle grows as an outpicturing of the expansion of our individual and collective consciousness. None of us need be alone.

Spiritual companionship is all around us waiting to be discovered. When we are willing to speak what we know, even in so-called mundane situations, a stranger overhearing what we say might well respond, indicating that he or she also knows that to be true. It is easy then for a conversation to begin on a substantive level. A friendship might grow from this and expand in different directions as you and this person open your world of friends to each other. We have experienced this time again.

Arleen made a comment to someone in the pool at the YMCA. She said she valued the bright sunshine in Arizona but even more she valued the Light within each of us that we can radiate forth. The woman in the pool responded immediately by affirming that view and saying that one day we will all radiate that Light to everyone and the world will begin to change for the better. Arleen and Paula became friends from that day on and expanded connections have resulted from the comment Arleen was willing to make to a stranger.

It is important to remember that there are awakened people everywhere; that we are not alone.

In 1987, we received a beautiful letter from B.F. in Ohio. He was a bright light who brought his joy with him wherever he went and we were blessed to have him in our work and Love Family. He began his letter with a small poem:

> Mmmm...
> Please, take a deep breath (and read this slowly)
> And imagine me,
> A spirit,
> With a big happy smile
> So appreciative, so thankful, and so joyful,
> About the two of you.

Bill had spent months overcoming impossible challenges with grace and unimagined success in his teaching contracts with NASA and the Department of Defense. His letter continued:

> I was teaching creativity and thinking skills to people who very much need them, and feeling the deepest satisfaction of being so in tune with my life stream. Then I awoke a few weeks later with pain in my psyche for about three hours until I reached a very quiet spot. I heard your names and called you for help with climbing up out of the pain. Thank you so much for your perfect help, for your commitment beyond time and space, to always be there for me should I need a guiding hand. Although we talk only every few years (tears), I need to know you are there (here.)
>
> And perhaps more importantly I need to know I can express my love to you. I love the people I work with very much, the NASA scientists, the business executives, the Department of Defense officers, but I cannot openly express my love to them. I am often overwhelmed with love for them, their struggle, but most of all their goodness. Humanity really is trying, although trying mostly in vain because of ignorance or perhaps fear.
>
> Thank you so much for having the courage to become the beautiful souls you are.

You said there are no answers to the 'why questions' concerning life, and I understand what you mean. And I think you will understand what I mean when I say there is an answer to the why question.

> For Arleen and Diane:
> Today
> I discovered the reason why,
> Why, the 'eternal smile' smiles.
> Why, life is so happy to be, everywhere.
> And why, of why,
> The heart of life
> Is
> Pure ecstatic bliss,
> Because it is all so pleased
> With you
> My dear one.

And if that's not a rational answer, then I don't know what is.

A short time after this wonderful communication from Bill, we learned of his untimely death in a car accident. What a loss!

Our Love Family extends across the continent and across the seas. Energy sharing knows no boundaries and carries love everywhere. In 1975 Irv Hershman of Los Angeles was hit by a car and hospitalized at UCLA Medical Center with a fractured right femur. He was in traction for six weeks. He called to tell us even though he knew we would be very busy because we were leaving for the Middle East. He was glad he called.

He later wrote to us that starting the following week, he began receiving thoughtful expressions and wondered how they could have known of his confinement so rapidly. The mystery was solved when someone drove 60 miles to see him and showed him the "beautiful, caring letter" that the two of us had mailed out to people who knew Irv.

Irv wrote:

> It was pure delight to receive all the cards, letters, visits, calls, and other expressions of love from so many. It made me happy to know I had so many concerned friends in my world. During my youth, I never envisioned in my wildest dreams that in my adult life I would have so many rich personal relationships. My recovery was hastened by healing waves of energy sent to me. This occurrence has afforded me the opportunity to "break" with the past routines and habits and to "realign" my ways of being with my world. In this endeavor the warmth, love, and support has been invaluable.

Over the years we have shared with groups of all sizes and ages. We have been keynote speakers at large conferences of savvy New Age folks, met with novices in living rooms, gone to schools to address kids of all ages and their teachers, met with couples, individuals and families, given sermons at Sunday morning church services, led spiritual retreats, been interviewed for newspapers, and appeared on radio and television. We have done sessions in over twenty states and three Canadian provinces.

Because we have always lived what we taught, we brought what we knew and what we had to offer everywhere, in all circumstances, as well as to each other so that we would continue to grow. We have decades worth of letters attesting to the value of what we have brought wherever we have gone.

This letter, received in 1976, from a sister-in-law, D.K., stands out because of the imprint made on her son John, then aged four:

> John was in the wading pool with a friend. I saw a bee land on one of the wet toys, but knowing how terrified John is of bees I didn't say anything. However, the friend spotted the bee and began flapping her hands. I thought, here we go...as John turns and says to the bee, 'I love you, bee. I won't hurt you.' He repeated it calmly several times...then the bee flew away.
>
> It sounded so much like you two that I asked John who taught him to say that. I was right. Thank you for caring about John and sharing in his growth in such a beautiful way.

We never know who is listening and learning from us; it behooves us to be our highest and best whenever we are conscious enough to set that in motion. We not only touch and imprint others; our expressions of energy reach far beyond ourselves and linger in the universe forever according to scientists. That should be sobering to all of us.

As we write of our years of going forth two-by-two, we are deeply touched by the written history that is contained in almost five decades of magazine issues, of articles and books written, and of letters and communication received. It is a whole life in a file cabinet that is bursting at the seams with Light, with Love, with applications of **The Love Principles**, with quests, with deep inner work, with joy and pain shared by us and by thousands of Love Family members. If anyone asked, "What have you done with your lives?" we can answer humbly and with incredible gratitude that we have touched many lives with unconditional love and created a support system for those on spiritual journeys.

Our Work Takes Form

We began our work at a time when the Humanistic Psychology movement was gaining strength and workshops were a popular format for exploring different approaches to human growth. We decided to call our workshops "Practice Sessions" in which we actively practiced how to apply the six **Love Principles** to real situations in the lives of individuals.

Practice Sessions

We began all our sessions with Toning, using an "ah" sound to fill the room with our voices, create a frequency for growth and exploration, and unite us in harmony through sound. We did this throughout all our years. It enabled participants to bring their focus into the room and to let go of the distractions of the outside world. A few people felt uncomfortable toning but they were free to stand in silence and let the warm sounds wash over them.

It wasn't until two decades into our work that we ran into objections that were very strange to us. It happened in Iowa. Some participants said they could not be present when we were toning because "It was the work of the Devil." Needless to say, the two of us were astounded, but then, neither of us was a fundamentalist Christian who had been indoctrinated with such input. We always made room for all belief systems, **receiving all people as beautiful exactly as they are**, but it became clear that not all belief systems made room for all expressions, in this case, of sound.

Following Toning, we would seat the group in a circle, each of us sitting on opposite sides of the circle, facing each other. This gave us a view of everyone in the room and also allowed all the participants to see each other. By sitting in the circle opposite each other we were making the unspoken statement that although we were leading the sessions we looked upon everyone as equals in the process.

We always invited participants to answer a question at the outset. For example, "What drew you to this particular exploration?" "What do you experience as your growing edge?" or "Give us your name, and share an example of how you **create your own reality consciously**." We did this so that people would introduce themselves with something of substance right at the outset, rather than telling where they lived or what they did for a living.

In writing this book, we are amused that in reflecting on participants going all the way back to the beginning, we can report on their growth processes and their spiritual contributions to the whole, but for the most part, we have no idea what they did for work or what degrees they held. We were focused on their individualizing process and who they were as beings, not the window dressing of their roles in life.

Opportunities to Share Multiplied

Immediately after sending out an announcement of our work, invitations began to come for us to share in both large groups and small. We were invited to make presentations at the Anderson Research Foundation in Los Angeles; at the International Cooperation Council in Northridge, CA; on the TV Show "Let There Be Light" in San Diego; at the Counter-Culture Conference in Isla Vista, CA; and at the Future Homemakers of America Conference at Asilomar, CA.

Our work seemed to grow in leaps and bounds. We had put forth our first communication in July, 1972. We had **no expectations** about how our work would unfold. By August, 1973 we had 350 people receiving *The Seeker* newsletter and over 1,000 individuals on our general mailing list of those who wanted to know where and when we would be conducting Practice Sessions or giving talks. A year later that number had quadrupled. In the 12-month time period we had taken part in 43 presentations and open dialogues on topics that included **The Love Project**, Parapsychology, Reincarnation, New Age Love, New Life Styles in the Age of Aquarius, the Naturalness of the Supernatural, the Gifts of the Spirit, Uniting Love Energies, Peace Begins with Me, and Love Works: A Jewish-Christian Dialogue.

During that first year, we facilitated 25 Practice Sessions in which the focus was always on the **Love Principles.** The majority were on weekends, 18-hours each; many were nine-hour all-day Saturday sessions; and several were three- to four-hours evenings. Our calendar continued to mushroom and before long we commenced traveling every single weekend, sometimes giving presentations mid-week as well. Other topics were added to the mix as time went on: The Power of One, Reviewing Your Past, Self-Healing, The Joy of Roots and Differences, Freedom/Choice/Non-Violence, Sex/Love/Cosmic Ecstasy, Bringing the Shadow Self into the Light, The Transformative Power of Conscious Love, The Nature of Private Worlds, Bridging the Psychological and the Spiritual, Consciously Registering the Frequency World, Standing in the Still Point, Living Life on Purpose, The Yin and Yang in Each of Us, The Value of Chaos, Living Lightly, etc.

We changed the focus of our presentations to match what was alive for us in our own growth and what was of special interest to the hosting group. It was almost by accident that we started doing Practice Sessions in living rooms with small groups. We started in our own small living room in Ocean Beach (San Diego), California and then people began to invite us into their own homes. A San Diego woman who attended a talk we gave in the fall of 1972 invited us to present the **Love Principles** to a small group of her friends in her living room. Of course, we said yes, and that was the beginning of the format that continued to serve as our primary way of interacting with people for over twenty years across the continent. We would probably never have thought of meeting in people's homes, but as we said earlier, we listened and we said yes to what became clear and what was in harmony for both of us.

We were also invited, often, into churches, sometimes to do three or four-hour sessions following a Sunday worship service, sometimes to offer a Saturday afternoon session, and sometimes to be the leaders of weekend Church retreats. We always presented the six **Love Principles** and invited people to practice embodying them.

Inspiration and Outreach

Following our beginning in living rooms and classes and churches in San Diego, we were invited to give the keynote address at the International Cooperation Counsel in the Los Angeles area and it was there that we met Randy Howell from Edwards Air Force Base, a loving man dedicated to *being the change he wanted to see happen* in the Air Force and elsewhere. He invited us to do a session at the base with the full-time and volunteer staff of the Social Action Center. Sharing at an Air Force base was a new experience for us and a delightful one. A week after we were there we were featured in the front-page article of *The Desert Wings* (the base newspaper). The article told of how we encouraged people to exercise choice in directing their energies, and that rather than condemning or complaining, everyone could **"be the change they wanted to see happen."**

The article went on to say, "One outgrowth of the weekend experience is a group of women looking at women's role at Edwards and in society with a view towards usefully directing their energies in the community... A second result of the weekend's activities is a new community action column entitled 'Sharings' that appears in *The Desert Wings* for the first time this week."

There were several letters to the General of the base thanking him for appropriating the funds to bring the two of us to do the session.

One Airman wrote a personal note to us requesting more sessions with us and saying that he had invited the General to attend the next one. He went on:

> Before the weekend...I was so obsessed with what was wrong with everything. Now I feel myself trying to see a more optimal way of [viewing] situations that happen to me. Instead of using everything within me to hate the situations...I'm...rechanneling the hate into a quietly strong and positive force. My morale has been so improved in the last two days that I myself can't believe the change.

Ann Gurley, who has remained a member of our Love Family over all these decades, and who is herself a dynamic expression of **The Love Principles** in action, wrote in gratitude for the new creative ideas we brought:

> Perhaps I cannot relate to you or anyone the great emotional impact which this weekend's experience has had on me. But I can tell you how the spirit of it will bring helpful results for our base...As a volunteer on the Hotline, I have been helped this weekend by the gift of a new tool...As a Christian I see the exact parallel in the philosophy and approach of **The Love Project**. The new element is in the wording and the purity of their presentation. It is this 'new' approach that can help me when I speak with persons who do not see religion as a viable alternative to their problems, but who may want a solution that works through the energy of love and positive living...I believe that a spirit of doing and wanting to help can be seen by others and will inspire them to become the change we all want to see.

Recently Ann applied her artistic skills to creating graphics for **The Love Principles**. We include them on the next two pages.

The Love Principles
Art by Ann Gurley

Receive all persons as beautiful exactly where they are.

Pathways to Inner Peace
Love Project Principles originated by Arleen Lorrance,

Be the change you want to see happen ... instead of trying to change everyone else.

Pathways to Inner Peace
Love Project Principles by Arleen Lorrance, 1970.

Create your own reality consciously, rather than living as if you had no control over your life.

Pathways to Inner Peace
Love Project Principles by Arleen Lorrance, 1970.

Our Work Takes Form

Have no expectations, but rather abundant expectancy.

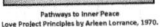

Perceive problems as opportunities.

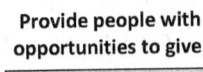

Provide people with opportunities to give.

Choice is the life process.

In every new moment of awareness, you can make a new choice.

Following a session on The Naturalness of the Supernatural at the First Congregational Church in Stamford, CT in 1974 we received a letter which confirmed our emphasis on embodying what we know and making it real in our lives. Audrey wrote:

> How much you have changed my life you will never know. It was while I was at your workshop that I saw color in auras for the first time. For many years, I have been a spiritualist and sat in classes for development, but somehow it was your **Love Project** that made everything come into focus...Every day I read my bible and prayed, but your presentation really opened up the way. I now feel God within me and know illumination.

Those who couldn't participate in our sessions were at least able to receive inspiration from our *Seeker* newsletter. In 1975, a United Methodist Minister in Los Angeles wrote to say that the newsletter "overflows with the love of its authors. It is a resource for my ministry I can't do without."

One of the remarkable things about our work together is that from the first session we facilitated together, we completely trusted each other. We always had plans for the session, but if one of us made a change mid-stream, the other simply trusted that that would work out. And inevitably it did.

In the first weekend we ever co-led, we were hosted by a group at a Methodist Church in Reno, Nevada. On Saturday evening, someone in the group began to talk about protecting ourselves by surrounding ourselves with white light. We did not resonate with the need to "protect" ourselves. We were focused on **creating realities** by *projecting* the energy we wanted to live in and **becoming the change we wanted to see in the world.** Of course, the change we wanted to see was unconditional love, but the group interaction began to spiral downward into disagreement and tension.

The two of us were at a loss as to how to transform what was happening when suddenly the doors flew open and a group of young people burst into the room singing, "They will know we are Christians by our love, by our love. . ." Our whole group joined in with heartfelt joy, and when the young people exited as suddenly as they had come in, we all dissolved in laughter at the irony and synchronicity. The timing could not have been more perfect. It was like being pushed out of the way of an oncoming bus.

We told the group, "We were all rescued by young people who understood what this session is all about: learning to love unconditionally." We reflected on the dynamic as an example of how things work in life. It is easy to get stuck in concepts and to cling to convictions rather than keeping the heart center open to let unconditional love energy flow. The two of us never forgot that experience. It was as though angels had intervened to rescue us.

From experiences like that the two of us learned to embrace many approaches to what we were trying to teach people and never to resist someone else's experience. We knew we did not have answers to all questions nor did we feel the **Love Principles** were the be-all and end-all of spiritual principles. We had to learn to trust the flow of events in our sessions, and to trust each other that we would be able to handle anything that came up.

We had a naïve conviction when we began our work that if we shared the six **Love Principles** with enough people, the transformational power of love would change lives in an exponential way. We did not think in terms of "earning a living;" we were focused on being of service. We had faith that if we were doing the work we were given to do, financial support would follow.

Therefore, for the first several years when people asked what we charged those who sponsored our sessions we said, "We ask that our travel expenses be met and that people be asked for donations rather than charged a fee." We did not want anyone to be turned away because they did not have enough money. We indicated that we were willing, in order to keep expenses at a minimum, to stay in people's homes and to eat meals with local people who invited us. When sessions were in California we drove our car to get there, carrying boxes of our books, **Love Principle** cards, and brochures announcing up-coming events. When we flew, we checked our boxes of books as luggage at the airport.

Surprisingly, over the many years we operated in that way, on only two occasions were our expenses were not covered. In one instance, we were invited to do a session in Montana. We decided to drive to get there, making a stop along the way in Yellowstone National Park. On the morning we were to leave Yellowstone, it began to snow. Fortunately, Diane had grown up in Nebraska and had learned to drive in snowy road conditions. As we drove north the snow grew heavier. By the time we arrived in Billings, Montana many roads were completely closed.

The man who had invited us to offer a workshop told us, upon our arrival, that he was sure no one would come to the session due to the weather. Sure enough, only one or two people showed up and the session was cancelled. Since no one participated, there were no contributions. The man who had planned the session apologized, but he had no money to offer. So, we ended up paying our own way to get there and home.

Another time we were invited by the minister of a Religious Science church to conduct a weekend retreat for his church members. We flew to Albuquerque, were put up in a lovely hotel where we were welcomed with a large basket of fruit and a bouquet of beautiful flowers. The retreat was held on Friday night and all day Saturday. When we left on Sunday we were surprised to find that there was no check to cover our travel expenses and there was no honorarium. We asked what had happened. The minister told us that by the time they paid for the hotel, the fruit basket and the flowers there was no money left over. And this was in spite of the fact that they taught abundance consciousness in their church.

But when you consider that we operated the same way for so many years, it is rather amazing that we ended up in the hole only twice.

One time we had the reverse of those experiences. We were invited to a tiny Unity Church in Columbus, Ohio. We were picked up at the airport and driven to a nice hotel. Then our hostess drove us to the church where we met the minister who gave us a very warm welcome. She told us how important it was for her congregation that we had come. They were a very new congregation and were in the process of building their church.

When we went into the room where we were to speak, there were only a few people present, four families and their children. We were horrified, thinking of what it would cost just to pay our airfare and the hotel costs. But the people were very friendly and excited about the evening and we gave them a full introduction to the six **Love Principles**.

At the end of the evening, our hostess drove us back to the hotel and handed us a check for a sizeable amount of money. We said, "What is this?" She said, "It represents the contributions that came in tonight." We said, "But there were only four families present." She said, "Yes, but they are the families who are building this church. They know about the importance of giving; most of them give about 40% of their income to the church."

We were dumbfounded. We said, "But what about our expenses?" She answered, "No problem. We took those out first." We thought of the Religious Science church that teaches prosperity consciousness and could not afford to give us anything after they paid the expenses for our accommodations. Surely this small group knew something they did not know!

Interesting experiences happened as a result of our seeking to save money by accepting invitations to meals and accommodations in people's homes. Early on we were invited to dinner at the home of some gracious people. The wife had spent a lot of time and energy preparing a lovely meal that centered on a roast. We had not thought to mention that Diane was a complete vegetarian. When we sat down at the table that the hostess had so lovingly prepared Diane knew she would not mention that she did not eat meat. Instead, she gave thanks for the meal and ate what was served.

That was a lesson in values. Diane realized

that honoring the gift the hostess was giving was more important than holding to her decision not to eat meat. In order not to do violence to animals by eating their flesh, she would have had to do violence to the feelings of a generous human being. She decided it was important to keep her priorities straight.

After that, we tried to remember to tell people that Diane did not eat meat. In those early years in the 1970's vegetarian eating was not common and often Diane chose simply to accept the hospitality offered rather than make an issue of her vegetarian preference. It seemed the more unconditionally loving thing to do.

An amusing incident occurred in Kansas City, Missouri. We went home with a couple who were generous enough to provide us with accommodations. They said, casually, when they showed us the room we would stay in, "We hope you do not mind the sound of cuckoo clocks; we have a collection." Well, indeed they did. All over the house, including in the room we stayed in, there were dozens of clocks. They went off at odd times, not all at once, so that all night long we were entertained with the sound of "Cuckoo, cuckoo!"

The next morning when the couple said, "We hope you slept well," we said we were very comfortable, not mentioning that we didn't get much sleep. Focused on gratitude for their generosity, we did not feel the need to mention the annoyance of the clocks.

Repeat Visits

Beginning in the fall of 1972, we were invited by Esther Lynn to give a Saturday workshop at the Southwest Counseling Service in the Inglewood neighborhood of Los Angeles. For several years we became "regulars" there and met numerous people who became lifelong friends and who participated with us in other sessions and events. We were indebted to Esther Lynn for her faithful "promotion" of our sessions by encouraging her clients to attend, providing us with multiple opportunities to share **The Love Principles.**

The Southwest Counseling Service was not in the best part of Los Angeles and our sessions always went from 10:00 a.m. until 10:00 p.m. Then we would drive home to San Diego. One night we started out and our car began to cough and sputter. We pulled into the next gas station only to discover that someone had put sugar in our gas tank. The attendants in the gas station were both friendly and polite in spite of the fact that we were definitely not from their neighborhood. They said it would take until the next morning to clear the lines and get us on our way, so we walked down the dark streets to a motel that was, shall we say, questionable.

The next morning, after sleeping comfortably in the rather shabby room, we had breakfast across the street and then walked back to the gas station. Sure enough, they had our car up and running and for a reasonable charge we were on our way again. We were glad we were practicing the **Love Principles** (*have no expectations but rather abundant expectancy, provide others with opportunities to give, receive all people as beautiful exactly as they are*, etc.) because we did not create anxiety about being strangers among strangers and people responded to us in kind.

Another time we had flown to Los Angeles because we needed to get home in order to fly out of San Diego early the next morning. When the session ended, Diane lingered, hugging people goodbye. Arleen got more and more anxious. Finally, she got Diane in the car. Irv Hershman drove us to the airport, accompanied by Jody Carter.

Arleen asked that Jody go into the terminal with us because she was convinced we would miss our flight. Sure enough, when we got to the gate they had just closed the doors and they would not open them to let us on. Out we went to see if Irv and Jody would drive us to San Diego. They did and they had a chance to practice the **Love Principles** while they mediated a process between the two of us. Arleen was definitely not happy with Diane and Diane really had no excuse for making them late for the flight, except that she was saying goodbye to people. After arguing and processing the whole way to San Diego (an hour and a half trip), Diane agreed never to make us late to a flight again. She never has.

Another group that invited us for many years to give Practice Sessions to their members was a community called Open End in Marin County, north of San Francisco. For over ten years we met yearly at Millie and Al Kline's home in Mill Valley. It was there that we learned a lesson that led us to change our policy of asking people for donations for our Practice Sessions.

There were several members of the Open End Community that came to our sessions gratis because we never turned anyone away who could not pay. One weekend we overheard people talking about going to EST weekends for which they paid $100.00. These were the same people who came to our sessions without contributing financially.

When we thought that over we decided to change our policy. We began charging for our Practice Sessions, with instructions to the hosts and hostesses that if there were individuals who wanted to participate but couldn't afford what we were asking they were to ask how much the person could afford and then tell them we would provide the balance as a scholarship. That has remained our policy to this day.

Publishing

Before we began our work in 1972, Arleen had been telling the story of the original **Love Project** in Brooklyn to groups of educators and students all over California. Diane urged her to write the story as a book, and in two months the manuscript was ready. We submitted it to Diane's publisher in New York and after several weeks of being read by a few editors in various departments, the manuscript was returned to us with a letter that said that in their opinion it wasn't a trade book. We took that to mean they didn't know how to sell it.

The Love Project was central to our work and we knew we would and could sell it to those who came to our workshops, so we decided to publish it ourselves. In the early 1970's self-publishing was not a big thing. It was called "vanity" publishing which seemed to demean the undertaking. We discovered quickly, however, that it was not easy to interest publishers in books we wanted to write for the work we were doing.

When *The Love Project* was rejected by one publisher, we decided to save time and trouble by **creating the reality** of a small publishing company called "LP Publications," for "Love Project

Publications." It was a way of **being the change we wanted to see happen**, and it turned out to be a very important and lasting vehicle for us. Just because others in publishing said "no" to us did not mean that we couldn't say "yes" to ourselves. Saying yes leads to finding new ways to move forward and to bring new realities into being. It is a fine way to live, in all circumstances: never to be daunted by rejection, or stymied by disappointment. There is always a way to accomplish a goal and it begins with saying "yes" to self.

The very week that we made the decision to form our own publishing company, we were at a **Love Project** sharing in San Diego. Arleen told the story about the manuscript and how we had decided to publish it ourselves when one of the women in the room jumped up and said, "I can do it for you in no time." Her name was Carolyn Worth, and she had access to an IBM Composer (an early computer). She gave her 20 hours of typing as a gift to us, and the book was soon ready for paste-up. Had we not decided to publish the book ourselves we would never have benefited from the completely unexpected services Carolyn had to offer.

The key to the new is to set energy in motion and allow facilitative help to fall into place along the way. Without Carolyn's composer work, it would have taken us a long and effortful time to produce the book. This was an example of our not being alone in the spiritual process. We shared our vision and hope, and by doing so we **provided others with opportunities to give to us**. Carolyn was a perfect example of Love Family cooperation.

We discovered that in order to put a price on the book low enough to encourage people to buy it, we had to print 2,000 copies! That was daunting, but we moved ahead in the confidence that the book would sell. (In fact, there were eventually five separate printings of the book.) We were blessed that the "printing company" we selected (recommended by another Love Family member) was a very small operation like ours, just Louie and his wife. He allowed us to pay for the print job in installments. We were always on time with our payments.

Our garage was loaded up with copies of the new book. Wherever we went we carried boxes of books with us and sold them to participants. We continued that practice for about 30 years.

Arleen started her own **Love Project**. Every evening that we were home, she sat in front of the TV addressing envelopes to school libraries all over the country. She addressed thousands of envelopes that we then, with the help of volunteers, stuffed with flyers about *The Love Project* book. That was a labor-intensive undertaking and the book began to sell at the rate of about 60 copies a week. We were delighted.

One response came from Peter Thompson in Ohio, a school librarian, who not only ordered the book but took it to Shady Brook House, a human growth center. They read the book and sent us an invitation to speak at Shady Brook, and that occasion opened new doors in ways we could never have anticipated. Once again, we had set energy in motion and it moved forward like a powerful locomotive. If there was any question about how to bring a new work into being, the answer was, simply begin. Then, **have no expectations.** As things began to fall into place, it was evident that we were not alone and that because we were coming forth, we were being met.

That first night at Shady Brook, Audrey MacDonald, a vibrant, light-filled powerhouse of a woman from Chagrin Falls, came to hear us. The next night she brought several spiritually minded friends with her. In very short order we were invited to give a talk at the Chagrin Falls high school. Then David Pointer, the minister of education at the Federated Church in Chagrin Falls, invited us to speak and to do a session there.

As a result of those first sessions we were invited back to the Federated Church every year, and sometimes twice a year, for twenty years! A bonus from the time in that beautiful community was that we worked with repeat couples and families over those two decades, designing explorations that stretched the participants to new levels of awareness. We watched the youngsters grow into adults who had a history with us and that brought even greater substance to their unfolding. We knew the families: their struggles and accomplishments, their joys and sorrows, their dreams for the future. It was extraordinary to have the privilege of serving an entire community over such a long period and being able to help them integrate their progress because the two of us remembered their unique histories. We could weave those histories into what was alive for them in the now and show them how that could serve them.

For most of those years we stayed with Audrey and Bob McDonald in their home in Chagrin Falls, though we often ate with other families, such as the Hissams, the Pointers, the Townsends, and the Dekkers who also put us up for many years. We continue to be grateful for and to our Ohio Love Family.

Love Works and Spreads Joy

It is amazing to look back on those days and to see how one thing led to another. **The Love Project** story needed to be told. The "problem" of publisher rejection of the manuscript led to the opportunity to discover self-publishing. This led to our becoming the promoters of the book so that we could clear the garage of 2,000 copies. The flyers we sent led to a talk, which led to a practice session, which led to 20-years of profound community work.

An important learning in all of this is to allow the natural order of the universal flow to take its course and to follow the path it opens before us. We find it much more efficient and effective than future planning emanating from our thinking process which requires great effort and investment with no guarantee of results.

Had we held expectations, they would have been very limited compared to what had opened to us. We had focused on offering a book and the **Love Principles**; the universe opened two decades of meaningful work for us.

We remained open to any and all avenues where we might reach forth with love energy. In 1973 Diane wrote to President Richard Nixon regarding his resumption of the bombing of North Vietnam and Arleen sent a copy of *The Love Project*. We had no expectations that he would receive our communications, and certainly none that policy would change. In fact, Arleen did receive a letter marked "personal" from the White House, signed by Rose Mary Woods, Personal Secretary to the President:

> The President appreciates the kind interest that prompted you to write and enclose the newsletter together with a copy of your book, which you warmly inscribed for him and Mrs. Nixon. He was pleased by your thoughtful comments and is grateful for the generous spirit of concern your work represents. With best wishes from the President and Mrs. Nixon for a happy Holiday Season.

Needless to say, the bombings and the U.S.

policy did not change. Love did not take over at the White House. We didn't send forth our love energy with that expectation. But we knew at the time, and we know to this day, that we (and all others who focus on peace and harmony in the world) made a contribution to lifting our group and national energy. It is vitally important to remember this and to continue embodying new realities. We are embracing the human race, and holding the field for the evolution of individual souls who stand as shining examples of what is possible.

The Love Project book traveled far and wide touching people, helping them to open their heart centers, and encouraging them to start **Love Projects** of their own right where they were. We received countless letters over the years from readers who changed their lives because of how they were inspired by the story of **The Love Project**.

Arleen reflected on how important it is to use the "materials at hand," namely ourselves and our ability to direct energy and mold reality. Arleen noted that we are all created in the image of the Creative Force (what some call God) in the Universe. She saw that what is invented by humans is designed as a reflection of who they already are: the telephone patterned on the workings of our ears, the computer as mirror of our brains. Entrepreneurial individuals reach inside the human being, design a replica, give it a name, patent it, and sell it back to all the rest of us who choose not to be, do, and use all of ourselves. What a joke on ourselves! What an invitation to be the more of who we already are.

The *Seeker* Newsletter

From the beginning, we sent out frequent *Seeker* newsletters to those who expressed interest in our work. Eventually the newsletter got bigger and we called it the *Seeker* magazine. By 1990, we had changed the name to *Emerging* magazine, because that seemed to capture the nature of our work, which was constantly emerging into new forms.

The newsletters and eventually the magazine spoke to people. Readers felt supported by the articles and inspired by our sharing our own growth processes. Each magazine brought expressions of wisdom that people could embody in their daily lives.

The Love Project Continues at Thomas Jefferson High School

In 1974, Arleen checked back with Margaret Baird, the principal at Thomas Jefferson High School in Brooklyn, to see how things were going since her departure in 1971. To her delight, she was told of a long list of accomplishments. Approximately 77% of the graduates went on the higher education, 125 students were members of

National Arista (a scholastic honor society), math and language programs were on the upswing, a college discovery program was in place, and they had developed Schools-within-the-School, a Co-Op program which was a work-learning experience in which two students hold one job and rotate working one week and going to school one week.

In addition, there was a separate Co-Op program for boys with police records who had been confined at the Riker's Island facility. When the program appeared endangered due to lack of available jobs, a Jefferson student, in true **Love Project** fashion, provided the Mayor of New York with the opportunity to give. Before Mayor John Lindsey left office, one of the last things he did was to find jobs for all those students.

The Mini-school at Jefferson was helping students *create their own reality* through programs of unique summer learning which encouraged them to stay in school and go on to college.

The Love Project as it was in 1971 had undergone many changes to meet the current needs of the school and the students; it was becoming a new and relevant expression of itself, employing **The Love Principles** to bring about continuing and productive change.

One teacher in El Centro, CA affirmed that **The Love Project** epitomizes a positive alternative to negativism and hostility:

Failure and loneliness are painful, they are easy; it does not take much effort to fail, it does take effort to succeed...The set-up of **The Love Project** provides circumstances of freedom and fearlessness, where conformity is not imposed, where interest is high, in which individuality is valued and where there is an active dedication to learning...**The Love Project** provides safety and an opportunity for the manifestation of the gifts of self and love. **The Love Project's** wide planning participation encourages the creative potential between the student and the teacher working together. Students can see more clearly the relevance of the goals and make a commitment to them.

Ten More Books

Once we had begun to publish, we kept it up! In 1974 the two of us co-authored a book called *Channeling Love Energy*. We had been teaching about energy since we began our work together, practicing directing energy in our weekend sessions. We focused especially on the power of love energy, how to open to it, and how to send it forth consciously for healing on many levels. One reader in Los Angeles wrote to say:

I've been inspiring myself with a close study of *Channeling Love Energy*. In my many years of reading books in the fields of spiritual and psychological self-understanding, one has never crossed my path carrying more simple, easy-to-get-at, lighted wisdom for us every day folk wherever we are now, than this of yours.

In 1975, we published a delightful autobiographical book by Arleen called *Buddha from Brooklyn*. There were many varied responses to the book. One reader from Los Angeles was deeply moved and in many ways, but initially found himself annoyed at what he experienced as a lack of humility. Reading further he realized that the book reflected his own struggle to become the "Buddha" in him. Another man wrote that he saw an old part of himself that never wanted to accept his own God-ness and would rather belittle his being as inferior, worthless, etc. He saw that he was preventing himself from living in his Godself by his own denial. He went on:

> When you talked, with purity and innocence, about shifting your vision so as to see with the Third Eye since you were a child, it reminded me that I had a similar experience as a youth and up until I shut off the process because I had misused it, getting involved with 'magic powers.' Having felt guilty about that, I had eliminated this experience from my current reality. Meeting myself there in your book...I relived the joyful innocence of this type of vision in earlier days and I made the choice, at that moment, to open my reality to include this process as well as any other psychic phenomenon that the Universe might choose to include.
>
> I am more consciously ***receiving myself as beautiful exactly where I am*** and choosing to manifest my Buddha nature in my conscious reality.

Arleen's spiritual teacher, Ev Nolt, found the book to be alien to her because "to verbalize certain facts of this state of consciousness is to crystallize them, to anchor them to the physical plane in words." She spoke of something Wendell Johnson had taught her at the University of Iowa, that all that we say and live is fiction. "The moment we verbalize, we are talking *about* something...you are stuck with your story which makes it an archeological artifact in a living, moving, being world."

A friend from Rhode Island wrote to say he was touched by *Buddha from Brooklyn*. He too, at first, thought the title a bit presumptuous, "but it is all a cosmic joke and you can be serious and laughing at the same time."

We have always been delighted with the varying responses that have come in response to our books and our writings in our magazine. While people are sometimes disturbed, they are also stirred. They go further and then share where they have come to. Each time someone does this, we are enriched, and our own growth is extended and expanded.

In 1976, we published *Musings for Meditation* by Arleen. It was filled with insights she had had over our first four years of work together. It was the kind of book one could open to any page to see what inspiration was there for the day. Readers loved it and kept it handy for when they had a free moment. Here are some examples taken from the book:

"As long as you have a question about whether or not to do something, don't. When, in your

decision not to, you begin to question 'Why not?' you are ready to do it because your questioning is in relation to the yes and not the no."

"Dreamers create realities that realists think are impossible."

"You are given more than you think you can handle because you can handle more than you think you can."

"Self-consciousness is working hard to see yourself through the eyes of others. Self- awareness is observing your process from the inside of you."

"Abundance is sufficiency; sufficiency abundance."

"War breaks out like acne on the globe when nations resort to adolescent measures to deal with their differences."

"When you have a question, it because you have an answer."

The pages of *Musing for Meditation* provided a lift of spirit and often pointed readers in unexpected directions.

Also in 1976, we brought forth *Cosmic Unfoldment: The Individualizing Process as Mirrored in the Life of Jesus* written by Diane. It was a small book she wrote in response to an inner prompting she had received while standing alongside the Sea of Galilee in Israel. Her inner voice said, "You will write a book on the life of Jesus."

Since Diane had spent over two years researching the life of Jesus, she thought it was unlikely she would write such a book. In essence, she said "no" to the inner voice. Within a couple of months her hands had swollen up and gotten stiff. She could hardly use them. She sat in meditation one morning and asked what the swelling was about. The answer was instantaneous: "You refused to write the book."

The next morning, Diane sat down in her Sanctuary of Silence with pen and paper in hand, ready. The material began to flow. It was not at all what Diane would have expected. It was a metaphorical or symbolic interpretation of the story of Jesus's life. This was another lesson of how important it is to **have no expectations, but rather abundant expectancy.** Diane's hands quickly recovered!

Readers were also surprised. Peter Thompson, from Cleveland, OH, wrote:

> I read *Cosmic Unfoldment* with great attention and loved it. The thought had never entered my mind that the human body is being symbolized by the cross, but it does make tremendous sense and we all do literally carry our cross with us during this life. I had also never fully recognized that all the figures in the Bible could be categorized as symbols and so it gives me an even different look at the Bible than when I read it picking out only those symbols that are of interest and concern to me. Many thanks for your loving contribution to the understanding of all of those who are ready to hear and understand the message of hope and love that is contained in this book.

In 1979 Diane wrote *My Journey Into Self, Phase One,* about the early years of her spiritual journey, and in 1980 we co-authored a book called *The Love Project Way* which spelled out how the **Love Principles** can be embodied in many life circumstances and carried testimonies from many who had been embodying **The Love Principles** in their lives and finding them transformational.

In 1981, the book *Born of Love* told the story in poetry of Arleen's rebirth to a "new" mother. It was the culmination of a lifelong search for a mother's love. Arleen had never experienced it in her childhood and yearned for it. She looked for it everywhere but was not able to find it until she ***received her own mother as beautiful exactly as she was*** and received her expressions of love as she had been able to give them.

When Arleen was willing to move beyond clinging to the problems she experienced in her childhood as deprivations and accept the responsibility for her reality creation of not ever asking for what she wanted, she was able to move to the opportunities that awaited her. She brought herself to the point of "being able to ask another if she would be mother to this new child, me, who was finally emerging unafraid. In a grace-filled response, her friend said, 'You honor me. You are only putting words on what has always been so.' She told me she felt more maternal toward me than her own children."

"As a poet," Arleen said, "I can never put words on what that experience meant to me, but it did confirm what I came to know and did find a way to communicate:

Who we are, need not be who we are
If we are finished with who we were
And make the choice to create the self
We now wish to become.

The poetry that appears in *Born of Love* was so deeply personal that Arleen could feel the experiences stirring in her again when she revisited the experiences. They came from so a tender place in herself that she almost wished she hadn't laid them bare in the world because they were of such a fragile nature. One letter we received at the time of publication told her it was all right to have allowed others into that hallowed space. We include it here:

> I own and treasure *Born of Love*, a book you wrote about the painful reality of not being mothered as a child. I needed that book to reconcile myself with my own unloved childhood. It enabled me to forgive my parents, in fact to love my parents for what they did provide for me. It has made me a more loving mother to my three adult girls. The book was in the form of a long narrative poem full of exquisite passages that touch me again whenever I read them.

Arleen reflected: "Even with this beautiful response, as I write today, looking back over those years, and the deeply personal and profound experience of having been 'born' to a new mother, I feel protective of the self of me who emerged then, and wonder if I should have been so disclosing.

"Yet, that is who Diane and I were and still are to this day. We are fully open about our experiences and totally willing for others to know the whole of us as growing individuals. It is a highly-held value of ours. Not only do we have no secrets from others, and therefore no worries about what we may have told different people about different things, but we also have no secrets from our own selves. We do not lie to ourselves, or cover up uncomfortable things, or practice denial, or squelch what arises in our awareness calling it unacceptable. We are open to the whole of ourselves, to each other, and to others. It is an incredibly simple way to live, an uncomplicated approach to a conscious life."

The value of self-disclosure was spelled out in a small booklet we issued in 1978 called "*Who We Are.*" A man from Illinois wrote to say that he found the booklet to be a really inspiring journey in self-disclosure, and telling-it-like-it-is:

> I am a little awed and more than a little envious of your forthrightness and boldness in saying so clearly, concretely and simply as possible where you're coming from. So few public figures are willing to do this and it is so much needed.

In 1982, *India through Eyes of Love* was Arleen's powerful story of our first Journey Into Self in India. It focused on releasing private world images of what we think should be in order to see things as they are and, through the heart center, receive all that is as it is. Many who travel in India see only poverty and overcrowding; they miss seeing the essence of God in the eyes of the people. India is a cacophony of sounds, sights, smells, and colors; it is a massive assault on the senses. It dares the visitor to ignore or avoid the basics that comprise the whole of life.

And one of the members of our 1981 travel group, wrote:

> It was especially well put that now you don't need to travel with your 'fix-it kit' and try to make repairs in the flaws of the world. Perhaps this over-all philosophy that runs through the book is the best part of all! You expressed it so well – everyone and everything needs to be 'as is' in order for the greater harmony to prevail – and that our part is to open to see its place in the whole. How great to put this out so clearly. Also, that we are to spend our time and energy to lift ourselves out of the struggle of polarities and into the bliss where all is one. You put it so beautifully when you said that we are not in charge of determining the whole, but only of the conscious unfolding of our individual facet of the whole. Wish that everyone could read it before traveling. It would be a great boost toward being able to leave that fix-it kit at home. Less baggage, better trip.

The period from 1978 through 1985 was a prolific poetry writing time for Arleen. She wrote at least one poem a day, and sometimes two. Her feelings ran high during those years and metaphors flooded into her consciousness along with images and phrases that went beyond the prosaic to grab hold of what was transpiring in her.

She found it practically impossible to be in India and not write poetry. Everywhere she turned another line appeared on the page of her inner vision. Because she was so thoroughly immersed in that land and its people, she needed the earthiness and the grandness of the poetic form to communicate what she saw and felt.

In 1985, we published a book of Arleen's poetry called *Images*, a collection of poems that caught the glory of nature, life, and the essence of God.

We had put out ten books in thirteen years. Not bad for a fledgling publishing company! We had worked with our IBM Composer to prepare the texts for publishing. That was a two-step process for which those who use high-tech computers today would not have the patience. Arleen would type a line, get a code from the computer, and then re-type the line after entering the code. Then the type came out justified. This was slow and tedious and if errors were made (and of course they were), we had to cut and paste the corrections.

Diane did the cutting and pasting. She also laid out the text on a light board so that it was camera ready for the printer. Our volunteers helped us keep up with mailing out copies of the books after we autographed them. Since we had to order

2,000 copies of each book, our tandem garage was half full of copies of our books. It was a good thing we had only one car.

Our books were a way of sharing our personal stories of growth as well as offering principles by which others might live if they were so inspired.

Two Books Published in New York

In addition to publishing our own books, Simon and Schuster published Diane's story of how to grieve consciously, *Life is Victorious! How to Grow through Grief.* Some said the book opened up things they had been avoiding, especially **giving others the opportunity to give**. They had been grieving but not sharing the process and so their relatives assumed they had it together and didn't need them. It made others realize that they were trying to rush people through the grieving process because *they* couldn't stand seeing them in pain. It opened others to the distinction between "little self" and Higher Self.

Arleen's book *Why Me? How to Heal What's Hurting You* was published by Rawson Associates in 1978. The idea for the book came when she heard her neighbor crying in her garden because her son had just suffered a severe stroke. She was so distraught she disavowed God because He had done this to her son. As Arleen listened to her lament, her inner voice called to her telling her to write a book about how to deal consciously with life traumas. She came into the house and announced to Diane, "I'm going to write a book on healing!" Then she headed for her desk and began work immediately. Amazingly, the manuscript was completed in two and a half weeks. Arleen recalled:

"It simply flowed. Everything I knew on the subject poured out of me. The most important theme was in the first two words, 'Why me?' When most of us utter these words, they come with a sense of helplessness or senselessness, and a reaching out for commiseration. When my inner voice told me to write the book, it told me immediately that when we ask the question 'why me' it should never be out of a sense of 'poor-me-ness' but rather because there are answers to the question which we need to find in order to set healing energy in motion.

"*How* the question is asked is the key. If, in the asking, the emphasis is on regretting being afflicted or on blaming outside elements or persons for having brought the condition into being, the dis-ease is actually strengthened rather than relieved due to the heavy investment of energy in ruing or accusing.

"Thanks to my inner voice, I could see immediately an empowering alternative: Ask 'why me' with eagerness and openness. Ask, 'What have I been given to explore?' or 'What is this asking me to change or to do?' or 'How did this begin? What is the meaning here? What are my opportunities?'

"Not only are we asking 'why me' with purpose and intention, we would do well to do the asking with gratitude and thanksgiving for the condition or the crisis. This is a way of affirming that in every hardship a blessing resides, in every dis-ease creative unrest is stirring, in turbulence churns the magnificent upheaval-like energy of growth-in-action. We have been given a gift that, when unwrapped, can lead to whole new ways of being. The dis-ease is the disturbance to the status quo which has grown stagnant. Breakdowns often lead to breakthroughs. Gratitude for the symptoms affirms that beneath them resides vital information for our moving forward in our lives to a next step or stage (and I would add, even if that next stage is beyond life in this body). In this sense, the dis-ease is really the healing of a deep condition which cries out to be seen and faced with love.

"To say *no* to the new that seeks to enter our lives is to create a problem. That 'no' *is* the problem. To say *yes* to the new, even though it seems uninvited, unexpected and even unwanted, is to open to the opportunities for growth and change. The 'yes' *is* the opportunity.

"Why me? Why *not* me?"

Arleen loved writing the book. She wrote it as an echo of the reader's own inner voice serving as a guide through a step by step process of identifying the opportunities and awakening the energy of healing.

People across the country wrote with praise

for how *Why Me?* had served them. The exercises in the book helped them to set healing in motion. A pastor spoke of how it helped him deal with depression and resentment. He saw how he had created that for himself and realized that he could now be part of a creating a new life. He appreciated the turnaround the book provided him. Others learned to be more tender with themselves. A woman in Sacramento found herself responding deeply and lovingly, reading for a while then stopping, holding the book close to her, "clasping it as something or someone precious, and weeping finally in release."

This letter came from Pennsylvania:

> Your book *Why Me?* has helped me to understand and elevate myself in ways that are unbelievable. Since I have been reading books on the subject of healing, none of them seemed to initiate or encourage me to really ask "Why me?" or to seek to be friends with my dis-ease. Nor did they aid me to come in contact with my Higher Self. Your book is the best I have read in the area of healing.

The two of us implemented the teaching in the book in our own lives with both physical and emotional conditions. It was the way we proceeded in all areas; if we teach something, we live it. We are palpable examples of the wisdom we know; as that wisdom shifts and changes, so do we.

Problems Are Opportunities

In the mid 1970's, during our expanding publication period, we had a major learning experience in a situation that called for full heart center energy as we dealt with a significant problem/opportunity.

Our publishing venture was proceeding nicely and we wondered if we should also publish other people's works. This idea came to us in 1975 when we were introduced to a man we shall call Aaron, a wonderful artist. We resonated to his work and its spiritual overtones. We both felt we were given inner guidance to publish a book of his.

Up until this time we approached our inner guidance as giving us direction that we would follow as each new indication was revealed. As this occurred we would move ahead with what we had received, one step at a time, no more, no less. This time our approach was slightly different. We stepped on the pedal of our enthusiasm and began to speed on our inner highway, rather than take things slow and easy. We made mistakes because we were enamored of the project we saw on the road ahead of us.

The mistakes we made served us long after the fact and we share them here as a possible guidepost for others who may be too quick to implement what they receive as inner guidance.

Instead of turning our attention to possibly publishing one of Aaron's books, we took a disharmonious leap of deciding to publish all of his works. This was similar to proceeding from getting a driver's license to becoming a race car contestant.

We had been drawn to one book, but Aaron felt that three other books of his were more basic and should be done first. In spite of our clear and specific inner direction, we let our minds take over and we concurred with Aaron because what he said "made sense." We were already not on the right road, the one on which we had started, but we didn't see that we were getting lost.

We went ahead with the project even when we had serious reservations about the nature of some of the written material in those first three books. It was not in complete harmony with our inner knowing. This should have been at least a red flag for us, if not a stop sign.

We had put out a request for money to publish the books and when it didn't come we ignored that clear indication and sought ways to modify our plans to "make" the reality happen. This move should have clearly showed us we had taken ourselves to a detour and could go no further on the road we had chosen.

Problems Are Opportunities

When this didn't stop us, a series of illnesses, accidents and periods of exhaustion occurred but we dismissed them. As we look back on this it is clear we had shifted our focus from inner directive to "our will be done." Big mistake.

Worse still, we failed to give significance to our own growing doubts about proceeding with the project. Others in our Love Family also expressed doubts about the approach to life in the books and how it did not line up with **The Love Project** approach to life.

We didn't listen. Instead we decided to wait and see what would emerge. We had grown stubborn by now, certain that new roads would open and we would be able to proceed merrily on our way.

We did not tell Aaron what was going on. We told ourselves we didn't want him to worry, in case it should all work out. We were lying to ourselves, to be sure, but we convinced ourselves we had the best of intentions. All of this might well have indicated that we may have initially misread the inner guidance. Instead, we compounded the issue impossibly.

We chose to *write* to Aaron telling him we could not go on with the project, rather than going to see him face to face. This was a violation of our own style of functioning. Once again, our minds had gotten in the way as we told ourselves writing would be fairer to Aaron so that he could have time to touch his own feelings and thoughts before making a response to us. As we write this we are astonished at how convoluted we had made this entire event.

By the time we did talk with Aaron, he had already created a reality of his own interpretations about us and our actions (how could he not?) which led him to file a summons against us in court, declaring that he was suing us for breach of contract, misrepresentation and intent to deceive and defraud, and demanding thousands of dollars in damages for failure to publish. We had clearly been driving recklessly and now we had crashed.

Taking Action

We packed up all the materials Aaron had loaned us as well as the work we had done preparing his books for publication and drove up the coast to meet with Aaron in person, which is what we should have done in the beginning rather than writing a letter. When we arrived at his studio, he was there with his lawyer at his side. His lawyer launched out on his presentation of why they were suing us while Aaron stood quietly at his side.

While the lawyer was talking, Diane quickly did an energy assessment and determined that he was functioning almost entirely in his throat chakra, and that Aaron was resonating in his solar plexus. Diane quickly moved her attention into her heart chakra and began to breathe deeply through that chakra, sending love energy to both Aaron and his lawyer. When the lawyer tried to hand her the legal document, Diane responded quietly and firmly, "We are not going to court."

As Diane explained what our intentions had been and how things had unfolded, she continued to send energy through her heart chakra, something we had not only learned to do ourselves but had taught many others. Before long, Aaron began to share from his heart center and the lawyer put the summons in his briefcase. After consulting quietly with Aaron, the lawyer left the studio and the three of us sat down for a genuine heart to heart sharing.

With Aaron's approval, we wrote a letter to all those who had made financial or other contributions to our efforts to publish Aaron's works, explaining to them briefly that we were giving up the project, enclosing an accounting of funds received and spent, and indicating that we would reimburse their contributions if they felt we had not put their money to good use. Only one person asked to be reimbursed.

This experience was a good lesson in the importance of taking only one step at a time, of always sharing process with people while in the midst of it, of distortions that occur in inner guidance when rational minds take over, of watching for every sign and heeding it, and of consciously and actively making choices instead of "waiting" for more clarification than we have already been given.

We were grateful for the learning. It enabled us to see clearly that it was for us to publish *only* what was a direct illustration of the power of love at work in life and of the way each of us can *be* that love embodied. That is the work we were given to do. Not any other. We were able to affirm that coming to this clarification through making mistakes was no "worse" than coming to it through making "right" choices. In that way, we were able to **receive ourselves as beautiful** in having made mistakes. It was merely another way to learn and grow, another way the universe keeps us on our path. **Problems are definitely opportunities**, and sometimes we are slow to acknowledge what the opportunity is.

Aaron wrote to us some weeks later saying, "I am glad the storm is over. It was brief – but very rough. Can't see how it could have occurred. I am working away–drawing and writing. It is flowing. One day in right time the stream will find the sea. If the work is right it has a place. We are friends. That is important for now. With my love . . ."

We were grateful for the power of the love force that enabled us to find a clear path through the disharmony so that our friendship with Aaron could be reaffirmed. The result was that we restored our relationship with Aaron to one of mutual trust, forgiveness, respect, and free flow of love energy. All without going to court.

Love As Unblocked Energy

Encouraging people to open their heart centers in order to live in unconditional love required redefining love for the majority of people we met. Most people believed they could never love someone they didn't like or agree with. Many who had learned of unconditional love in their church upbringing had interpreted it as turning into a doormat, a misinterpretation, surely, of Jesus's injunction to "turn the other cheek." And many told us they simply did not want to **receive all people as beautiful**. What about Hitler, for instance?

We accepted the challenge and almost immediately began to teach people to look at their interactions as an exchange of energy. Both of us saw, in our experiences of awakening, that everything is energy and we are therefore energy beings. Whenever we interact with another, we either share energy or block it. In the simplest terms, unconditional love can be understood as unblocked heart center energy.

Energy is life-giving; without it we could not thrive and grow. Our heart centers function like the sun, to use an analogy; they give off rays of life-giving energy that can be called love. In the same way as all living things need the sun for life and growth, human beings--in fact all living things--need love. Many studies have shown that human beings cannot survive without love even if they have proper nutrition.

To stay with this analogy, if we close our heart centers the effect on those with whom we interact can be inhibiting, impeding their further growth. Of course, no single one of us is the only source of life-giving love energy for a given human being. However, in circumstances where large groups of people conspire to deny love to individuals or groups, the effects are often devastating.

A woman once shared with us that she had been raised in a very confining religious group with extremely narrow beliefs and ways of living. As a young person, she rebelled against the constraints and as a punishment, she was shunned. The practice of shunning is the harshest kind of rejection because one is not only thrown out of the community but is energetically isolated, even ignored. This woman told us that she had spent the rest of her life trying to recover from the effects of that excommunication, and even though when we met her she had been far away from the group for over forty years, she could still feel the stunting effect of being banished. This is an example of denying someone the benefits of the love force.

Learning to Register Energy

To teach people to acknowledge themselves and everything in the world around them as energy, we taught people about deep breathing. Most people are relatively unaware of breathing because it occurs so automatically. However, breath is our most direct access to the flow of energy through our fields. It is the only function of the autonomic nervous system which we can consciously control.

It is obvious that the breath energizes us. When we are "out of breath" we cannot continue to function physically or mentally until we "catch our breath." When we learn to direct the breath consciously we can begin to direct the energy flow. This is a method that has been taught for thousands of years in the science of Yoga as well as in other esoteric methodologies, and the two of us use it daily in our own lives. We have taught people to breathe consciously in our Practice Sessions as the most direct access to their own energy fields and to becoming aware of themselves as a whole self in body, mind, emotions, and spirit.

Once any of us awakens to knowing that we can actually direct our energy flow and make a difference in the immediate circumstances confronting us and even in the world at large, our perspective on who we are as conscious beings changes and we begin to touch the power of creating realities and influencing others. This ability is best executed when we imprint the world responsibly, with heart center direction, asking what is wanted and being of service to others with a focus on creativity, beauty, and alleviating suffering.

Arleen first learned the power of breathing consciously and directing energy when she stepped into the fray of burgeoning violence at Thomas Jefferson High School. Using the strength of her will, she separated the two boys who were on the verge of destruction. She never said a word. She touched the boys with the energy of her heart center and they turned and walked in opposite directions. As a confirmation to Arleen, that very day she was "given" **The Love Principles** and **The Love Project**. (Refer to the whole story in chapter three, starting on page 23.)

Years later, Arleen had another memorable personal learning experience in relation to breathing and directing the energy flow when she discovered one morning that she was doing neither! During a tennis match, she discovered that her body was trying to imitate Lego construction. She would start walking and the knee would do its thing quite separate from the foot or the ankle. She would swing at the ball and the shoulder claimed domination over the move, ignoring completely any relationship to the arm, hand, wrist, etc. The entire body was functioning as if constructed of separate parts and pieces. She took the opportunity to observe this separation. The main element missing was energy flow; this disenabled Arleen from functioning as a whole being.

Extending the observation from the body to life in general, Arleen was glad to have this kinesthetic experience of how people live in separation from one another, with imaginary lines drawn around them to encapsulate their differences. This false view of themselves enables them to argue, to go to war, to kill each other, to *make* love rather than live in merged heart centers. She saw that another way to talk about the primary opposing forces of good and evil is to call them by other names, Union and Separation.

Arleen had no energy flow moving through the whole of her that morning. Instead, the life force bounced from one part, one joint, to another, as if she were thousands of separate beings wearing her clothes. That is how the not-yet-awakened members of the human race live: millions of separate beings not realizing they are all one being in the same lighted attire of the One Self.

Once Arleen returned to full energy flow, she immediately felt connected to her inner self, to the world of the One being, to the energy world in which the cosmic influences dance and imprint all that is manifested.

Arleen was grateful for the seeing of this, and that she has made it a constant practice to see the More in every action and event so that every day becomes a learning experience as the truths of the Universe are revealed.

Touching and Sensing Energy

In our sessions, we helped people extend their sense of touch in order to discover that they *are* energy. By rubbing their hands together and then separating them by about an inch, people could feel the energy being emitted by the hands as radiating heat and sometimes as magnetism. An expansion of that exercise was to have people rub their hands together and then to approach another person's head very slowly, for instance, to see how close they would have to come before they could feel the energy radiating from the head.

These practices were augmented by standing in front of a person with eyes closed to see how close you would have to come before you could sense the other's energy and how far you would have to move away before you would lose touch with it.

We used these and many other exercises to enable people to be sensitive to the energy of others and to their own energy. It was not commonplace to talk about or practice with unseen frequencies four decades ago. Some participants jumped right in, eager to learn something new; others were reticent or even quite skeptical.

In one session a rather tall, athletic man, call him John, was lying face down while two participants gave him what we called an "energy massage." His physical body was never touched as hands facing palms down traveled from the top of his head to the soles of his feet. We did these energy massages so that people could begin to sense their energy directly rather than through the sense of touch.

John assured everyone during the process that he felt nothing. His head was turned to the side and rested on the floor as he looked at the group gathered round him. When the two who were massaging reached the back of his knees and slowly proceeded toward his heels, John's legs lifted off the ground several inches. They had levitated and he was not aware of it.

When John sat up he proudly announced that he had felt nothing and was denigrating the "experiment." He did not "believe" in "energy" and therefore could make no room in his conscious awareness for a different experience. When the two women who had witnessed his legs levitating and the two of us assured him of the event, he refused to consider the possibility. Beliefs held in the private world are sometimes more powerful than actual experience. In those cases, even seeing is not believing!

Other people tried to dismiss the experience of "energy," saying it was just heat radiating off the body. But, of course, energy produces heat and it is important to recognize that, because when the body loses heat we can warm it up with deep breathing, rubbing the body, and toning.

The Power of Toning

To tone is to use breath and the voice to move energy through the field, as taught by Laurel Keyes (See her book *Toning,* DeVorss & Co., 1990). It is very effective for warming the body, as well as for moving blocked energy and thus promoting healing. We taught Toning in all our sessions because it has been so useful and effective for the two of us. At the beginning of a session we invited the whole group to tone because it is a way to be in touch with the energy of everyone in the group at once in an impersonal way. It doesn't take long for a group to come to a harmonious energy exchange with toning.

Toning is also a very effective way of moving solar plexus energy when an individual or a group is emotionally upset. Toning clears the mind efficiently, without needing to mentally process anything. And Toning, we have found, helps us to connect with universal, spiritual energies since sound was, according to all great Wisdom Traditions, the first creative act and once a sound is made, it reverberates forever throughout the universe as scientists have proven.

We were delighted to learn on our trip to Australia about the practice of healing by Aborigines. They teach that there are several essential elements to healing:

First, there is the energetic reconnection that

occurs as hands are passed through the etheric body where the memory of the perfect pattern is held. This jogs the memory of the cells into acknowledging the true nature of their healthy state, and they begin to realign with that state.

Second, moving hands through the energy field without touching the physical body removes any shock that has been experienced. This prevents swelling and bruising.

Third, chanting (or Toning) and singing reinforce the restored harmony, guaranteeing no pain and no aftereffects.

Fourth, once the healing is complete, no more energy, time, or attention need be given to the injury. The circle of the event is closed and no one refers to it again.

Finally, there is only one source for the healing and that is the power within. How we feel emotionally about things is what really registers. It is recorded in every cell of the body, in the core of the personality, in the mind, and in the eternal self. Therefore, if the one injured or ill is open and receptive to receive wellness and has faith in a state of full and immediate recovery, then it can occur.

We taught a similar process in our Practice Sessions that focused on healing and self-healing. We taught people how to promote healing with Toning, first by clearing the field and then by focusing on areas of congestion and using the voice to move through the blocks. We also showed participants how to slowly, and with conscious attention, move their hands over a strained or injured area to set a healing process in motion. As one moves the energy with the magnetic pull of the moving hand, the congestion or block in the afflicted location eases or breaks up, and soon, the pain is gone or at least greatly diminished. Both Toning and use of the hands to move energy are practical applications of our knowledge that everything is energy. If the energy is blocked or congested it causes pain, stiffness, or discomfort and eventually can manifest as an illness. Moving the energy invites release and healing.

The two of us not only brought these methods to our Practice Sessions, we used them continually in our life together. One morning Arleen was cutting a bagel with a very sharp knife. It went through the bread and into the fleshy part of her palm causing a deep gash. Blood started pouring forth into the sink. Diane came over immediately, took hold of the injured hand and moved the energy by holding her own right hand a few inches above the wound. She continued to move the energy for about 15 minutes. During that time, the bleeding ceased and the pain subsided. When Diane finished, the two of them looked at the palm and saw that the gash had completely closed. In its place was a very thin line, about an inch long. There was not even any red along the line; it was slightly whiter than as the rest of the skin, as if it had been perfectly sutured by a medical professional. The scar remains to this day as a reminder of the healing power of moving energy.

Similarly, one time Diane was at home alone, working on rearranging books on tall shelves. She climbed up on a ladder to reach the books. At one point she stepped off the ladder onto a metal bookend, which made a deep cut into the sole of her foot. Diane sat down on the nearby couch and held her foot. The telephone was across the room and she did not want to step on the carpet transferring blood as she went. She quickly decided to use her hand to move the energy and stop the bleeding. She worked for several minutes until the bleeding stopped and there was no more stinging in the wound.

By the time Arleen came home later that afternoon, the only evidence of the incident was a scar on the bottom of Diane's foot. It remains to this day.

On another occasion Diane woke up on a weekend morning with a stiff neck that was so painful she could not move her head. Not wanting to disturb her chiropractor on a weekend, she sat down in the living room and focused on the neck with her voice in Toning, moving from below the stiffness, through the area and releasing the energy through the top of the head. In a very short time, the neck relaxed and the pain went away. Such occurrences were frequent in our home over the years.

There is no magic to this approach; anyone can do it. Diane once helped free one of her nephews of his bad cold (sneezing, watering eyes, stuffed nose, and feeling bad all over) by holding him on her lap and moving the energy out of his field with her hands, which passed over and around his face and head without touching him. He was soon up and playing and feeling good, so his mother asked Diane what she had done. Diane explained. Dorothy told her many months later that when her husband came home from playing hoops with friends, having sprained his ankle so that he could hardly walk, Dorothy said, "Let's try what Diane did for Tom." She sat down and began to move the energy around Jim's ankle. Before long, the swelling subsided and Jim was able to walk on the foot with no pain. Dorothy said, "It really works." And it does.

This same phenomenon takes place in relational interactions. If Betty closes off from Judy, puts up a block, no energy moves between them. Their communication is disrupted, sometimes severed. When the two are willing to examine the rift and they take deep breaths and open to the possibility of interacting, they can be said to be having "a change of heart." By opening the heart center and allowing unblocked energy to flow both are able to open to new possibilities with each other. Unblocking energy is often the shortest route to resolving conflicts; it eliminates the need for confrontation, explanation, rehashing the past, and searching for new ways to meet. Unblocking the energy is a direct pathway to union.

The Heart Center

Once people become aware of energy and the breath they can begin to identify the various energy centers, called chakras in the Eastern philosophies, through which they receive and send energy. It is very empowering to have this information and we have been introducing the chakras and teaching people to tune into them consciously since our beginning years of working together.

The Heart Chakra is an energy hub that supplies energy to our entire field and can be visualized as focused in the center of the chest near the physical heart and the lungs. The word chakra means "wheel" and helps describe the movement of the energy. The Heart Chakra circulates the life force throughout our energy fields and is therefore appropriately associated with the heart and lungs that circulate blood and oxygen to the entire physical body. We can focus on it as a booster and bring replenishment to ourselves in times of overload or diminished life force.

In contrast to what is often *called* love, which is focused on *getting* what we desire, Heart Center love is motivated by an *urge to give*. Rather than wanting to *possess* a lover or to *receive* love, Heart Center energy arouses a desire to *give* to others what will bring them joy.

The forces in the Heart Center also awaken an urge to understand the larger dynamic of things, to see the big picture, to understand others and what makes them function as they do, to know why things are as they are in the world. In Heart Center energies, we become aware of how little we really know and how little we understand about others and the world around us.

The Love Principle that is associated with the Heart Chakra is **receive all people (including self) as beautiful exactly as they are.** Notice the principle begins with "receive," not "accept" or "like." To receive we must open to others, taking in their energy and then releasing it. It is as if the Heart Center has a revolving door: the energy comes in and passes right on through. As a consequence, we are able to fully experience others but we are not "stuck" with them or with their energy. Instead, we are free to *choose* what responses to make.

In the Heart Center, we stay balanced; we are not thrown off balance by the words, actions or even withdrawal of others. From our balanced state, we can make conscious choices about **the reality we wish to create** and about **the change we want to be** without any need to change others or even receive acknowledgment from them.

The energy pouring through an open heart center is vast and seemingly endless. There are no limits on how the energy can be expressed and no boundaries on how far is its reach. In 1978 Arleen wrote of this incredible love and energy in a poem entitled *Being Magnificently Unsatisfied:*

I suffer Joy pain...
> *the incurable ailment*
> *of not*
> *of never*
> *of not ever*

being able
> *to say*
> *to show*
> *to express*

The Love –
> *My God,*

The Love –
> *that rushes through my being*
> *like the rapids of river*
> *on journey without end.*

I
don't know how
to tell you.
The rose opens so full
> *so flat against the air behind it*
> *in the stretch of its scent,*
> *in the velvet of its field.*

I
cannot stretch far enough

        to say it all.
        The butterfly touches so lightly,
        so gently, the gift corsage of God.
My
touch is too loud
        for the softness of my soul.
        Wheat waves its caress
        upon the blue of morning sky,
Rainbows leap from earth to heaven's eye,
But I
        I
        haven't found the way
        to match the inner call.
        I suffer Joy-pain; I cannot say it all.
The ailment is incurable.
'Tis the reason I am here in human form:
        to struggle deep within this well
        of wonder,
        to reach beyond my grasp,
        to run in circles in a field of flowers
        in the exultation of my love
        which carries me closer
        to the source
        of the symphony of my spirit.
I
don't know how to tell you
of my love.

The Other Energy Centers

The Heart Chakra is only one energy hub in our individual fields. There are six other primary chakras, each one of which empowers certain aspects of our functioning in the world. For example, the Generative Chakra is the source of all sexual and reproductive energy as well as creative physical expressions such as athletics, dance, construction, and cooking. This Chakra is the home of the **Love Principle** *be the change you want to see happen instead of trying to change anyone else.*

The Solar Plexus is the center in which we register all feelings and develop our sense of self as a powerful and creative being in the world. It is in the energies of the Solar Plexus that we feel our emotional connections with others and our sense of belonging. It is easy to see why the **Love Principle** *problems are opportunities* connects with this chakra since we register our feelings of distress here as well as hope and happiness.

A simple example would be responding or reacting to a situation that evokes strong feelings. When functioning unconsciously, it is easy to be thrown into emotional upheaval. The solar plexus, where feeling energy churns, can become a pit into which one falls. Because there are no "handles of awareness" to grasp, there can be a plunge into upset and no view of how to extricate oneself. In the same situation, a conscious person can observe the descent and shift the energy from the solar plexus into the heart center where life force can more easily flow, or into the generative center where something can be set in motion using that energy for constructive action. A conscious person can begin to look for the opportunity in the seeming problem and not get bogged down in despair.

The Throat Chakra provides energy for our mental processes: thinking, speaking, and hearing/listening. Needless to say, empowerment in and through this energy center is critically important in almost every situation. Through these energies we make rational connections with others and are able to invite cooperative evaluation and interaction. The **Love Principle** that relates to the Throat Chakra is ***provide others with opportunities to give.***

The Third Eye Chakra correlates with the center of the forehead and energizes all perception, both external and internal. We associate external perception with our eyes, but the processing of perception in the brain is essential to the external seeing. Internal seeing includes visualization, imagination, and understanding (as in "I see"). This is the realm in which we ***create our realities consciously.***

The other two Chakras are at the polar extremes of our energy fields. The energies of the Sacral Chakra help us to feel our connection with the planet on which we live and the physical surroundings that "ground" us and give us a sense of "place." This chakra links with the coccyx and the **Love Principle** *have no expectations, but rather abundant expectancy.* The other polarity is called the Crown Chakra and is associated with the top of the head and above. It is our connection with the subtle or spiritual energies of the cosmos and with the thread that ties all the **Love Principles** together: *Choice is the life process. In every new moment of awareness we are free to make a new choice.*

Back in 1978 we wrote the following:

We know from our own experience that one of the qualities that characterizes the life force is love. Love is that property of attraction or adhesion that enables the universe as we know it to exist. All forces of attraction—gravity, magnetism, sexual attraction, preferences, likes, curiosity, mating instincts among animals, etc.—give evidence of love at work in and through the life force. Without love, the union of two polarities—as positive and negative ions uniting to release electricity, or protons and electrons to produce an atom, or male and female to give birth to a new child—would not occur and life as we know it would cease to come into being, into manifestation.

We also know that each of us is an expression of the life force. Therefore, it is in our nature to be loving. When we love you, we are doing what is natural to us, what is easy.

It takes no effort on our part to love you. We simply leave ourselves open to the force that gives us life, letting it fill us and flow through us. As long as we do not struggle with the life force, or block it or interfere with it, our love for you is not only effortless, it is boundless.

We choose to **create the reality** that love *Is*. As long as we are alive, we are also alive with love. That love draws us to you as naturally as magnets with opposing electrical charges. Therefore, we relax and let life express love in and through us. We simply love you. [From a booklet called "When We Love You ... ," LP Publications, 1978]

Unconditional love, then, is energy that brings us together and unites us in life-affirming association. This is the love we have sought to teach for over four decades, and that others are sharing widely through their own lives.

In 1977, Arleen had an experience which exemplifies the power of love as unblocked energy. Here is her description of the event.

We sat around discussing bussing. Yetta and Jack were tossing out stereotyped statements about the violence of Blacks, the hopelessness of everything, and the fault of the system and government, about which we can do nothing. [Writing about this today, in July, 2017, it is almost shocking to see that with all the change there has been, little seems to have changed.] They said,

"Individuals can't make change." Liberals in the room were enraged by their comments, and the arguing jumped back and forth like a hard-hit tennis ball. The players were really into the game.

"You can't change anything," Jack repeated. Yet, he went on to relate to us that he donates several hours a week in a nursing home and Yetta told us that once, when faced with a Black man holding a gun on her, she treated him as a human being and came out of it without a scratch.

The liberals returned the volley. "You see! That just proves what we've been trying to say." Yetta lobbed back over the net with, "That case was one in a million. The rest of them would just as soon kill you."

I re-examined my participation. I had been engaging in the same way as everyone else. We were into our minds. I had been contributing nothing new or different. I shifted gears and consciously sent forth love energy from the heart center. I said to Jack, "The most important thing I'll go away with from this engaging is that you are making a vital contribution at the nursing home. That is *being* change."

That simple affirmation constituted a turning point. Jack warmed up, became appreciative, and began saying loving things.

Group members began to tell Jack about **The Love Project** and how it turned violence in a ghetto high school around to make the school a center of love and caring. Jack crossed to the sales table to buy *The Love Project* book so he could come to know the whole story. He *wanted* to know.

Yetta came up to me. She wanted to talk, personally, intimately. She said, "What is it about you? There's something different, unusual about you."

Having no answer to her query, I went instead with my own thrust. "You two misrepresent yourselves. You throw out what sounds like negative rhetoric and yet you are both very loving. Why not share the loving and if you must share the other, share it from the point of view of what a struggle it all is for you, rather than as blanket statements which do little more than evoke equally blanket statements in others?"

"You are a very beautiful person," she said.

"Thank you. But, you know, when I was a young street kid in Brooklyn, I was no different from those who disgust you with their 'bad' behavior. I was a roughneck, a neighborhood bully, often foul-mouthed, and almost impossible to reach because of my cover of toughness."

"You're kidding."

"Hell, no."

A long pause followed. Then Yetta said, "You radiate light. I need to put on my glasses. I can't look in your eyes. They hypnotize me."

"What you see in me is in you," I replied.

"You have an important message for millions.

You should live a long time. Your life has worth. You are precious. I don't want you killed."

"My life would be totally worth it if, like you, I will be loving when facing death."

Bowing her head, she said, "Thank you."

"Yetta?" She raised her head. "My life is well worth it. *You* are my reason for living."

"You have given me a great gift. You have reminded me of the wisdom I once knew and forgot: that all people are beautiful, that there is hope for everyone."

"And you, Yetta, have given me the special gift of affirming for me that truth and love make miracles."

"You speak truth," She said. "It radiates from you. It made me change. It made me remember. You are the like the child I never had and I am your child as well. Together we have given birth to a child between us."

This is the power of unblocked heart center energy.

We have found that as people begin to think in terms of energy flow in their own fields as well as between them and others, they can better understand how they can have a beneficial effect on others while remaining centered and at peace in self. Being unconditionally loving is as simple as breathing along with others, sharing life force, and freeing others to choose how to express their own energy.

Expanding Our Repertoire

Presentations to Large Groups

Our intention from the beginning was to touch people with universal love and to inspire them with the six **Love Principles** to choose a life of love. Ours was a very personal approach. We liked to meet people individually and by name, and we were happy to share our personal lives and experiences in exchange.

From time to time we were invited to give talks to large groups at conferences. We were grateful to Leland Stewart for inviting us to speak at the conferences he organized for the International Cooperation Council (ICC) in Los Angeles, CA. Twice we were keynote speakers to crowds of over one thousand.

This was our least favorite format, however, even though we welcomed the opportunity to share the principles with more people. What we didn't like was two-fold. First, it was difficult to involve the audiences actively, and we were both convinced that people learned more, and more quickly, when they participated. Even with large groups of a thousand or more, we always invited people to partner with someone sitting near them, or sometimes even to break into small groups. Our objective was to have them try out the **Love Principles** in interactions and to share from their personal perspective and life experience. Because we are both enthusiastic and outgoing, we were usually successful in getting people to interact, but there was no way we could get around the room and be present to them individually as we preferred.

That leads to the second thing we didn't prefer about speaking to large groups: we usually met only a few people in person, namely those that chose to stay after the presentation to speak to us individually. We were grateful for those contacts and we tried to compensate by asking people to give us their names and addresses if they wanted to receive more information about our work. That invitation always brought to us hundreds of names, but it was not the same as speaking with people one on one. For that reason, we tried to offer a small workshop as a follow-up to a large presentation.

It was on one of those occasions of addressing a large conference that we learned a lesson about hugging. We both thought hugging was the best way to let people experience that they were embraced in unconditional love. However, after we finished our presentation at one of the ICC events, the next speaker came on the stage. Diane approached him to give him a welcome hug. His whole body stiffened and his face turned red. She quickly realized he did not want to be hugged. It was a revelation to us both that some people might not want to be hugged. From then on, we approached people with the question, "Do you hug?" sincerely giving them an opportunity to say, "No," or "Not really."

Several times over the years we were asked to speak in worship services, often in Unity or Religious Science churches, but occasionally also in Episcopal or Methodist churches and of course at the Federated Church in Chagrin Falls, Ohio. In almost all those cases, we also gave workshops so that people could engage with us and with the **Love Principles** more extensively and actively.

By 1977, five years into our work, people we met and worked with were taking **The Love Principles** into their own communities and creating their own **Love Projects**. Cliff Marks in San Diego suggested we print the principles on small cards that people could carry with them as reminders. All these decades later that little yellow card is still being distributed and it has traveled around the world, many times.

By the fall of 1977 we had facilitated about 133 Practice Sessions and over 64 Experiential Seminars. We led over 140 Open Dialogs and reached between 7 to 10,000 people in the process. Over 245 individuals participated in our Journeys into

Self in San Diego, and we took over 150 people on foreign travel experiences: three trips to the Middle East, one to Guatemala and Mexico, one to the British Isles and one to South America.

Our active sponsors grew to 600. Nearly one fifth of those receiving our newsletter were non-monetary sponsors because we did not exclude people who couldn't afford to pay for the services we offered. Others who could afford to contribute to our non-profit corporation sent part or all of their monthly tithe money to **The Love Project**. We published five books, amounting to 19,000 volumes, and made significant distributions to libraries. All the work during those five years was done without paid staff and with the assistance of a group of faithful volunteers. The first year **The Love Project** finished in the black was 1977, five years into our work.

It should be noted here that all this was accomplished without advertising and before the Internet existed, before mass digital communication, before all the media outlets such as Facebook, Twitter, YouTube, and the like. Our expansion took place person to person, by word of mouth, by mail, workshop by workshop, presentation by presentation, and through our books and our magazine. We can only imagine, 45 years later, what the exponential explosion of outreach might have been if all of the above had been available. But it wasn't, and looking back, we are grateful and astonished at our progress.

Consciousness Coaching

Initially we were both convinced that we needed to meet people only once, introduce them to the six **Love Principles**, give them a warm hug, and send them on their way. However, people began to ask for variations on the Practice Session theme. A woman from Pennsylvania suggested that we do private consultations. We had never thought of that and we said, "We wouldn't even know what to charge." She suggested that we begin by charging $25.00 for an hour's private consultation with the two of us. We agreed and were surprised at the number of people who came to us for what we began to call "Consciousness Coaching." We helped people to see how, by applying the six **Love Principles**, they could move forward in their personal and spiritual lives in more life-affirming and positive ways.

About ten years later a movement started across the country called "Coaching," and people set up training programs to teach people to be "life coaches." We do not claim to have started that movement, but we were certainly among the first to call ourselves "coaches." We did that to distinguish ourselves from those who were trained as psychologists and therapists. Our training was as teachers and we wanted people to be clear about what they were signing up for. We were teachers of how to live life consciously, how to make choices, how to live in unconditional love, and how to become the more of self that was waiting to be revealed. We knew a lot about the subject because we were practicing it ourselves every day and being very successful.

Our focus in the coaching sessions was not on the past; it was on how to move forward from the present. Looking at **problems as opportunities** meant we focused on the positive rather than on dissecting the problem. We asked people what they wanted to bring into being in their lives and helped them to see how to **create that reality consciously** and how to **be the change they wanted to see happen.**

We have continued to do Consciousness Coaching over all these years, sometimes working alone, sometimes together. We have coached both individuals and couples. Our focus is always on taking positive steps into the future based on the desires and intentions of those who seek our help.

We usually encourage people to do a series of six sessions so that they have time to find clarity regarding the challenge they want to address. We have enjoyed the opportunity to watch individuals grow and mature in their ability to take responsible charge of their lives and to feel empowered to do so. We have always been grateful to June for suggesting and requesting that we do private sessions, something we might never have thought of ourselves. The fee for the coaching has increased during these decades but the focus and work remains constant and the results are quite satisfying.

We provided coaching for one couple facing divorce. He needed and wanted out; she was deeply wounded by the pending dissolution of their long marriage. They were in a heated dispute and considering hiring lawyers. We suggested they come for coaching. We did a series of sessions together during which they were able to explore their hurts, their needs, and their purposes as they looked ahead. By the end of three sessions they were applying the **Love Principles** to their situation, to themselves, and to each other. They came to a very amicable resolution emotionally and financially. We were all grateful that they were able to arrive at a place of harmony on all levels.

Arleen has done considerable coaching with teenage boys. She has an affinity with their inner struggles and is able to help them move beyond angst and away from trouble. She helps them find ways to love themselves and their family members. The work with them involves harnessing the burgeoning hormonal energy that is in need of redirection and application to life purpose.

Diane has done a lot of work with grown adults who lacked adequate instruction about life in society as they were growing up. She thinks of it as "raising adults" and she values the opportunity enormously.

Together we have done some more extensive coaching that has enabled individuals to examine lifelong patterns that they want to change and then to move beyond them as they learn to receive themselves as beautiful. It is one of our great blessings to be beside people as they grow spiritually and apply what they have come to know in their practical, day-to-day lives. We all need to know that we are not alone as we walk our spiritual paths.

Writing Workshops

Responding to requests, Arleen offered writing workshops in which she led participants into the realm of the right brain, giving them the opportunity to further awaken their creativity. In a nonjudgmental atmosphere, a safe space was brought into being, an environment with no restrictions or criticism. A variety of stimulating and unusual assignments stretched and inspired writers to go beyond their comfort zones.

The writing workshops garnered rave reviews. Participants exceeded their dreams in being able to express themselves and to break down mental blocks that had previously squelched their creativity.

Weeklong Journeys Into Self

Other people requested longer Practice Sessions. We began to offer weeklong sessions with one day of focus on each of the six **Love Principles** and a culminating day focused on the theme that ties the six principles together: ***Choice is the life process. In every new moment of awareness, you are free to make a new choice.***

We were blessed that a Methodist Church in our small community of Ocean Beach in San Diego offered their Fellowship Hall for our use at no cost. Large groups of people from 30 to 40 came to the sessions for several years. Later we were invited to offer the weeklong sessions in other parts of the country as well.

The sessions were always interactive. We would introduce the **Love Principle** that was to be our focus for the day. Then we would guide people in a series of live interactions with each other that afforded them opportunities to practice applying the **Love Principle** as they engaged with others.

We observed, and participants reported, two profound elements in a weeklong session. 1) The depth of the experience was cumulative, packing a wallop of powerful energy when people least expected it, and 2) the effect of another person's experience on the observer could be as great as if it were happening *to* the observer. This was a great way for participants to discover the value of companionship on our spiritual journeys.

People reported that new possibilities rushed

in and old wounds closed in the light of powerful healing. We utilized all kinds of activities to bring the experiential side to life, including Toning, movement to music, drawing and coloring, sculpting our bodies into shapes that communicated to us, mirroring each other's movements, journaling, sharing in partnerships, and writing poetry.

Tears, laughter, and insight all flowed equally. Participants reported their discovery that it is very difficult to move beyond being critical of self if the self you use to praise yourself is the same one you find lacking! Another insight shared was that we create hurt in ourselves in order that we might focus attention on ourselves for the healing process. The hurt is not the dis-ease. Rather, it is the lack of attention in the first place.

Some participants came suffering the pain of unfulfilled relationships, or were heartsick over love lost, or were weakened by their inability to acknowledge their wholeness. There were also participants who came, not because they had something specific they wanted to heal but because they wanted to go deeper into self in a joyful, loving environment. There was plenty of opportunity for that, as well as camaraderie and fun.

There were moments of surprise. We had met a man named Ray at an ICC conference. He was unusual in that he stood at the back of the room moving in gestures that were something like Tai Chi, though the movements were of his own invention. Because he was different, most people avoided him. We embraced and welcomed him.

It turned out that Ray lived in San Diego. He showed up on our doorstep more than once, usually saying he came just to get a hug. We always welcomed him and brought him in. Eventually he told us his story. He had been a pilot with the Air Force during the Korean War. One day he was sent out on a foray to bomb a village. He did not feel he could do that because innocent people would be killed. So he tried to fly his plane off the planet instead. When he returned to the base, he was confined and then sent home for psychiatric treatment. Eventually he was given a medical leave.

Ray shared experiences with us such as hearing voices and seeing disembodied people. We always *received him as beautiful just as he was.* When he asked if he could come to one of our weeklong Journeys Into Self, we said, "Of course." He came on a scholarship.

At the first session when Ray stood behind the circle and began to do his movements, we explained to the group that Ray would do what made him comfortable since it was not easy for him to be in a group. We invited people to *receive him as beautiful*. Ray shouted out, "Don't worry. I am certified insane." The group laughed, but in an easy, friendly, and receiving way. Ray had a good week in the Journey Into Self and other participants in the session had a good learning about making room for all kinds of people and their unique expressions of self. At the end, Ray told us, "I was misaligned. Now I am at peace."

During another session, the two of us had an opportunity to "trust the process," to "remain true to our intuition," and to practice the knowing that "perfect love casts out all fear." Following a highly intensive experience we had designed so that participants might have an awakening, a participant, call her Sue, journeyed below the surface of an old wound, going deeper into the unhealed festering than ever before. She spent the afternoon not fully connected with where she was; she had *become* the energy of her trial and was reverberating with waves that comprised its tribulation. She had moved from the emotional aspect to what we might call an energy event, or energy opening.

Sue was ministered to by loving people in the group, caring for and about her. Some worried about her and described her (to us) at various intervals as "spaced out, out of control, not able to be responsible for self, needful of being watched." Yet, this was *not* Sue's experience of herself and we confirmed that throughout the day.

We monitored Sue but were not worried about her since both of us had had openings of our own and trusted the higher frequency energy that orchestrated such openings. There was a woman in the session who was a licensed psychologist. She spoke to us at the end of the afternoon, calling us into question for not intervening to "do something" about the woman's experience. She suggested that we should have called 911 or had the woman committed for observation at a psychiatric clinic. We tried to talk with her about spiritual openings, but her professional training had taught her to be careful of situations for which she could be held liable.

We trusted our knowing. We were not pre-programmed to look for symptoms or to make diagnoses. But we were fully armed with our intuition and we trusted that above all else. From our personal experiences, we knew that we don't create for ourselves more than we can handle at any given moment. We also knew from personal experience that suffering in the personality self is not irreparable. If we guided Sue in her process on the level on which the data was being presented we would be aligned with something that was "wrong" in her life rather than focusing on finer frequencies and love energy where a healing was in process and was something Sue needed to do for herself. We kept the energy flowing in the room, continuing to cast out fear, inviting perfect love as we commenced the evening session.

Surrounded by a holy, caring environment, Sue touched the core of the distress that had been lodged in her for a long time. Slowly, with tears flowing, the suffering part of self in Sue began to emerge. She could see that part of self and bring it up to embrace it. As it rose to the surface, Sue looked into the face of the old fears and torment that had long dwelt in bondage. Looking at them face to face, being able to see them, they no longer ruled her life. Breathing deeply and freely in her newly found sense of grounding, Sue could love them; she could be beside them in her wholeness.

A miracle was worked that night because what was presented on one level of consciousness was dealt with on another, and because rather than being "committed to a facility" Sue was allowed to do her process and have an opportunity to commit to her own Self.

We checked in with Sue later that night to see how she was doing, giving her more suggestions for how to be present to herself as she moved through the aftermath of her energetic opening. By the next morning, she was settled in herself in new ways. She was free. Many years later we heard from Sue; she was married and doing well. We were glad we had trusted ourselves and our intuitive reading of her experience. Years later she wrote again:

> I just wanted to say hi, and to let you know that because of my decision to meet you both, and grow spiritually, life hasn't been the same. There are few days that pass that I don't think of you two. I was talking in general with my son (now 27) last night. I reflected back to the time when I met you both. He then accessed your names on the computer. I was thrilled to hear of your move to Arizona. Thank you for listening to one of so many you impacted with your never-ending love and wisdom from one to another.

It is important to say that if either of us had had a doubt we would not have proceeded as we did. We would have done something different. We were not in the habit of putting people at risk, but we did value allowing individuals to risk going deeper and potentially freeing self.

Most people reported that they went away from the weeklong workshops with a very practical sense for how to use the **Love Principles** in their daily lives and how to observe themselves in interactions so they could make conscious choices about how to respond and how to **be the change they wanted to see happen.**

One man wrote to say "… because you have touched me and loved me and I touched and loved myself, I can and do receive my rejection of self as it is and thereby affirm and receive my beauty in this ongoing process … I affirm the more of me by taking care of and loving me." A woman from Ohio reported, "There were so many gifts from so many people. Being allowed to process pain without some well-meaning soul trying to 'make it better' was a gift from the whole group." And a woman from California said she came to see her mission through the experiential processes we did. "I am here to touch people's lives lovingly and to **be the change I want to see happen** … Those times in life when I berated and belittled myself for mediocre performance in certain areas of life sprang from that personality self that feeds on what the world terms success. Success for me now is living the **Love Principles** … free from doubts and uncertainties." Another man shared "I am confirmed as being a man: total, complete, integrated – masculine has united with feminine, my polarities have touched and now, I Am."

Some attendees got their batteries recharged, others learned more about who they truly were and the gifts they had to give. One said, in her written evaluation of the week, "I've never before been loved so much. This Journey into Self was the most touching experience of my life yet."

A main emphasis in our weeklong Journeys was on activating greater potential, discovering new aspects of self, adding to the quality of life, bringing new life to relationships, and opening to untapped avenues of wisdom. We knew that people would be able to support and facilitate the emergence of others into their spiritual potential as they learned to love unconditionally.

Following the 1977 Journey into Self we had letters from almost everyone expressing their gratitude and their delight in where they now were in their lives. Here is a typical comment:

> What a wonderful group we were. My problems can seem unbearable when they are also seen as unique. And so, I give my special thanks to those who bared their souls so that I could see that ***I am not alone***...All of us were encouraged to trust, to open up and be ourselves. Our culture trains us along the lines of Collette's 'Rien d'ailleurs ne rassure autant qu'un masque.' It means, nothing provides as much assurance as a mask. It is a tremendously freeing concept to realize that when I drop all my masks, it is then, and only then, that *I* am loved."

Others Spread the Joy

By 1978, we had received numerous reports from Love Family members who had created their own **Love Projects** in large and small ways. Audrey McDonald made it her mission to scatter "mustard seeds," her name for the little yellow cards with **The Love Principles**. She ordered them in bunches, sent them through the mail, left them on tables in public places, all the while *having no expectations* about who or how they would be received. She was convinced, "**The Love Principles** are all anyone really needs."

Many other people distributed the principle cards in similar ways and we often received letters which said "I found this little yellow card and want to know more." Others printed **The Love Principles** on their holiday cards. One man in Maryland incorporated **The Love Principles** into his Business Management Training courses as effective guidelines for business persons. Another man in Ohio, worked with Transactional Analysis, in training and in therapy. He worked out a correlation between the **Principles** and the tenets of T.A. so he could share them with clients as a part of his training.

A Methodist Minister in Ashland, Ohio spread the **Principles** among his congregation by using our **Principles** posters, sharing our books, and referring to them from the pulpit of his church. Another Methodist minister in San Jose, CA gave out the principle cards in his counseling sessions for over five years, as did a retired Methodist minister in Inglewood, CA whenever he was invited as a guest preacher. Ordained ministers in Unity and Religious Science Churches did the same, linking the **Principles** to the teachings of their churches.

Other Love Family members used **The Love Principles** in inspirational talks and training sessions with Blue Bird and Campfire Girl groups, in women's groups among those seeking to release their creative potential, and in classrooms across the country.

A Roman Catholic brother had been using **The Love Principles** regularly in his preaching. Other brothers in his order became interested and decided to put the six **Love Principles** on a silk screen and share them through their Christian Family Catalog of inspirational pieces called the Abbey Press Catalog (begun in 1867 and still functioning today). It is distributed to over a million families. They called **The Love Principles** "Pathways to Peace."

It was very important to us that people so benefited from the power of **The Love Principles** that they not only lived them but wanted to share them and to incorporate them into their own work. We encouraged the free use of the **Principles** because we knew of their meaning in our own lives and wanted them to be available to as many others as possible. As our Love Family members distributed them in their own unique ways, the two of us continued our ceaseless travels every weekend to all parts of the country and the continent that would invite us. We can't remember saying no to anyone who extended to us the privilege of sharing what we had to bring to enrich the lives of others.

Journeys Into Self in Foreign Countries

From the beginning, we were eager to take people on trips out of the country, and thus out of their comfort zones, where they would have opportunities to practice the **Love Principles** actively in circumstances that were stretching and challenging. We began with trips to the Middle East and Egypt and gradually expanded our horizons until we had traveled to over thirty countries, some of them more than once.

For the first twenty or more years of foreign Journeys Into Self, we planned our own itineraries and then hired travel agencies to execute the plans for the trip. We held group meetings each evening except when travel did not permit. We suggested a **Love Principle** to work with for each day and then invited people to share the experiences they had had in which they had been able to apply the principle in order to keep their Heart Chakras open and the unconditional love energy flowing through them.

There is nothing like foreign travel to present challenging situations. One of our first Journeys Into Self was to Egypt, Jordan and Israel. When we were visiting the Egyptian Museum, we took a group of women to the ladies' restroom. Having traveled in the Middle East before, Diane knew we were not likely to find restrooms along the way of our excursions, so she urged people to use the one in the museum. There were stalls for privacy, but no toilets to sit down on. Instead there were holes in the floor designed for people used to squatting, and instead of toilet paper there were faucets and little cups to hold water to use for washing yourself. The women at first refused to use the facilities. Diane encouraged them, saying they would be sorry later. Finally, most of them acquiesced. The others had to squat by the side of the road later.

The discussion about **problems are opportunities** that evening was dynamic. We relished the opportunity to urge people to practice the **Love Principles** everywhere and under all circumstances.

On our last morning in Egypt, several people ate eggs for breakfast. The eggs were apparently bad because by the time we got to Jordan and were on a bus driving across the desert to Aqaba, several members of our group were violently ill with food poisoning. They were lying on the hard, wooden floor of the bus, in the aisles, writhing in pain. Of course, there were no rest stops along the three-hour drive, and stopping by the side of the road was inhibiting because there was no cover of any kind: no trees or bushes; only open, flat desert as far as you could see.

The group rallied to comfort the ones who were sick and to seize the opportunity to keep their Heart Chakras open. Those who were ill had to **provide others with opportunities to give to them** over and over again, learning to receive without resistance. Arleen was one who was violently ill, and she found that allowing one of the group members to care for her was about the hardest thing she ever remembered doing.

Guatemala

On a Journey into Self to Chichicastenango, a large indigenous town 87 miles from Guatemala City, our entire group had a profound learning experience. The town lies on the crests of mountaintops at an altitude of almost 2,000 meters, and 98.5 percent of the population is Mayan K'iche. Although there is a large Catholic church in the town square and the drinking of alcohol is forbidden by the priests, one week of the year the population celebrates a native holiday and festival during which time the men are allowed to drink. As our bus pulled into the outskirts of the town we had to slow down because men were lying drunk in the roadway and their wives were rushing from their humble homes to pull them out of harm's way.

The travelers in our group had a broad spectrum of responses to the scene before us and we spent the evening's meeting focused on the different realities we had each created: from amusement, to shock, to being appalled and judgmental, to delight in the custom, to curiosity, etc. We went around the circle asking all members to share their initial response. We did not comment on anyone's sharing but let each contribution form a grand interweaving of **reality creations**. By the end it was clear that holding opinions about the behavior of others is fruitless and often separating, and that there is room for every view and every expression when we are unconditionally loving. The cultures from which we come are determining factors in how we act and how we respond to others, and there is a place for all of them.

The British Isles

In 1976, we took a group to the British Isles. A picture that remained imprinted on our minds was of our whole group sitting in a horse-drawn cart, laughing hysterically with their heads thrown back, as they watched Arleen, ever the photographer, back up to get the whole group in the frame and stepping in a big pile of horse manure while not looking where she was going. It was a mess, but she did get the photo!

We covered a lot of ground including the Cliffs of Moher in Ireland and wonderful pubs with music and dancing; the Scottish Highlands where we encountered a lone Scotsman in a kilt, seated on a hillside with his dog at his feet, playing his bagpipes for no one in particular; the new age community of Findhorn where everything was organic and the community members work with devas to grow giant organic vegetables; to the blessed sounds of the King's College Choir in Cambridge; to a deeply touching experience at Coventry Cathedral.

Following that Journey Into Self we had letters from the Idaho farmer and his wife. She wrote in wonder that 28 diverse personalities could be welded together by the power of **The Love Project**. "It has to be experienced to be believed. Repercussions may be felt for years." Her husband, a U.S. postal employee, sent a classic response to capture what it was like to venture into the world with a group practicing **The Love Principles**:

> In late June when letters postmarked "**Love Project**" came through the mail, I was the victim of many jibes at the post office. Finally, the postmaster asked, 'What the hell is this **Love Project**? Anything I could use?' 'Might be, I quipped, knowing of his new female interest. Learning how to love!' Wasn't that a bag of truth! Little did I know how close I hit the nail on the head.
>
> The spirit of Arleen and Diane was contagious. We all know that a busload of ordinary people cannot be cooped up for 22 days without an occasional flare-up. **Love Project** members are the exception. As the days passed we could see the magic working. It was a terrific experience.
>
> Because of this I am not sure if Ireland with its rolling hills, castles and friendly people was as great as it seemed. Nor if Scotland with its braes and lochs is

really a fairy land. Or if England with its Stonehenge, Stratford on Avon, or London really was a land of enchantment. An air of sadness prevailed the last morning as we tried to put into words our tender feelings and failed. As the 747 flew us safely home we tried now and then with difficulty to say goodbye. Thus ended a trip I can never forget.

Every country of the world is different and offers something unique for the traveler. We chose to revisit several countries for different reasons. Israel has more to offer in terms of our shared cultural beginnings than anywhere else. We took groups to Israel three times. Italy is rich in physical and cultural beauty and has a jovial population that is fun to experience. Spain is rich in heritage and affords the opportunity to hear beautiful Spanish spoken. France has provincial charm, big city eloquence and art treasures. South America is a virtual smorgasbord of beauty and diversity. We could say something wonderful about every place we have visited from Scandinavia, to Australia and New Zealand, to China, to the Baltic States, to Russia, to Japan, to Indonesia, to Nepal and Tibet, to Africa, to South and Central America, and so on.

India

One country stands out for us as a haven of spirituality: India. We have taken groups there four times, once for six weeks, never for fewer than four weeks. India is exotic, vast, rich in tradition, embracing, and often overwhelming. Her greatest asset is her ordinary people who carry a knowing of God in their hearts, a light in their eyes, and a welcome that combines openness and innocence. While outer poverty may greet the ordinary tourist, it is the soul-consciousness that walks in the beings of the people in the streets that calls the two of us to return (both to the country and to that quality in our own selves.) India is the polar opposite of the United States in many ways; it offers spirituality as its wealth rather than material accumulation.

Traveling in India is always an adventure and invites constant use of the **Love Principle *have no expectations but rather abundant expectancy***. We were on our way by bus to Rishikesh, a pilgrimage city, on one of our trips and we kept seeing big billboards advertising a brand-new hotel with air-conditioning, which happened to be the hotel in which we were scheduled to stay. We encouraged our group to ***have no expectations*** in spite of how alluring the billboards made the hotel look.

Sure enough, when we arrived at the new hotel, the manager invited us to have a seat in the lobby. He proceeded to inform us that he was "very sorry" that Rishikesh was in the midst of a drought and there was no water. Consequently, no laundry could be done. As a result, they had no sheets and no towels. The rooms were very clean and the mattresses were spotless (it being a new hotel and all) and we really didn't need towels because there was no water for washing or bathing. But some members of the group did not believe they could sleep without a sheet to cover them. Needless to say, this provided us with plenty of material to examine **problems as opportunities** and for **creating our own realities consciously**.

As group leaders, we were given the only room in the hotel that had a sit down flush toilet. We could sit down but given the drought there was no water to flush the toilet. Morning and evening an old man, at least we thought he was, climbed the many floors to our room carrying a large bucket of water to fill the toilet so it could fulfill its potential. By the way, we later discovered that the man was really only middle aged, but given the very harsh living conditions in India, he appeared to be an old man.

Our room had a neighboring roof outside our window. Periodically a cow would walk by on the roof. We had been in India long enough not to be surprised by this sight. Cows are revered in India; they walk the streets in between every sort of vehicular traffic and always have the right of way. They are enthusiastically joined by goats, chickens, dogs, carts, raggedy children, and the occasional elephant.

By the way, we discovered the air-conditioning that had been so widely advertised for our hotel was actually electric ceiling fans. But it didn't matter, since there was no electricity.

In 1979, while in India, Arleen wrote extensively in her travel journal:

India is a threat to all we keep covered and hidden inside. Its oppressive heat burns through the shields we have carefully placed in self to hide our deepest sensitivities from others and from ourselves. India's intensity of life in the streets disenables anyone from functioning in a blasé approach to the next moment. India demands that we see, that we experience, that we live more deeply.

There is a way out. One *can* be a stranger here. One can *remain* an outsider who will soon finally be going home–leaving *them* to *their* way of life. One can go from here insulated with complaints about how they don't do it right here. Then one doesn't have to look keep inside of self to see what of India resides there.

Mother India greets each of us as her child. Like any good Mother, she sees *all* there is in the child--from its excretions to its accomplishments. Mother India embraces the whole of life. She rejects nothing. India is synonymous with vulnerability.

One is brought up short here. Thrown into the den of one's own spirituality and left to be eaten alive by one's own contradictions. It *is* true that everything simply *is* and that everything is in its perfection *as it is*. Acknowledge that, or go home and work still more on the resistance in you that separates you from the whole ... In humility, in simplicity, in life stripped bare is found the seed of Divinity awaiting Its blossoming in consciousness—in all of us. In the throngs of India, I saw in face after face what the religious seek, what the rich strive to buy, what the ambitious yearn to accomplish. India is an open lotus inviting and welcoming all those who shake their heads in compassionate ruing of her plight.

India is starkness itself. It is profoundness that shocks and demands that the polarities of life be honored and cherished equally. It is life—the struggle eternally seeking Itself.

India is tough for many to handle. It rends the skin of its personality and lays bare the flaming substance of life. India's physical needs shriek out loudly into the endlessly echoing hallowed halls of existence. And yet, the cry is not "fix this, change this, make this better." It is, rather, open further the eye that sees, expose to me the revelation of holiness in all that is.

Diane reflected:

To walk among the people on the streets in India was for me an experience of walking in the conscious Body of God. Each person was like a cell of that body, and each—no matter what his/her social class or the condition of his/her physical body—was conscious and present to me. Never had I walked among a people who were so consistently present in their souls when I looked into their eyes. To walk consciously in the Body of God and to be acknowledged by other cells of that Body, to be seen by them as a soul, experienced by them, was one of the most profoundly moving experiences of my life. I am different for it.

In India, the conscious Body of God—the body we call humanity—walks, breathes, lives and dies on the streets, in the open, where it can be encountered, touched, interacted with, known and loved as a Body, not as fragmented parts of that Whole. I saw the Body—what so many before have called the "teeming masses" of India—and I was more profoundly moved than ever before in this life. I *saw* the Body of God and found it whole, balanced, graceful, sensitive and very beautiful.

The body of God in India is mature. It has been developing as a culture for well over 6,000 years. It has been fed by some of the most profound religious literature and trained by some of the most enlightened spiritual leaders ever developed anywhere on earth. No wonder the Body is agile, strong, filled with grace, and devout—expressing reverence for life in all forms. No wonder the individual cells of the Body, representatives of its soul, are *present* in their consciousness.

The individual cells of the Body of God in India—what we call persons—reveal their maturity in the refined quality of their skin, in the graceful lines of their physical structure, in the delicacy of fingers and toes, in the size, depth and beauty of their dark eyes which seem to be pools of infinity. Their bodies are like fine works of art and when

I focused on their inherent beauty, gasps of awe, wonder and admiration escaped from my mouth.

When we returned to India in 1982, Diane wrote:

To step off the plane in New Delhi was for me like easing myself over the bank of a deep river. Into the flow I went--the flow of universal heart center love energy. That energy moves with slow, powerful force through the group psyche of India, and although individual Indians may be unaware that it is so, deep love shines in the eyes of nearly every person one encounters. Love flowed beneath me, around me and through me. No effort was required. It was natural and easy just to love.

Sometimes the scenes in India seem surreal and too overwhelming to grasp or to fit into a familiar frame of reference. It is easy to wonder, as did Arleen in this poem:

Is it real?
   The view before me –
   The thatched village at dusk,
   The sleek black bodies in the sun's
      farewell glow,
   The thick palms crowding to reflect on
   the surface of the gnat-dancing water.
Is it real?
   Perhaps a life-size postcard.
   I check in the corner for a stamp, and
   seeing none, I know the scene is living.

No place to write your name,
 to mark it air mail.
I am here, and in it.
 It is real, this view before me.
Oxen shaking painted horns,
 round-bellied pots belching steam,
Black mantillas of flies
 laid across open food,
Pedestrians crisscrossing as if playing
 checkers on the board of the streets.
It is real.
 No postcard could hold
 this much bustle in its borders.
No words I could mail could set you in the
 center of the sights, the smells,
 the sounds.
It is real.
 There's no stamp in the corner –
 only the stamp of life,
 and its imprint that lasts forever.

In all, we made four journeys to India. Each was a powerful experience that never failed to stretch us to more awakened places in self and to expand our consciousness. While in India our groups were privileged to have meetings with enlightened or powerful individuals who enriched us with their presence. On our second trip in 1982, forty days in length, we were granted a private audience with Prime Minister Indira Gandhi who graciously responded to our questions. Everyone was impressed with her simplicity and her presence of being.

In Bodhgaya, we spent an hour with Vimala Thakar, an Indian spiritual master and teacher of spiritual awakening. She was deeply influenced by both J. Krishnamurti and Mahatma Gandhi and therefore embodied the essence of enlightened consciousness and social responsibility. At the age of five, the awareness of something beyond dawned on her and she was never the same. She became an activist and a philosopher and it was a privilege to be with her and to hear the truths she had come to know: "Nothing in life is trivial. Life is whole wherever and whenever we touch it, and one moment or event is not less sacred than another."

On the same journey, we were granted 20 minutes with Swami Chidananda of the Divine Life Society in Rishikesh. He stayed with us for two hours (!) and helped set a profound tone for our whole group. He reminded us, "Real happiness comes out of peace. When the mind is tranquil and serene, peace, bliss, wells up from within you. You do not have to manufacture happiness, for it does not lie outside of you. True happiness is right where you are sitting. You are yourself happiness. Happiness is your essential nature."

It was Chidananda who told us the wonderful

story of a man who spent his whole life in a spiritual community environment where his devotion was great and his needs were very small. On one occasion, he traveled to a big city and stopped in a large modern shop where he stood transfixed. The clerk asked him if something was wrong. The man replied, "No. I am being amazed at all the things I can live without!"

This sentence has lived in us to this day. More and more there is more and more we can live without.

On our third trip to India, Nepal and Tibet in 1990, we visited the Darjeeling Monastery and had the rare privilege of a private audience with His Eminence Venerable Thugsay Rimpoche (Abbot,) a four-and-half-year-old child in monk's clothing who had been confirmed by the Dalai Lama as the reincarnation of the meditation master who had established the Monastery and had died in 1983. It was a remarkable experience to be in the presence of the revered child who accepted from each of us a *khatag* (a ritual cloth that is offered as an expression of respect), blessed it, and placed it around our necks.

We also had an opportunity to hear the firsthand account of a family who fled Tibet by foot after the Chinese took over. The hardships they faced and their determination to reach India where they could be close once again to the Dalai Lama were impressive indeed.

India is a place of learning, a place of lessons,

a place of heart. In Calcutta, we visited the Kali Temple and reinforced the wisdom that this world of ours is a world of polarities. Kali is the Goddess of Destruction and without her there can be no Creation. The two are halves of one whole. This reminder must live in us every moment because Creation and Destruction are happening all around us all the time. We must receive both the good and the bad, the holy and the evil as equal and not struggle to eliminate one as lesser than the other. The struggle is useless; it leaves us weary and frustrated. Everything simply is.

Near the Kali Temple we visited the Institute for the Destitute and Dying, established by Mother Teresa. Volunteers walked about ministering, bringing water, gently touching the heads of those who lay about on straw cots, crouched in positions of pain or waning life force. The energy in the dismal rooms was respectful, upbeat, full of love and caring. There was no fear of disease or dying; only a high regard for the human beings who had been found on the streets, dying alone. A definite contrast to the Kali energy outside, which comprised dozens of ragged children who clawed at us, begging for attention, food, or rupees.

We finished our 1982 journey in Sri Lanka where Arleen was in serious danger of being detained (perhaps permanently) while the rest of the group boarded the airplane. Arleen recalls:

This was an experience that required a lot of breathing and all my years of experience as a professional actor. When we arrived in the country, I forgot to declare how much money I was bringing in (personal funds and over $800 in group tipping money.) The customs official wrote "nil" on my card. When I was ready to depart, this was challenged and the officials wanted to see how much money I had on my person. Five officers took my passport, my bags, and took me to a distant office. Three officers joined us there. They had all the authority and they had me! My blood pressure rose a bit as I continued to focus on breathing deeply. My mind was going a mile a minute. They could arrest me, hold me for falsifying documents (even though I had said loudly that I made a mistake, that it was an omission), and they could confiscate all my traveler's checks.

The eight uniformed men hovered around me chattering rapidly in Singalese while my carry-on belongings were being spread on the table. I addressed one of them, insisting on making eye contact, saying, "Do I look like someone who came here to break the law? I made a grave mistake and I am terribly sorry." He shook his head in understanding but made no commitments.

Then, the Number One man arrived. The eight officers all began talking to him at once and I joined in trying to make my case. Number One was angry and cold; tourists had been driving him crazy all day. He wanted no part of me and huddled with his men.

Suddenly, my stomach sank. I remembered

that in addition to the $700 now on the table, I had the other $800 in another traveler check folder. I would never be able to explain that. I was cooked.

I dared not panic and instead moved my energy into positive action. I joined the young officer searching my purse and proceeded to help him, actively cooperating. In the very small open area of my purse, our hands danced, though he did not know I was leading. He would move to one side searching and as he did, my hand slid the other billfold the other way. Back and forth, maybe four times, with eight men hovering, until he became focused on a case with a few gemstones I had purchased. I willingly took it out for him and closed my purse. I opened the back compartment for him to search but all of them were now focused on the gems, all garnets and a handful of tiny white sapphires thrown in as a gift. The men were all leaning over the table, examining the stones and receipt of purchase. They were highly suspicious of me and examined everything as if my true nature would somehow be revealed in secret code in the receipt.

My heart pounded and my eyes darted around the room looking for a way to change the dynamic. I reminded myself to stay alert and to observe what was transpiring to see how I could **be the change I wanted to see happen**. Suddenly the second in command addressed me in a loud voice. "Madam," he said, "This receipt says you paid 2500 rupees for these stones (the equivalent of under $300 then.)" "Yes," I said, "That's true." The men continued to circle the table and utter comments I could not understand. I had no idea what they were observing or getting at; I couldn't see how to enter the event with them. Then, I was asked again, this time with an emphasized question mark at the end. "Madam, you paid 2500 for these gems?"

Suddenly I saw an opening, a way to turn all this around. I gasped, seeming almost to faint. "Oh no," I shouted with despair. "Don't tell me I overpaid!" There was an immediate shift in the room. Eight men peering at the stones. My acting skills kicked in as I was about to give the performance of my life. Aghast shopper! Play the role fully. "Have I been taken? You're kidding. You don't mean it? Please tell me it isn't true."

No other issue was present in the room. The second in command lifts the gems and breaks the ice. "I can't tell you but we have a man who can." I beseech them, "Please call him. I must know." Actually, I couldn't have cared less. "Please call him!" Suspense builds. The man comes. He looks. He sneers, "Indian stones are soft." He dismissed them. "Not nearly as fine as Sri Lanka." The eight men gather closer as do I. The man lifts the gems. He looks. He shakes his head and puts it down. Not a sound in the room. "You paid too much, Madam."

I let out a cry. "Oh no. It can't be true. Where

were you when I needed you? You must do all my shopping with me!" The second in command squawks out loudly like a crow. "Take him, take him. We don't want him." The other men join the chant, "Take him, take him." The room erupts in laughter. I know the crisis is over. I laugh with them. The second in command looks to the chief who is behind me. He gets the word. He speaks. "We'll let you go this time, Madam, but you must be more careful." I agree.

I express gratitude, a lot of it. I shake his hand and offer my hand to the chief. He will not take it. He waves me away. "Go, go, Madam." I put my hands together and give him the God-greeting, gather my things, and leave. I have rarely been so glad to be finished with an event. I learned a lot from it and I told the second in command so. They were doing their job, and well.

I am grateful for how it all turned out, and for the laughter to free us all from the bondage born of regulations. In the future, I will fill out all spaces on all declaration cards—even where they ask my weight!

In this experience, Arleen used as many of **The Love Principles** as she could, especially ***problems are opportunities***. Sometimes when in the midst of a problem, it is not easy to see what the opportunities might be. In this case, a lot of listening, observing, and breathing were required. Arleen used all her energy to ***create her own reality consciously*** to get herself out of the situation. She could have no idea how it would turn out, so practicing **having no expectations but rather abundant expectancy** was a key factor as she **provided the others with the opportunity to give** her clearance to leave. Having the **Principles** at the ready in consciousness makes for productive ways to keep energy flowing and moving in a positive direction.

Each time we traveled to India we were deeply imprinted by the culture, the people, the spirituality, and the inundation of the senses. In Arleen's poem "India, You Are Mary," she seeks to capture the essence of the experience of spending time there.

> India, you are Mary. You cannot hide from me.
> Within the borders of your womb, Christ-ness is set free.
> You wear a tattered shawl beneath which millions huddle,
>   Living in your streets in chaos and in muddle.
> The rags upon their backs are all they own.
> Yet, how much less they have to shed along their journey home.
> God is in everything ... and equally,
>   In bellies hung with starvation,
>   looking pregnant with death about to be born.
> And in those bloated by abundance,
>   for whom we might equally mourn.
> When I was young, my cup was filled with pain.
> Hardship's heavy drapes were hung that I might learn its name.
> As I look back to the past from which I came,

I see Grace, having cleansed myself of misguided shame.
I bow to then in gratitude for showing me the good in all that's been created.

I'm ready for your impact India, I won't be overwhelmed or inundated.
The world is a balanced polarity.
For richer and poorer, wedded to the One,
In sickness and in health is each day begun,
   in the singular body of humanity.
I come to you India in wonder and to bless.
I'll not create rejection of anything you possess,
Certainly, not the hunger and pain you tenderly caress.
I'll not turn away from suffering.
To all there is, I humbly say,
Yes.

India, you are Mary.
You cannot hide from me.
Within the borders of your womb, Christ-ness is set free.

It is impossible to share here the many fascinating experiences of insight from our four long trips in India. There was a wealth of learning for us as Westerners and as individuals longing for spiritual growth. It was difficult not to return to India yearly, just for refresher courses in all we are missing in our culture.

A primary factor in traveling to foreign countries is the chance to experience the global community first-hand. This becomes more important as the global ties grow stronger and more evident each year. To be able to appreciate differences and see the beauty in them while recognizing that people are just people wherever you are is a priceless gift. And to break out of the isolating view of our own country and culture as the "best," rather than as just one of many, is an essential transformation of consciousness for living in the Oneness that true spiritual perception reveals.

China

In November of 1999 we traveled to China with a group of 19 eager explorers for 25 days. The majority of us went with images of China gathered over the years, but it is fair to say that the principle **have no expectations** was probably the **Love Principle** theme for all of us. China presented us with unending paradoxes and contradictions; our mental images and preconceptions were challenged at every turn. China is one of the most ancient and highly developed cultures in the world, yet over a ten-year period (from 1965 to 1975) their Cultural Revolution sought to wipe out their entire cultural history.

In the West, we have heard a lot about the destruction of the Tibetan culture by China, but in China we discovered that what the Chinese did in Tibet they did to themselves as well. The intention had been to bring China out of feudalism and into the 20th Century with one blow. We got to witness the emerging modern China. The repeated horrors of their history are balanced by the magnificence of their creativity, ingenuity and industriousness that enables them to rise out of adversity into new expressions of who they are.

The experience made deep impressions on all of us.

Central European Capitals

Our trip to Central European Capitals in September of 2000 was our first experience with merging our Journey Into Self group of eight with a larger, commercial tour group. We weren't sure how it would work, but it actually provided us with more opportunities to interact with other people. On bus trips and walking tours our little group intermingled with the larger group. When we had choices for excursions or free time, we went as our small group or sometimes two or four of us together. And, of course, we had our gatherings in the evenings for sharing our experiences as we always do on Journeys Into Self trips.

Not only was this trip beautiful and educational, but it was also healing for at least two of our group. One woman had suffered the taunting and humiliation of being the brunt of Polish jokes as a child; therefore, she never liked her name or being Polish. We started our tour in Poland, first Warsaw and then Cracow. Sandy wrote after the trip, saying:

Our group session helped me. Listening to

others and speaking up helped me move out of the quagmire of guilt and shame. My people are not a perfect people, yet they resisted the Germans and Warsaw paid a great price. Yes, I am of Polish descent. Yes, millions of Jews were exterminated in Poland. Yes, I have hurt people. My silence has created harm. I can't change that. And I choose to forgive myself and my ancestors for the harm we have caused others. I choose to forgive myself and others, for how else can I move forward to wholeness? And isn't this what this trip was really about?

Arleen remembered she had once written an article for *Emerging* called "A Holocaust begins with a Polish Joke." She reflected that she had always been disturbed by jokes told at the expense of others. The jokes were demeaning and stereotyping; they were jokes at, not with.

Polish jokes, for example, depicted Poles as blockheads. Yet, circa 2001, Poles formed labor unions under an oppressive regime; this was an act of great courage. And during Hitler's march across Europe, Poles refused to cooperate with him, for which they paid with their lives. Such brave and principled people are not blockheads.

The so-called Polish jokes could have been told without mentioning "Polish" at all because they really referred to how human beings generally could be literal or stupid. A Polish joke could lead to a Holocaust because when we diminish people through jokes, we render them expendable, and unworthy. We dehumanize and objectify them, making it easier to exterminate them.

Many today disapprove of being "politically correct," but the practice really relates to honoring people and cultures, and acknowledging how they view themselves. It is about respect. Polish jokes are disrespectful. They are an example of self-created superiority by those who dismiss others as inferior; they contribute to discrimination. If we listen to those jokes we are as guilty as if we were telling them.

People do make fun of themselves through humor, but that is different from when others tell jokes about them that are meant to degrade. We need to realize the power of the spoken word and how we imprint the whole world each time we open our mouths.

Another group member was a boy in Germany when Hitler ruled there. He chose to travel with us to Europe in order to face his memories and the mixture of feelings he still had about those times long ago. Our group sessions were an opportunity for him to be received in love as he explored his memories and mixed feelings.

The whole trip was eye-opening and broadening, which is the point of our Journeys Into Self abroad. This kind of travel is a way to expand consciousness into our global village and to find our place in the emerging whole.

In the middle of the deep and meaningful,

Foreign Journeys Into Self 289

there was also humor. The funniest experience occurred in Budapest. Five of us decided to try the famed Turkish baths. Since taxis would take only four, Sandy, Cathy, and Mary went on ahead. The two of us followed in another cab after going back to our room for swimsuits.

We didn't see the others when we entered the baths, but we were immediately swept up in the prevailing procedure. The attending matrons spoke little or no English. They handed us skimpy pinafore-type garments that would not have covered the bodies of anorexic girls, and then led us to a change stall where we were to lock up our clothes and valuables.

Using mostly pantomime, we inquired if we were to put the pinafores over our swimsuits. The matrons vigorously shook their heads indicating *no one* wears swimsuits. We felt sufficiently foolish for having asked.

So, the two of us took off all our clothes and then laughed uproariously as we surveyed each other in our little pinafores which ran down the inner center of our bodies, tying around the back, and leaving breasts and hips hanging out for all to see.

We exited the stall and reentered the center hallway leading to the baths. There we stood side by side as Cathy, Mary and Sandy emerged wearing their bathing suits and no pinafores. All five of us were shocked by each other—we two unable to understand why they were in bathing suits, while the three of them were overwhelmed by our attire, or lack of it.

The five of us began roaring with laughter and nearly collapsed from being unable to catch our breath. We clutched at our bellies (the two of us had more to clutch) and finally had to be reprimanded by the matrons. At which point all five of us stripped off pinafores and swimsuits and joined the nude Hungarians in the baths.

To this day, if one of the five of us mentions Budapest, we immediately dissolve into laughter. We suppose you had to be there, but it truly stands out as one of the funniest travel experiences ever.

The Baltic States: Estonia, Latvia and Lithuania

Late in August of 2001 we went as a group of eight on a Journey Into Self in Russia and the Baltic States. We were in Estonia on September 11, walking through the streets of the beautiful old city of Tallinn. Two women in succession rushed up to us, asking if we were Americans and telling us that we should get to a television because our country was under attack. We thought they were exaggerating. We could barely comprehend their urgency and anxiety, until we arrived at our hotel and immersed ourselves in images of the planes plowing into the World Trade Center. Yes, we were under attack. But it wasn't just the United States under attack; it was humanity around the world.

Everywhere we went we saw the imprint of the tragedy on the faces of those we passed. Because we were visibly Americans, expressions of compassion poured out to us from every shopkeeper, salesperson and resident on the streets. On September 12, we toured in Riga, the capital of Latvia. We were driven past the American Consulate where Latvians had lined the street with bouquets of flowers. Their president had declared a national day of mourning for the tragedy suffered in the United States and we attended their memorial service at the National Cathedral where we were surrounded by Latvians who spent their lunch hour in sympathetic alliance with Americans. Our ambassador and his wife were there but very few other Americans. The goodwill expressed to us continued when we went the next day to Lithuania. The world had come together as one being to embrace the planet with love enough to begin to heal the gash that had ripped open its heart.

As we continued our travels and made our way home, we felt fortified by a palpable unity formed by millions who, in their goodness, were standing up to terrorism.

Imagine our surprise when we returned to the U.S. to find people living in fear of foreigners when we had been lavished with concern and caring while in foreign countries. The contrast remains with us still. It seems that the actions of a few, devastating as those actions were, led many people to distrust and fear all foreigners. The opportunity had been there to claim our place among the peoples of the world who have suffered great devastation and loss and who are determined to unite with others in one global community.

Italy

We were a small group of six on our Journey Into Self in Italy in August of 2003. The trip was planned around the intention to attend performances of a special theatre group in Milan. However, the troupe changed their schedule and were traveling out of Italy while we were there, so we had an opportunity to practice the **Love Principles** *Have no Expectations, but Abundant Expectancy* and *Problems are Opportunities.*

That theme played out in several ways as we traveled. While in Rome the temperatures broke all records for summer heat; we drooped with perspiration, looking disheveled in our wrinkled travel garments. We admired the Italians who always looked like they had just stepped out of fashion magazines, both men and women.

While in Florence one of our travel group had her purse stolen with all her documents, including passport, and money. She became well-acquainted with the Italian authorities through the adventure.

And when we got to Damanhur, a spiritual community situated about two hours from Milan, we were put up in accommodations on the grounds of the community. It continued to be exceptionally hot and our rooms had no air-conditioning and no screens on the windows, so we were challenged to live in harmony with mosquitoes unless we wanted not to breathe!

But all such challenges are welcome when we are focused on spiritual growth, because we get to practice moving beyond our preferences and our personal habits in order to adapt to and even welcome the new. In so doing we expand our own consciousness and develop our skills for living in the moment.

On a later trip to Italy we had many wonderful adventures, but the most amusing came in Verona. We arrived at what was supposed to be an easy entrance with our trusty car but couldn't find the way in. Mind you, it is a large old city with visible walls, but never mind; we drove around the outskirts several times, asked numerous people, but seemed to end up outside the walls after several tries.

When we finally got inside and parked the car, we began to look for *Information*. We followed signs and asked many people for directions, and we went around the same territory so often we began to feel the city was only ten blocks wide and long. No matter how we turned, we experienced *déjà vu*. The signs and the people would direct us to "*I*" for Information, but when we got close there were no follow-up "*I*" signs to point the way. We finally spotted a small flat sign on a bank building. It was so well hidden it seemed to shout, "*Gotcha*"!

After spending time seeing the sites in the center of town, we decided to return the next day for a tram ride. But getting out of town was no easy matter. We were less than ten minutes from our hotel, but as the GPS tried to guide us we kept running into streets that were closed off. Besides, none of them had names and those that did were too faded to read. The GPS had us laughing quite a lot. While it didn't express annoyance, it did say with emphasis, "Recalculating," every time we took another wrong turn. First, we would be 250 meters away from a left turn, then we would end up 750m and be told to turn right instead, and then left, and then right. It kept adding five minutes more to our projected arrival time until we were 25 minutes in transit and still lost. Diane said she now understood why Romeo and Juliet killed themselves in Verona; they tried to elope but couldn't find their way out of town. We were not that desperate and planned to try our luck again the next day.

We had a fabulous day of sightseeing the following day. We got to see everything on our list, including Juliet's balcony (so-called). There was one attraction we skipped: Juliet's Tomb. *Juliet's Tomb?!* A tomb for a fictional character? Of course, the same could be said of her balcony, but there it was easy to guess that the tourist industry chose one they could pass off as the Capulet's residence, with a long, high, sturdy trellis of greenery for Romeo to ascend. But a *tomb*, for a fictional character? To top it all off, the tour book said that the tomb was empty! Duh! Of course, it was empty; Juliet never existed. Sigh. Juliet's tomb.

Our GPS was sometimes less than effective. It didn't take us off at the exit to Venice and then was completely befuddled about where on the planet we were, constantly recalculating and wanting us to use a roundabout in the middle of a speeding highway. We went a long way out of our way because there wasn't a next exit for many kilometers, but, as if saved by the Italian gods, or the Great Mamma Mia, when we got back on the road to return to the long lost exit, we were within a few meters of Mestre and our hotel.

Australia and New Zealand

Our Journey Into Self "down under" was one of the most outstanding of our many years of travel. New Zealand wins the prize for the most diverse and beautiful terrain: caves with thousands of glow-worms, geysers that rival those at Yellowstone, enormous green-blue alpine lakes, rugged mountain wilderness areas, beautiful valleys, the Milford Sound (fjord), sun-drenched, golden farms with herds of sheep, cattle and deer, and an incredible diversity of trees, ferns, bushes, wild flowers and grasses. New Zealand was a feast of beauty. It was like experiencing what the planet was like before humans overpopulated and polluted it. What a privilege.

Australia offered its own diversity, from the large cities of Melbourne and Sydney, to the Outback and Ayers Rock (Uluru) to Desert Gardens and the wetlands of Kakadu Park, The Great Barrier Reef and an enormous rain forest. But perhaps most important for our Journey Into Self was the opportunity to learn more about the Aboriginal culture in Australia. Our approach to self-healing was expanded by what the Aborigines practice, and it was in New Zealand that we learned about the healing properties of emu oil, which we have been using on our joints and benefiting from ever since.

It was not a new experience to have a tour member suffer an accident, but when Marilyn slipped on the bottom step of the bus at the airport in Darwin and severely fractured her ankle we were loath to leave her in Darwin. But she needed the hospital, and she spent nine days there, missing the rest of our tour and then having to purchase a first-class ticket to get home because of the cast on her leg. We not only missed her on the rest of the trip, but we felt phone contact to be inadequate as a form of support for her. But such are the occasional challenges of travel.

Vietnam, Cambodia and Thailand

Some travel experiences, more than others, underline the importance of world travel. We are certainly aware that many people cannot afford to travel abroad, but those who can, help to cultivate the global consciousness that is so essential to our future.

In January of 2005 five of us toured a part of the world that we had previously known primarily through news reports about the effects of war. In addition to our touring, we took advantage of the weeks in these Asian countries to talk with other travelers from around the world. What we discovered was that, to a person, these world travelers were ecologically conscious and concerned. Aware of pollution of air, earth and water, these people valued policies on the part of their governments that aim to improve and protect our global environment.

Everyone we had a chance to talk with shared a conviction that war will never resolve the problems that are at the root of terrorism. All seemed to feel that poverty and the disparity between the rich and the poor are the most direct cause of terrorism, and all recognized that no matter how we would classify ourselves at home, in relation to the world's poor, all foreign travelers are rich.

Most people felt that religion is a divisive force around the world. The travelers were surprisingly broad-minded about religion, expressing tolerance for nearly all practices and beliefs as long as they are not imposed on others.

Our sense was that nothing contributes more to broad-minded thinking and nonjudgmental values than world travel.

Our hearts and minds were stretched and opened by visits in North and South Vietnam, where we heard about and witnessed the horrors of a war that seems to have been pointless. Nevertheless, the resilient population has moved on from the past and is focused on building a better future. Cambodia was too poor to be focused on building the future. They were relying on their ancient past and the tourists it attracts to see them through troubling times. Thailand provided us with an example of how the past can be woven into the present as the future is emerging. There was much to appreciate and much to call into question.

South America (twice)

South America is a vast and beautiful continent replete with an incredible diversity of terrain and cultures. We were blessed to visit on Journeys Into Self twice, with a thirty year interval. That was a revealing experience. While we were growing older, other people were discovering what a fabulous continent this is to visit, so we found the infra-structure around popular tourist destinations, like Machu Picchu and the Iguassu Falls, had grown enormously to accommodate the great increase in sheer numbers of tourists.

The challenges presented to us for our Journey Into Self were numerous, especially on the second trip, where we had an abundance of opportunities to practice all **The Love Principles.** It was a lot of work in consciousness, but that's what we had wanted when we set out.

Japan

Our visit to the Hiroshima Peace Park and Museum made an indelible impression. The museum presented a history of Japan's war-making and its abuse of Korean and Chinese slave labor. It also documented how the Japanese people suffered under the severe constraints of war regulations that restricted civilian life.

It then gave a history of the United States' decision to bomb Japan, starting with the drive to create an atomic weapon before the Germans did, and proceeding with the motivation to get Japan to sign a treaty with the allies before Russia declared war on Japan. The United States was worried that Russia would end up as the most powerful military force at the end of the war. So, in consultation with our allies, the U.S. decided to bomb Japan into submission by using our newly developed atomic bombs. We had used the greatest minds of the time to develop the greatest weapon of mass destruction.

The two of us had been trying to remember when we first learned about the bombing of Hiroshima. We were surprised that we did not know of it as children (we were in the first and second grades then) or as teenagers. In the museum, we read that the U.S. enforced a media blackout on the bombings of Hiroshima and Nagasaki. As a consequence, even the Japanese did not learn about the fate of their people for nearly a year.

As we saw photos and read stories told by survivors and listened to video-taped testimonies from survivors, we saw once again how absolutely brutal and inhumane our weapons of war are and how immoral it is that the leaders of nations can make decisions that result in the murder of thousands, even millions, without being held responsible for their actions. There has to be a better way for us as humans to resolve our conflicts than to go to war.

There were hundreds of Japanese children at the museum. The older generations see it as their responsibility to educate the young so that no other nation ever has to suffer an atomic attack.

Bali

While we have long been aware of racism in the United States and in other nations, we encountered the dimension of inculcated self-hate while on the island of Bali. Arleen had a conversation with a beautiful Balinese woman who responded to a compliment by saying, "I not beautiful. You beautiful. You white. I black. I not beautiful." Arleen was saddened to see the self-loathing of dark skinned people. These Indonesians cut off the crust of white bread because brown is not good. We had met similar in-culture racism in Southern India where every billboard had the face of an almost blanched out Indian to sell a product.

It became clear on this trip that racism will never disappear as long as the concept of race remains. We all began in Africa as the one and only human race, which was, in the beginning, black. The skin color phenomenon changed as humans moved into different climates affecting tone.

Racial identification didn't begin until the 1700's when Carolus Linnaeus, an expert in natural sciences, devised the formal two-part naming system we use to classify all life forms. Europeans of the time were obsessed with devising a classification system for plants, animals, and humans. Linnaeus obliged by classifying humans into four primary races and *arbitrarily* defining them by culture and personality. As a European, he not surprisingly defined *homo sapiens europaeus* as the keenest of mind, while *homo sapiens afer* were lazy, careless and cunning. He had never met American Indians but classified red people as cheerful and resolute, and Asians as proud and greedy.

Thanks to this, and people's desire to be better than others, there was mutual and universal agreement about racial differences (where there had been none before because there was only the human race). This delineating enabled people to label others as less than human.

Biologists joined the party and went on to narrow the (nonexistent) races into Caucasoid, Negroid, and Mongoloid. This has made it even easier to identify each group. Although scientists no longer uphold the "idea" of race, culturally the myth is perpetuated and false separation is sustained. The two of us practice removing the myth when we walk down a street and a person (of any color) is walking there. We erase the mythological imprint which has us reporting to ourselves, "There goes a black person," for example, and say instead, "There go I."

The Balinese woman was entrapped in the myth. We knew that only by changing our concepts can we change the way we see the world and the phony realities we have created.

Deeper Inner Growth Work

For several years we traveled across the continent every weekend doing Practice Sessions and giving talks. Through those sessions, we met thousands of people, sold lots of our books, and developed our large mailing list. The years were stimulating and exciting, but there came a time when change was beckoning. We grew tired of being on the road constantly. But more than that, we began to feel that we had more to give than describing the **Love Principles** to a parade of new people who were dabblers in New Age offerings. We were going deeper in our own personal growth and we wanted to provide that opportunity to others. We had gotten a taste for that in our weeklong Journeys Into Self and in our Journeys Into Self abroad.

As with making any major change in a mode of functioning, we knew there would be consequences. In cutting down our exposure we would be doing less "headlining" and would therefore reduce our name recognition. We would meet fewer people, sell fewer books, attract fewer sponsors to our work, and reduce our income. Why would we do that when we had a good thing going? The answer is simple. Our purpose was to follow what called to both of us on inner planes. Yes, we were entering the unknown but we were willing to take the next step and discover what awaited us.

Changing Names

We, Arleen and Diane, are also known by our spiritual names. During the course of our work together, it came to each of us, at different times, to choose a name that spoke of our spiritual essence, names that matched how we knew ourselves in the finest frequencies of Self.

Arleen shared her spiritual name in 1975 in a small announcement in the Summer, 1975 edition of the *Seeker* newsletter.

Arleen's story:

The choosing of the name came after I had spent time reviewing correspondence with my spiritual teacher, Evelyn Nolt. I saw that Ev often addressed her salutation to "O Shining One." I noted that this was how Ev named and thought of me during my spiritually formative years, 1969 to 1970, just prior to receiving **The Love Principles** and beginning **The Love Project**. During that period, Ev would write letters with suggestions of books to read and avenues to explore, as well as responding with wisdom to my many questions as a fledging on the Path.

As I reread these letters I suddenly realized that my spiritual name was "O Shining One." It was my direct link to my soul lineage in the Deva Kingdom. Rather than have people call me by a lengthy name like "O Shining One," I chose to be called OSO, using the initial letters of the words.

By now I am known by multiples of people as OSO and whenever anyone calls me by that name, I remember to shine. It calls forth the essence of my True Self.

Bearing the Light of the Wisdom Tradition; Diane's story:

By 1980, eight years into our work, I had cleared my personality of so many patterns that I began to notice that when people called my name I didn't recognize immediately that they were speaking to me. It was as if the name no longer resonated.

Then my inner voice began to suggest, subtly, that I take a new name.

I resisted at first because at that time there was a kind of fad going around in New Age circles of taking new names. I had never been one to go along with fads. However, the inner voice persisted and one morning it spoke authoritatively and loudly, saying "Take a new name!" I acquiesced.

After going through every name I could think of in both English and Spanish without finding one that felt right, I began to draw on Hebrew names. When I came upon "Mariamne" my whole being resonated. I asked Arleen to say the name to me and when my heart sang in response I said, "That's my new name."

It did not occur to me that most people would not know how to pronounce or spell the name, which is a derivative of "Mary" that was quite common around the time of Jesus. For example, Herod's wife was named Mariamne. But this was a choice based on an inner process, and when the name Mariamne did not seem to go well with "Pike," I found my way to "Paulus." I had always felt an affinity with the apostle Paul and that surname felt good to me.

By December of that year, I had come to the awareness that taking the new name represented my readiness to take my place publicly as a teacher in the Wisdom Tradition. It felt like a "coming out" of sorts, as if for the first time I was allowing my real Self to be seen.

On New Year's Eve, 1980, we invited a group of our San Diego friends to gather in our home in Ocean Beach for a naming ceremony. We taught everyone to tone the name Mariamne after explaining why I was taking the new name. Following that ceremony, I sent out a formal announcement that I was taking the name "Mariamne Paulus" and I have used that name for my teaching and writing ever since that time. In this book, we use the name Diane throughout for consistency.

The Wisdom Teachings
Diane continues:

Shortly after my awakening, I went to the senior minister of the Methodist church where I was working to tell him of my experiences. He listened attentively and I knew he resonated with my account. However, when I finished he said, "You will learn not to talk about those experiences. People will not understand." As I passed through the doorway on my way out of his office that day I felt an inner directive surge in me: "I will find a way to talk about experiences of awakening."

I was first introduced to the Wisdom Teachings by Laurel Keyes with whom I thought I would open a center for spiritual study in Colorado. She brought the teacher Vitvan and his School of the Natural Order to my awareness. [sno.org]

I was thrilled to know of the continuity of spiritual teachings through millennia because during my experience in South America I had realized just how polarizing religious *belief systems* could be. The Wisdom Tradition was built on personal experience and direct perception of fundamental and universal truths rather than on beliefs. I was certain I would find a way to speak of my experiences in that ancient tradition.

The Wisdom Teachings about the process of creation, the nature of God, and the place of human beings in the stream of evolution were entrusted in ancient times only to those wise ones who were able to incorporate the truth of the teachings into their own lives and thus to open their own direct perception of the same reality.

As we were writing about this, Arleen was pleased to note that this was the exact process that had occurred for her when she was "given" **The Love Principles** on that ray of Light. She had gone to "classes in her sleep" but she could not remember the teaching until she could open to her own direct perception and embody the wisdom in her own daily life.

In ancient times, only a very few human beings ever evolved sufficiently to be able to receive the transmission of the Wisdom Teachings. The masses were content to turn to the wise ones of their cultures to receive guidance and direction.

As the human group psyche evolved, the masses demanded to share in the power represented by knowledge. Consequently, during the past 6,000 years there has been a split between exoteric religions, in which the teachings have been presented in a diluted form to the masses as belief systems, and esoteric traditions, which preserved the Wisdom Teachings in their pure form.

In the shadow of each current world religion one can find an esoteric tradition being preserved by a few faithful disciples. Among Muslims, there are Sufis; among Jews, Kabbalists; among Hindus, Yogis; among Chinese Buddhists, Taoists;

among Tibetan Buddhists, Masters. In Christianity, early Gnostics (those who "knew") were declared heretics. As a result esoteric Christian societies didn't surface until the nineteenth century and they were never acknowledged as valid by mainstream Christianity.

The Wisdom Teachings are divided into two primary branches, the first being a body of knowledge about how the universe works. This body of knowledge is called a divine science because the principles revealed are beyond human perception and understanding. All seers, those who perceived directly the nature of things in our universe, have been in agreement about the fundamental nature of God and man. To this day, a study of the Wisdom Traditions cross-culturally reveals concurrence about this Divine Science.

The second branch of the Wisdom Teachings is the practical application of the Divine Science in the life of a given individual. The methods taught were threefold: doing work alone through meditation, thus discovering the powers within self; doing work alongside others through group study, thus coming to understand the symbols and the divine science; and doing individualized work with a master, thus developing the powers uncovered in meditation and learning to embody the teachings in everyday life and action. This process leads to both *knowing and becoming*.

I realized that I could be a conduit for the Teachings, offering at my own level of understanding and in modern language a synthesis of the many traditions I had studied. It is easy to understand why I trembled internally at the prospect of taking my place in the long line of Light Bearers. The task was formidable, but I felt ready.

A School of Consciousness

So that I could begin to present the traditional Wisdom Teachings, we decided to offer classes at our home base in San Diego for local residents. The classes would last six or eight weeks with time for reflection and application of the learning in between each class. My first class offering was "The Private World: How We Create a Sense of Separation." That was followed by "Learning to Love Yourself," "Facilitating the Individualizing Process," "The Process of Transformation," "Kundalini: The Awakening Creative Force," and "The Structure of the Individual."

After the first series of eight classes, people who lived outside of San Diego began to ask if they could have recordings of the classes. From then on, we recorded each session and invited people to sign up for the classes in person or by recording.

This phase of the School of Consciousness continued for four years.

The Theatre of Life
Arleen continues:

Soon after we decided to offer deeper work in consciousness in 1980, I felt the pull of my previous life in the theatre as a professional actor and director. A voice inside encouraged me not to let all my years of training, talent and theatrical experience go to waste. I knew I did not want to return to a career in the theatre and I wondered what shape this awakening would take. I decided to start by rereading the books by my "Guru of Method Acting," Constantine Stanislavski. I was astounded by what I found in *An Actor Prepares*, *Creating a Role*, and *Building a Character*.

When I had first studied those books in classes with my acting teachers, Irene Dailey and Uta Hagen, the focus had been on the emotional life of the character in a play and on the importance of the actor truthfully immersing self in the role. By the time I returned to the books more than a dozen years later, I had had my breakthroughs in consciousness. I discovered pages of teaching in Stanislavski's books that I had glossed over or had never noticed before because I had not then had the eyes to see. Since my acting teachers were not focused on the spiritual aspect of Stanislavski's offering, they never pointed it out.

What I discovered was that Stanislavski was

an awakened being who followed yogic philosophy, knew about the energy world, and focused on teaching the actor to merge in finer frequencies with the character in the role he/she was playing. The parallels between Stanislavski's contribution and my spiritual studies were remarkable.

In his three main works I found the seeds for taking his contribution to another level: just as an actor creates a role for the stage using multiple techniques, so a person could consciously develop the role (or roles) of his or her daily life and make choices about what characteristics to embody, what feelings to feel, what physical expressions to live through, what voice and speech and movement to create for the self in the world, and how to direct the character/personality known by his or her name from the consciousness of Player, that governing aspect of self that can create anything at will.

This was what was calling to me from my past in the theatre. I had a vision of a way to facilitate the conscious evolution of the Self in a creative and dynamic way, The Theatre of Life. Once the vision came, I allowed it to germinate for a few years so that the approach could begin to take shape.

I designed six Acts for The Theatre of Life program, each with its own focus and experiences, all designed to consciously create the life being lived.

Act One: *Who Am I?* I Am the Player who creates my Personality/Character

Act Two: *How Am I?* I Create an Environment for Becoming

Act Three: *What Am I?* I Am Energy, Expressed through Feelings

Act Four: *Why Am I?* My Life Has a Purpose Aligned with an Unknown Super Objective

Act Five: *On What Instrument Do I Play Life's Music?* My Body is My Instrument of Expression.

Act Six: *I Am.* I Can Consciously Create a Life Role and Have Creative Jurisdiction over my Personality Expression.

Groups were limited to 16 and sessions were 14 days long. Diane tied the experiential aspects of The Theatre of Life together with the wisdom teachings and led out each morning with meditation and a comprehensive presentation. After a lunch break, Arleen led the group through a series of exercises designed to put into practice the techniques that she presented each day.

The Theatre of Life program continued uninterrupted for over 20 years. Often, we presented two or three Acts during the course of a year. We first offered Theatre of Life sessions in San Diego, but eventually we also offered them in Ohio, Pennsylvania and Ontario to make it easier for people who lived in the East to participate. Participants reported profound positive and conscious changes as a result of the work.

Soon after the first group graduated from the Theatre of Life we began offering Graduate Theatre of Life sessions, called Mastery Sessions, at first in San Diego and later in other parts of the country and in Canada. We found that people appreciated the opportunity to practice the techniques they had learned and to share the progress they had been making in their lives.

Embodying the Wisdom

In all our work over the years we stressed the experiential in addition to the dissemination of wisdom. We were devoted as teachers to the embodiment of learning. We considered it too limited to take things in on the mental level and be satisfied with a conceptual grasp. It could be compared to studying about the process of walking, even buying classy shoes to wear, and then remaining seated, never getting up on your feet and moving into discovery.

For decades, we have observed that people go to lectures or conferences with well-known New Age Speakers, take notes, and then talk *about* the ideas that were presented. So many of these people never change in themselves, never apply what they hear, never awaken. The process, in professional theatre, is called vamping till ready. But if you are never ready, never willing to jump in with both feet, to challenge yourself to become more than who you are comfortable being, you never step into the spotlight to do the dance of conscious living.

When Players came to do The Theatre of Life they had to immerse themselves in the whole process. They had to absorb what was taught and to live what they learned. Sometimes people would begin to do that immediately and with each Act they added to their unfolding and growth. Some people came, entered a deep unresolved place in self, became frightened as they sensed a major shift was coming or was required of them, and they quit. Although we were sorry to see them go, we knew that only they could take themselves to the next step, and if they weren't ready, they needed, alas, to stop where they were. Some of these people came back years later and picked up where they left off. They were ready to move on and they did. There were others who went through all six Acts and are still digesting what they learned and working at making the shifts in self as they are able.

The process of awakening cannot be rushed. The kinds of growth about which we are speaking is akin to approaching the edge of a precipice and being ready to leap into the unknown with **no expectations and very abundant expectancy.**

Many who completed the six Acts of The Theatre of Life made major leaps in consciousness and became the more of themselves that had been waiting to emerge. They are out there in their communities functioning as change agents and Light-filled influences on those with whom they come in contact. Nothing pleases us more than knowing that we contributed to their unfolding process. They continue to grow on their own because they have the tools they need and they know themselves as the Player who brings new realities into being every day.

You can read about the entire program in the book *The Theatre of Life*, by Arleen Lorrance, and put some of the exercises to work in your own life. Here are descriptions of the six acts to whet your appetite. The Theatre of Life is not just a metaphor applying theatre techniques to a life being lived. It is a revolutionary way to come to know who you really are and how you can live your life consciously. It is a total spiritual package which allows you to have "creative jurisdiction" over what you bring into being in every moment.

Act One

In 1982 the two of us offered the first Act One of The Theatre of Life which focused on the question, Who Am I? This is the most basic spiritual question to be answered. Too many in "New Age" work talk about "having a Higher Self," a Self which is there to guide them to greater knowing and finer frequency functioning. But there is a basic flaw in this widely accepted approach that is not just a matter of semantics. For example, if one "has" a Higher Self with whom to consult, who has it? Clearly it is the personality (what in Theatre of Life we called the character). If that personality/character says it has a Higher Self, then by definition it is always functioning from a denser energy, or lesser perspective, and reaching into the higher realm for guidance. The basic flaw is the identification of personality/character *as* the self.

In Theatre of Life, in Act One, this flaw is dealt with directly. The teaching is that one *is* that Higher Self, or as it is called in the approach, the Player. Arleen, as Director, would emphasize daily:

You are not the character you appear to playing in the world. You are the Player who brings that character into being each day. You put it on like a costume and wear it in the world, on life's stage. This character has a basic or habitual way of functioning. It doesn't need to be aware of what it is doing because it has multiple patterns it employs in daily life which allow it to proceed on autopilot. The character you think you are is the one that thinks it has a Higher Self. In fact, that Higher Self, the Player, *has* the character and, when functioning consciously, uses it to traverse the stage of life, express feelings, perform tasks, and interact with others.

Once you come to know, "I am not the character but rather the Player who brings the character into being," you are able to have *creative jurisdiction* over everything you do, say, think, or feel. And, clearly, the extension of this is that you, Player, can create new characteristics for yourself at will, even new characters, at will.

This is one major theme throughout the work of the Theatre of Life. It is a ground-breaking way of knowing self. It was ground-breaking for the two of us as well. Prior to The Theatre of Life, the two of us also talked of having a Higher Self, even though we knew that we were more than the personality who appeared on life's stage on a daily basis. The Theatre of Life was a breakthrough to speaking of an awakened life consciously because it shifted our perspective to functioning *as* the Self I Am rather than identifying with the personality and its characteristics.

In one of the experiences in Act One, participants had to audition for their own personalities to see if they could keep who they thought they were. A participant would share an emotional experience with the company. Then a few others would "audition" for that role by retelling the emotional experience as if it were their own, recreating the feelings, the voice, speech, and gestures of the one who first told the story. Then the original person would audition for her/his role by telling the emotional experience once more, consciously recapturing how it was first told. The Theatre of Life company would then vote on who gave the best performance of the story, who best embodied the original teller and presentation.

Deeper Inner Growth Work

During a few of these auditions, someone other than the original person was better and "won" the right to play that character. The ones who "lost out" came to see that they had not portrayed their own personality consciously and could not therefore recreate it. The impact of this was revelatory and everyone in the company became more alert to what they were bringing into being rather than simply living through a series of patterns that repeated themselves while the individual was on automatic.

Knowing and functioning as Player enables remarkable things to occur. During an Act One, one of our participants was dealing with a severe condition in her back that made it difficult for her to bend over or to sit for long periods of time. This condition had been going on for years. No medical treatment or intervention had seemed to help. In the midst of one of our experiences of shedding the current personality and creating a new one using random articles of clothing, she brought "Thor" into being. He was strong and perfectly healthy, and certainly without any back pain. We all watched in amazement as Nan turned, twisted, bent, and danced as Thor, all the while experiencing no physical difficulty. At the end of the experience, Nan retrieved her own clothing and personality, returning to self as she had known herself. She was immediately afflicted with the same physical pain and restriction. The next day, the group used a few articles of the created character's clothing to bring it into being again. Once again, as Thor, Nan had no physical problems; the problems returned when she recreated her familiar configuration.

There was tremendous learning in that experience for everyone. Nan's issues were not psychosomatic; they were "real." But the question that loomed was, just where does the dis-ease reside? In the body, in the psyche, in the energy world, where? Nan's healing with the embodiment of Thor was an example of something that is beyond the ken of most people. We see the body as real, as form, but the body is really units of energy that have been brought into form. Nan and her doctors saw her units of energy as malformed in a condition of physical illness. Years of work trying to fix the perceived form did not achieve the desired goal. When Nan, as the creator of her personality's reality, took on the expression of Thor, she configured the units of energy differently, thus rendering herself free of any physical limitations.

As the Theatre of Life company, and Nan, viewed in amazement this phenomenon that had occurred before all our eyes, we each became aware of the power of our consciousness to **create new realities** even on the physical level. We recognized how much we humans have yet to open to and discover beyond the reality for which we have collectively settled, and how much we have to learn about "how" to **create new realities**. Having creative jurisdiction over our physical bodies is an enormous challenge.

The level of work was so high it thrilled us and confirmed our decision to offer longer sessions that took all of us deeper into consciousness expansion.

Participants saw that when they move into private world interpretation on the character level, they move out of the actual energy of an event and into a pattern. From the point of view of Player, entirely new perceptions and choices open up. One participant saw clearly that *fear is a misinterpretation of an opportunity*! Others were grateful for the larger perspective. "I will never be the same two days in a row, unless I choose to be and create it." Others discovered they could go into experiences without planning. They could stop the mind and wait for something to emerge. A woman from Ohio felt "re-born into an entirely different sense of self ... I learned that my character is expandable and flexible, not set in concrete. I can embody the characteristics I choose and withdraw energy from aspects of character that no longer serve." Others felt that participation in this work gave them the feeling of emerging from a fog and viewing life in all its dimensions for the first time.

Act Two

The work in Act Two was focused on the importance of creating a physical environment that enhances our spiritual growth. One of the projects was to create the background for a painting observed in an art museum and then to embody the character who was permanently painted into that background. Carol selected an elegant woman who was immersed in a flower garden. As a result of her experience in that project, Carol realized how important it was for her spiritual growth that she have a garden she could work in to nurture flowers and vegetables. Since that time, she has had the joy of two or three different gardens in which to blossom.

Other people were challenged to create new environments on the inside of their homes. When Natalie moved into a new condominium, she started without any furniture so that she could feel her way to discover what would serve to nurture her spiritually, rather than choosing items only for their external beauty and serviceability.

Act Three

The focus in Act Three was on feelings, learning to choose which ones to create and use to empower personal expression. Most people assumed that feelings "just happen" and that they could not make choices about them. Learning to discriminate between energy that stirs in the solar plexus and the shape we give to that energy made all the difference. We don't *have* feelings; we create them!

Participants discovered that reality is entirely subjective because it is filtered through each individual's past history. One Player acknowledged that "the more conscious we become, the less filtering we will do and the truth will be what emerges in the moment for us. What we believe to be true is the reality for us. If we don't create it consciously, it will be created unconsciously." Many saw that breathing enabled them to create and express feelings that fit for them in the moment rather than disempowering themselves by reacting.

Scott would no long hold back feelings, worrying about what people will think about him. He saw that feelings are the bridge between the heart and generative chakras and recognized how empowering they are. "Never again will I allow myself to settle into 'comfortable' unconsciousness."

Elizabeth had arrived from New York. She felt like a trapped, angry, shrunken soul walking around in a city full of things that bothered her. Every day was a struggle; very little made her happy. "I came to Act III in a very depressed and hopeless state wherein I thought there was no way I could change my life, no way to be happy, no way to love myself. I wanted to change but I didn't understand how. Now I have learned that I have the power and the agency to take charge of my own life and that it is far simpler than I ever anticipated."

A Player who worked as a psychologist summed up her experience this way: "In both my professional and personal interactions I have observed a true shift energetically during the past month. I see others and myself in a very new way. In the past, I believed in the Oneness in our universe. Today I experience this Oneness as the connection in energy that moves in every living cell and finds expression uniquely in each individual person, kitten or daffodil, as if for the very first time. Now, *this* is living consciously. *This* is life."

Act Four

In Act Four the group spent time mapping out their lives as plays in three acts in order to discover the theme of their life play and the underlying life purpose. To enter into the theme more actively, people were assigned scenes to embody from well-known theatrical plays.

Andy had discovered he was not very good at listening, especially to women, and Rita knew that she had crippled herself in her past relationships by not standing up for herself and her own interests. Then, partnered in a scene from "The Far Country," they played characters that enabled them to move past their limitations. In the course of the rehearsals, they began to care about each other. After the two weeks, they continued to explore together, and today, years later, they are living together in a mutually rewarding and enhancing spiritual relationship.

A primary focus in Act Four was on learning

the difference between adapting to life and in relationships and accommodating, diminishing self by giving up what is important to you in order to keep the peace.

To adapt is to be true to yourself while giving to another. When you adapt, you reach to the other and seek to meet half way in the exchange. To reach is to be responsive; to be responsive to self, first, and then to the other. You are responsive to the frequencies you are registering and you reach forth from those, being true to the natural order process that you are experiencing within your own consciousness.

To accommodate is to abandon self in order to please the other and keep from making waves. When you accommodate you are responding to what the other wants, what the other needs, and leaving yourself out of the picture. While this may feel virtuous since you are thinking of the other rather than yourself, you are not really giving of yourself to the other. You have left yourself behind and have made yourself into what the other desires. You might as well not be there.

This perspective was important to many who had previously been like door mats in their relationships. They became whole persons, trusting their intuition and honoring themselves. They became more self-confident and less self-conscious.

The import and imprint of the Acts were progressive. Participants began to see that The Theatre of Life was integrative, a grand mix of spiritual wisdom and growth techniques, a large enough construct and a large enough purpose to weave it all into a very powerful and empowering whole.

Act Five

Act Five was about learning to express more consciously through the body as an instrument, exploring variations in tempo and rhythm, and using the voice more effectively. These tools were then applied to the creation of three different versions of the personality self, each representing a different context in the Player's life. Participants were to assign each version characteristics, values, and patterned ways of functioning in that context. They gave each a specific objective on which to focus and wrote a soliloquy for each one which they would later perform for the company.

Through the conscious creation of three different faces of self, Players could more easily come to know their creative power and that they did not need to function solely through the personality they always believed they were. As they proceeded, they made notes of what they were learning about themselves as they brought new bundles of characteristics into being.

One Player reported: "For several years I have been aware of repetitive behavior patterns but never understood the dynamic of how they would appear in the scene, full blown, and play themselves out." Now that she knew about how to activate chosen characteristics she saw that she had the tools to live consciously, "...a skill that will change my life."

Another proclaimed, "I have a new self-image: creative life artist."

Act Six

The culmination of this profound work came in Act Six when all participants were invited to create a new and more conscious version of themselves as personalities. They were given a partner (a clone of themselves) to shape and direct so that they could learn how to direct their own character rather than being identified *as* that character. The results were both amazing and lasting. Once they had the experience of being "in charge" it became difficult to revert to a subservient or even victim position.

They were able to break up limiting patterns and move beyond comfortable (but not necessarily useful) ways of functioning in the world. They began to see who they really were as Players who had creative jurisdiction over all aspects of their lives.

The length of the Acts allowed for practice and integration, stretched people beyond mental understanding of concepts to actually (and concretely) creating the expressions of Self they chose. One Player was asked by friends, "So who is the real you?" She didn't know yet but she was prepared to keep going. "The story is not over. I am listening."

Players reported that they did not know of any growth work that focused on people individually and addressed their uniqueness while allowing them to learn in a group interactively. One Player called it a Humanities course for the Self. She came to see herself as "the architect, builder, and maintenance crew of my life."

Clouds Gather

In the 12th year of our life and work together, clouds began to gather on the light-filled horizon. As we know, the nature of this plane of existence is polarities. Change is inevitable and is a necessary factor in our growth processes.

Arthur Mason was a man devoted to finding truth and living it. He had done a lot of work with us and brought his joy and intensity to every session he attended. We will never forget, nor stop laughing over the prank that he and Sid Stave pulled during one of our workshops. They were to spend the night at a friend's home. We had given them specific directions and assumed they had found their way. The next morning Arthur called, sounding harried. He said, "Did you say turn left on Balboa?" We were aghast that they had been driving around all night, until we realized that Arthur was making a joke. We laughed so hard we cried.

Arthur died January 17, 1984 at age 66, the year the clouds began to gather. By March 24 of that year our beloved friend, actor Sam Jaffe, made his transition at age 93. His dignity, his fervor, his kindness, his intelligence, and his beauty of soul remain imprinted upon us to this day. Also that year, Love Family members began dying of AIDS, some before we even understood the disease, others as the illness became more widespread.

It seemed there comes a time in every life when people you know and love begin to die. But there was another death in 1984 that had a profound impact on Arleen; it was the death of her former husband, Richard Lorrance. His death was a hard lesson to learn about the destructive nature of cancer and about how it feels when one suffers the loss of someone whose being has been interwoven with your own.

By this year 1984, Arleen had the wisdom to know that death was simply a transition into ongoing life, but she had not experienced what it was to be present to a loved one who was being tortured by life prior to the blessing of death. Hence, wisdom and agony stood side by side. Arleen wrote about her emotional upheaval in the midst of Dick's horrendous end-of-life ordeal. So many who are the caregivers, experience their own agony and many of them don't have the words to express their own personal trial. Arleen had the words and the ability to describe and to give passage to the intense energy. She shares these excerpts from her journal, speaking for all those who wish they could.

In December 1983 Dick was diagnosed with testicular cancer which had already metastasized to his bones. He wanted to live and had tried every form of healing he could find. We met once a week, playing golf together, and engaging in tender and gentle exchanges. In June of 1984, six months after his diagnosis, he responded to me differently and all at once, I knew that he was dying.

He drew me to him...
>*holding me to his body,*
>*breathing me in cell into cell,*
>*holding me close*
>*in the midst of fairway*
>*newly alive with morning sun.*

He reached across the arm's length
and the years of separation,
>*taking my head to his chest*
>*as we stood beneath the leaves*
>*and the carefree bird song.*

He drew me to him
>*and I knew that he was dying.*

Time had grown so short
Nothing could keep the wine of his life
>*from the parched of his heart.*

He held me to him,
I held him in return,
>*and we remembered,*
>*love that knew no equal*
>*long ago.*

He drew me to him.
I came.

So tender, so fragile a moment.
In other times, a beginning.
Now, the beginning of Goodbye.
        June 13, 1984

Cancer is an incredibly powerful life-death expression. Its swiftness is as surprising as a river abruptly awakened into rampaging fury. By August, radical changes had occurred.

I saw him from the window:
  Bones, covered with the barest reminder of
    pale skin.
I gasped.
A slender wail of almost silent agony
  escaped from my fallen mouth.
It pierced the air for a single second,
  leaving me behind in a shroud of
    despair.
Where had the cancer gone with him?
For here remained
  but a whisper of once booming strength.
Once fleshed robust
Now little more than ostrich in legs and arms.
His shoulders hung upon a wire hanger
  with no courtesy of life-cloth to embellish
  them.
His head

> *still full with knowledge and poetry*
> *sat strangely large upon a skeleton of fragility.*
> *Each step he took, a dirge;*
> *Each gesture effortful.*
> *I gasped again*
>   *overcome with inner sobbing,*
>   *hidden,*
>   *as I went to him.*
>   *27 August 1984*

Talking with him by phone was so difficult. He was so weary. Cancer is such a formidable adversary.

> *Your voice is muffled*
> *Slurred, as if your words shuffle slowly*
>   *adorned by an old man's slippers.*
> *Drugs have claimed you.*
> *Tablets of kindness*
> *Thieves of consciousness*
> *Soothing your pain.*
> *You talk to me as from within a closet*
> *Your life-force hung at the rear*
>   *deep behind the garments of who you used to be.*
> *The pills are strong*
>   *in potency and irony.*

> *They ease the agony*
> *   to prolong life through deadening.*
> *I reach for the you who remains*
> *And cannot find you*
> *   in the dense fog of medical sustenance.*
>   *17 November 1984*

By November, Dick had had a spontaneous fracture in his arm and shoulder and was in hospital for radiation to heal the fracture and ease the unbearable pain.

When I entered his room, he was standing at the phone dialing me. He didn't know I was coming. I didn't recognize him; he barely looked like a human being standing there. He turned when I entered and said immediately: "I was just trying to call you. Can you help me? I want to die. Can you help me get something?"

He was wild with wanting to die, desperate. His doctor had told him there was no hope, and his pain was too great for him to bear any longer, even with morphine...I didn't know what I could do.

I paced in the same cage with him, helpless as was he.

I had brought my poetry with me. I wanted to read it to him, to share my process with his illness, and of the love I was feeling. But my eyes went blurry with tears before I could read the first word and Dick could not listen either. He said:

"I've too much to deal with, with my pain, to have you share your grief with me. I love you too much and your pain would be too great for me." I put the book aside.

He paced again. Shuffled was more like it, because of the drugs and his very swollen ankles. I bit my lip to contain the tears that fought to envelop my face.

Again, he pleaded with me to help him die. His eyes darted to the pull of an inner pain-master that allowed him no rest, demanding that he perform suffering life movements ... Finally he sat on the bed. His body took up so little room.

The radiation had claimed most of his hair. What remained of his skin barely creased over his bones. It was all I could do to keep from screaming over what was left of him. And every centimeter of what was left resounded with pain. How inhumane can our legal system be that we would force a person to continue when all that is left is an agony that will not cease until the body finally dies, finally yields to the devouring disease.

During the visit, a clinician came to take blood. They had a conversation about how Dick might end his life. 10 ccs of insulin would send him into a coma and lead to sure death. Someone could get it for him in Mexico.

Dick's wife, Vivian, was coming to pick him up. He wanted me to go.

He asked me to help him get dressed. Each

article of clothing had more substance than the parts of his body they covered. Who had stolen the fullness I had once held in my arms?

He said goodbye several times, each time with a gentle kiss. I told him I loved him. Then I left, barely able to see.

In the parking lot, I sat in my car screaming and smashing the steering wheel. I screamed for half an hour and all the way home.

Every feeling I had was involuntary. It was as if reason had left me entirely and circumstance was a battering wind that did with me as it wished.

Diane wasn't home when I got there. How could I do what Dick wanted? I felt ripped in half–wanting to grant his urgent, desperate desire to be free of the agony, yet not knowing how moral or ethical such an act would be. I didn't think I could do it–leaving aside the 'murder' aspect. It was Catch 22. I had two choices, it seemed, and both represented something over which I could choose never to forgive myself. I screamed more–unendingly it seemed.

For about five hours, spiked emotional boots were walking up and down the inside of my being. I ached all over and my eyes were swollen with tears of helplessness. The phone rang. It was Dick, speaking hoarsely and hurriedly.

He told me to write down exactly what I was to get in Mexico. He begged me to help him. The voice sounded lost in his body–pulled by heavy chains of pain into the barren canyons of what remained of who he used to be. I told him I didn't know if or how I could or couldn't. I had no words. His life felt like a dry autumn leaf in my hand. He hurried off the phone. I stood alone in a room that had turned grey and felt anger rise at the harshness of life. Dick's dignity had been taken from him. That is what he had always valued most. The cancer took his dignity, but ironically not yet his life ...

By the time Diane got home, a part of me was too tired to leave the chair where I sat telling her of the day, and another part was like a person aflame, running wildly in an attempt to stifle the hell that was eating me alive.

Diane wept with me and offered to go to see Dick and meditatively help him to lift up and out of his body. I called him and offered that but he wanted something chemical. Drugs had overrun his awareness and he couldn't talk anymore, suggesting we connect tomorrow.

The pain of all that is fresh as I report it now. I can't help but think of all the people who suffer alongside loved ones who are being tortured by diseases that take their time in taking the person's life. In most states assisted suicide is still forbidden and the one who is asked to aid in the dying is thrown into a precarious situation. I loved Dick. I wanted to help him. The law forbade it. I was no longer his wife, but even then, I don't know how I would have responded.

So many who are the caregivers experience

their own agony and many of them don't have the words to express their own personal trial. I have the words. I had the words, the ability to describe and to give passage to the intense energy. I speak here for all those who wish they could.

The next day at 5:10 p.m. Dick called.

His voice was high with the falsetto of painkillers. He called to say he had made all the arrangements. He didn't know when it would be. He told me he had had no business asking what he had asked of me—that he had taken care of it now. He thanked me for doing what I *did* do for him. He said, "Let me go in peace." I told him I wanted that for him and that I loved him. At the hospital, he had told me I would probably not see him again. Now he told me we would probably not talk again. And he said, "Goodbye." I felt so grateful to be released from an untenable dilemma.

When Dick liberated me from the request to help him end his life, I knew that to be another act of his great love for me. His asking me in the first place was an act of love, a recognition of the major role I still played in his life, though more than a decade had passed since the completion of our marriage. But this call from him was an even greater offering because he made it from the midst of his excruciating struggle, and because he wanted to leave me unburdened by any guilt for not being able to participate. It was a supreme gift from him, wholly worthy of the years of love we had shared together. It was like a full turn on the circle of who we had been and still were together, in spirit.

Thus began a week permeated with the odor of madness, because day after day there was no news and no contact. I wanted to call but the conditions were bizarre. We had said goodbye. I wanted him to feel free to go, without tugging on him, keeping him here. Yet I wanted to be supportive and to know what was transpiring. I waited. I put my feelings on hold and waited. It was like saying goodbye to someone who was going on a trip and then having the trip be delayed indefinitely.

On Monday, November 26, I called. A friend answered, the one who would help him make the transition. Another fracture had caused paralysis of his lower body. He was in hospital getting radiation. Vivian was with him. I reached him by phone the next morning.

Dick's voice was even more high-strung. He could die if his doctor would give him the highest legal dose of morphine but no one would do that for him. It was so crazy; we can't over-medicate *dying patients because they might die!* Hospice gave me the names of doctors who might be able to help. I called Dick again on Wednesday, November 28.

His friend was with him and about to take him home. He said: "Don't call me until the day after tomorrow." He said he had things to take care of tomorrow and reiterated that I must not call tomorrow but wait until the day after.

I did wait the two interminable days and sought the comfort of loving friends. By November 30, I tried calling as Dick had said to do. There was no answer on the main line and his line was busy all day.

I had a vision of Dick that afternoon. His face was full of healthfulness; his cheeks and skin had a rosy color. His eyes were closed. He looked at peace—as he had so often in our marriage when his head lay in sleep on the pillow beside me ... Turning my attention to him I heard only pure silence, as if it was all over.

I hoped for closure and kept calling uselessly all weekend. My mind jumped about as if a bee were trapped in it. Finally, Sunday evening, I called Dick's dear friend Milt in Rhode Island. It was he who told me that Dick had died on Thursday. He was shocked that no one had told me. Now, relief and grief set in for me.

This has been a long sharing. But Dick's life was more than a few paragraphs long. He gave me the best of himself. He taught me so much about loving. He devoted himself to my flowering into wholeness. He was a man of principle and dignity. And he found something in me of nourishment for himself.

I wrote a last poem.

A flock of grief filled the sky.
Tens of widow's scarves
*   Beating wings of black*
*   in dirgeful crossing*
*   of the empty horizon.*
Death flew over on the day you died.
Winged pallbearers hung mid-air
*   behind your ascending soul.*

Personal Crises

When you are committed to spiritual growth above all else, and when you perceive your relationship as a crucible in which to gain freedom from your personality patterns and blocks, then rough spots are almost certain to appear. Ours came in the mid-1980s after 12 years of living and working together.

For over a year, the two of us engaged in an intense process that was both difficult and revelatory, and often emotionally painful. We hope that some of what we learned will be useful to readers who are in relationships and who want to use those as a way to enhance personal and spiritual growth.

In 1984, Diane entered deep internal waters and had a hard time finding her way out. A woman whom we shall call Louise (not her real name) had moved to San Diego to take classes with the two of us and Diane was immediately drawn to her. Her "rescuer" sense of self came to the fore. Diane felt she could help this woman and she wanted to do so. Today she would say that she felt "driven" to do so.

The fact that the urge was so strong should have been a wake-up signal to her, but it was not.

She was "hooked" in various ways that will become clear as we recount the events of that year.

It had happened in the past that one of us was drawn to a particular person and the other not, drawn as friends or because one of us felt that she had unique gifts to bring to this other as a teacher or consultant. When one of us would pursue such an attraction, she would share with the other, as we went along, what transpired in the one-on-one meetings and we would then both benefit from what occurred as the relationship developed.

Diane deviated from this 12-year practice and that was the beginning of our difficulties. For over a year, Diane kept her meetings with Louise private and never told Arleen anything that transpired. She would say only that this was important for her to do and she wanted no interference from Arleen.

Arleen was very uncomfortable with this but she backed away, and, unfortunately, for the wrong reasons: reasons that lived on the character/personality level. She had had a strong feeling early on that what was taking place was not in harmony but she did not share that energy registry with Diane. Instead, she descended into her solar plexus where she became entrapped by her own feelings.

Because we were both very strong individuals, we sometimes protected ourselves with defensiveness or stubbornness. When we moved into those qualities, our heart centers were not very open and we were at odds with each other.

Even though Arleen sensed trouble in the beginning, she knew that Diane was an independent spirit who didn't like to be told what to do, or to be criticized, or to be controlled in any way. Arleen backed away because of fear. She knew that if she pushed Diane a breach might open up that would disturb their work and union.

Arleen had a controlling aspect to her own personality. She didn't want to activate that but she didn't see how to address the driving energy in Diane. She might easily have said that it seemed inordinate and overwhelming, that the lack of revelation about Diane's sessions with Louise was not only a departure from the way they had always functioned but also that it felt like a violation of who they were together. But Arleen said none of this, taking an uncharacteristic "chicken approach" instead. If that was all she had done it might have been all right, but instead she nurtured upset which can easily fester and set the mind to thinking all kinds of useless, even dangerous, things.

It is almost inconceivable that two conscious people could have gone so astray and that neither of us thought to use any of the **Love Principles** we had been teaching and practicing.

Sometimes all of us ignore what we know. When we do that we invite potential chaos. The two of us had a spiritual union that was a wonderful vehicle for keeping a check on the ego, but each one in the union needs to be open to feedback and criticism. Neither one of us was open to that at the time. Diane felt a deep need to respond to her inner promptings and she didn't feel she could trust Arleen to honor what she was feeling. Arleen felt cut off and allowed an ominous sense to build in her. She did try to get Diane to share with her but that did not happen. Diane pushed back, accusing Arleen of being controlling and jealous of her affection for Louise. Arleen did feel jealousy rise in her because she had been cut off. We each retreated to protect self.

Things escalated. They always do when we don't face issues head on and immediately examine what is transpiring. It was certainly a lesson to us.

Egos Take Over

Diane took Louise under her wing and began to spend a lot of time with her. Louise was very bright mentally, but she suffered from low self-esteem and from a failure to form intimate relationships. Diane was determined to befriend her to provide her a way out of the low self-esteem. Diane didn't see at the time that she had an ego investment in the undertaking. Diane believed that "she," the personality Diane, could *change* Louise. She was doomed to fail from the start. She had an inflated sense of herself and her ability to "fix" what was ailing Louise.

Both of us knew that it is never possible to "rescue" another. Each of us needs to deal with our issues or weaknesses and nourish ourselves so that we can be stronger and/or change our behavior and personality patterns in order to move away from a debilitating or destructive course. Something in Diane's personality structure took over and she ignored this basic truth and pursued with a vengeance.

This should have been a clear indication to Diane that she had slipped out of identification with Self as Player. It was there that she had long known that nobody has solutions for other people's problems. **The Love Principles** would have helped her to stay clear of the deep waters, but in her personality/ego she was not focused on those principles. She was responding instead to an unconscious urge to rescue this woman.

The energy Diane felt seemed too powerful to be driven by this lifetime alone. Looking back on what occurred, Diane feels that she must have had unfinished business with the Louise soul, or someone like her, in a past life. That led to the compulsion, something she "had" to pursue and did not want Arleen to try to stop.

Arleen sensed that what was going on between Diane and Louise was not healthy and she started to distrust Louise.

At this juncture, Arleen took a step that happens in many relationships, a step that further exacerbates what is transpiring. Arleen loved Diane, wanted to trust her, and didn't want to lose her and the fine work they had created together. In Arleen's mind what was happening couldn't possibly be Diane's fault, so it must have been Louise who was the disrupting factor. Once she made this shift the "evidence" easily piled up for her. Louise was evil; Arleen had no question. Louise was the Devil and Diane was caught in her sway.

On the personality level, self-serving fictions are easily created. The personality lives on the level of soap opera and drama is a key ingredient. While it all plays well on television, the process can be excruciating in "real" life.

Eventually we reached out to a psychologist friend for therapy, but Arleen was focused on changing Diane and Diane seemed unalterably determined to move headlong into the maelstrom she was creating. The therapy did not help.

This would have been a perfect time for both of us to see that we had each taken serious missteps, that we were not functioning as Player (Higher Self) because we had very little jurisdiction over our runaway characters. We had each gotten caught in a downward spiraling energy and we couldn't seem to climb above it. We certainly did not apply any of the wisdom we knew or any of the **Love Principles**. We were blinded and continued to be carried by the psychic tornado.

Diane complicated things further by referencing what she felt to be knowledge from a past lifetime in her efforts to free Louise from her low self-esteem. Caution! This is what is known in spiritual circles as mixing levels. What we learned in past lives cannot be translated literally into a current life. The result was a disaster on many levels.

Diane continued to assure Arleen that her interaction with Louise was not a threat to their union but Arleen felt as if she was being abandoned. Finally, Arleen confronted Diane saying that this interaction with Louise was deeper than any of her other teacher/student relationships, that she was entrapped and had lost her way. Arleen's words struck like a thunderbolt. To deny this would be to tell Arleen that her highly valued intuition was no longer valid. Diane could not and would not defame Arleen's intuition. Hence, Diane acknowledged how off-track she had gotten by mixing levels and life times and by trying to free Louise from her low self-esteem. Arleen had felt betrayed for almost a year and although it was helpful to have Diane admit she had been wrong to cut Arleen off, there was a lot of pain to be healed.

Louise also felt betrayed when Diane told her she had been off-course in her relating with her because Diane was a trusted friend and teacher and now it seemed the "teacher" had lost her way.

The soap opera had reached a climax and emotional upheaval reigned. It was hard for us to see how to move forward. Recovery time was needed.

Arleen felt stymied because she knew that Diane was fragile. She felt she had to navigate very carefully. She had never experienced Diane as so unstable and in such a precarious state. Her fall into despair seemed to be the polar opposite expression of her fierce pursuit at the beginning of the relationship with Louise. The same intensity of energy was present but now she seemed lost.

Diane was lost, but in the depths of her own subconscious energies. It was as if she had stepped into quicksand and the only way out of it was to go through it. She was driven by something inner, not pulled by or at the mercy of anything outer, neither circumstances nor persons.

She was in intense inner turmoil. On the one hand, she felt she had to pursue this relationship with Louise; on the other, she was totally committed to her partnership with Arleen, and she recognized how much pain Arleen was in. She could not find a way to reconcile these two commitments inside of herself, nor with the two of them. She felt torn apart emotionally, yet unable to extricate herself from the situation she had created.

Getting Out by Going Through

One night Diane walked down to the ocean and cried out for help. Looking up into the sky, it seemed she was shown a star in the distance far off to her left and she heard an inner assurance, "You are on the right path." She was not surprised by this assurance, because she felt absolutely compelled to pursue the path she was on, though she didn't understand why.

Symbolically, the fact that the star was on her distant left should have spoken to her of how deep into her subconscious mind she had plunged. It was "right" for her to be on this path because she had chosen, as part of her spiritual work, to unencumber her psyche of anything that interfered with a clear registry of higher-frequency intuition and guidance. Although she was in a quicksand of emotion, it was still "right" for her to continue going forward because the emotions needed to be cleared up and out. She saw this in hindsight. At the time, all she knew was that she needed to continue doing what she was doing.

On another walk along the beach, while in great emotional pain, she heard herself say out loud, "If there is more I need to have burned out, let's do it now. Let's get it all done." To her objective mind it seemed crazy to invite more pain, but again, she felt compelled to get clear of what was causing this internal conflict.

The whole experience was no doubt an example of a deep karmic lesson that Diane needed to learn. Such lessons are difficult to endure because there is no way to understand them on the objective level with the rational mind. All one can do is trust that the inner urge, which appears disastrous on the outer, is serving an inner purpose that will become known eventually.

The experience was so intense that it was as if she was walking in the dark, pulling on a thread that indicated the way ahead. So much was this the case that Diane has very few memories from that whole time period of several months. It was worse than being in a fog; it was like being in total darkness.

Looking back, Diane could see that she was so deep into her own dark night of the soul that she ceased to be aware of Louise or the dynamic between the two of them. The event occurring was entirely about "me with me, about my personal consciousness and my personal subconsciousness."

Perhaps this is true of most events we experience. Others may be present or involved but the process, on its deepest level, is about self with self and what the individual needs to learn.

The culmination of this internal pain came while we were in Florida doing sessions. While conducting our workshop during the afternoon, Diane began to feel as if her heart were splitting down the middle. After the session, as we were driving south together, Diane began to scream and cry. Arleen told her to pull the car over and stop, which she did.

Then Diane experienced such a wrenching that it was as if her heart completely split apart as she screamed and convulsed. It was like having a fit of some kind. Then an incredible silence descended and, in the aftermath of that wrenching pain, she felt free. Whatever deep bond was creating the conflict within her broke when her heart split in two, symbolically, and she was left with the commitment she was living out in this life.

That commitment was to walk two-by-two with Arleen while clearing her personality of patterns that interfered with the flow of unconditional love and while sharing that process of unfoldment with others as a teacher and companion. It appeared that a commitment in a past life to the Louise soul had become an obstacle to further growth for Diane in this life. It dragged her down into personality instead of freeing her from it. Diane regrets that she was not able to come to that clarity sooner.

This painful event in our lives required a cooling off period, a time for us to calm our emotional turmoil and to rediscover our centers so that we could pick up the pieces and get on with our lives.

In the midst of Diane's dark night, she found that none of the approaches to personal and spiritual growth she had learned and taught served her. She looked for a new way to move through and past the internal conflicts she had been facing.

Arleen was taking time to heal her great upset and slowly getting her life back together.

Although we don't know the specifics, Louise moved forward with her life.

The two of us had been planning, before this crisis erupted, to take a four-month sabbatical break in Europe. We had made all the arrangements for volunteers to live in our house and handle our affairs. Arleen insisted that we go forward with our plans and we flew to Paris in December 1985. After a month in France we drove into Spain where the healing of our trauma began as the new way of healing Diane had been seeking came to the fore.

Life Is a Waking Dream

In 1970, Diane had had a vivid experience of remembering a lifetime when she was the Mother Superior of a Convent of Carmelite Nuns in Spain. She had seen, in the recall, many specific details about that lifetime, including what the terrain around the convent looked like. It was so clear that she was sure she could find her way there if we went to Spain. Neither of us had ever been to Spain and we knew essentially nothing about it, but we trusted Diane's intuition implicitly.

Diane did not know the precise location of the convent, but she felt intuitively that it would be in the northern part of Spain. Just after crossing the border from France, we spread a map out before us. Diane breathed into her lower abdomen where the knowing about the convent seemed to lodge. Then she put her index finger down on the map. She asked Arleen to look in our guidebook for towns in the vicinity of where her finger had landed. One of them was called Soria.

Arleen read the description of Soria. She said there was a Carmelite Convent there, founded by St. Teresa of Avila in the sixteenth century. Adrenaline rushed through Diane's body and the two of us got goose bumps all over, as if we realized that this could be it. We were full of expectancy. What if we were actually to find Diane's convent?

When we started south toward Soria, the road took us higher and higher into mountains. The land got rockier and drier. In the recall, Diane had sensed that the convent was in high country, though flat, with dry, rocky soil. As we drew closer, the terrain was exactly as Diane had seen it. Soria sits in the center of a high, arid plateau.

Diane asked directions at the Tourist Information Office. A quick walk through the center of town took us to a building on which there was a plaque that read: "Convent of the Barefoot Carmelite Mothers, Founded Personally by Santa Teresa de Jesus on June 2, 1581."

During the drive toward Soria, Diane's rational mind kept saying, "You know, this is really crazy. You can't have a so-called past life recall and then expect to find the place. You know nothing about the Carmelites, have not read anything about them, and you know nothing about Spain." But her strong feeling that we would find it won out. It did not surprise either one of us to be standing in front of a building from the very period Diane had remembered in that experience fifteen years before. It was a meeting of inner and outer realities, of the known and the unknown.

We stepped inside. A small sign informed us that we were too late in the day to visit. We thought "visit" meant to see the ancient building that had once been used by the nuns. We surmised it had been preserved as a historical site. We made a note of the visiting hours and retired to our hotel.

Meeting the Mother Superior

The next morning we arrived at the convent shortly after 9:30 A.M., the beginning of morning visiting hours, which lasted until 11:30 A.M. Diane rang the bell. A tall man emerged. "We would like to visit the ancient convent," she told him eagerly.

"That's impossible," he replied. "They are cloistered." "You mean the nuns are still using it?" Diane asked in surprise. He nodded, adding, "And they are entirely cloistered."

Diane asked to speak with one of the sisters. The man rang a bell. We heard footsteps in the inner courtyard. Then a voice spoke from behind a dark window. The old caretaker told her that some women wanted to speak to one of the sisters. He motioned Diane to the window and then left us alone in the reception area.

Diane stepped up to the small opening, grateful that she spoke Spanish fluently. "I have come from the United States," she began. "Several years ago I had a vision of a convent such as this—I believe it was Carmelite—and I have come looking for it." From behind the dark window the nun answered, "Just a moment, I will get the Mother Superior."

Perhaps you can begin to sense how the "real world" and Diane's inner experience began to merge. She was to be given an opportunity to speak to the Mother Superior; in her recollection, she had been the Mother Superior.

The Mother Superior pushed a key through a small window. She directed us to a second-story parlor and told us she would meet us there. When we entered the parlor, we found two chairs set on either side of a round table, under which there was a small heater. The nuns, we learned, had no heat in the convent, but they provided that comfort for their guests.

The table sat in front of a large, grilled window without glass. Soon the shutters were opened on the other side of a matching grill. There was a foot of space between the two grills. A light went on, and the Mother Superior greeted us. She was dressed in a dark brown habit, just as Diane had worn in her recall, with a white cloth fitting close around her head and neck, and a black veil over her head. She wore glasses. Her round face and eyes peered eagerly at us. She said, "Now we can talk."

Diane had been hoping that the Mother Superior would allow us inside the convent, even though she fully understood the nature of their cloistered life. But when she saw the Mother Superior, she became totally absorbed in the vividness of the moment and all prior thoughts and desires fell away. At the same time, any sense of herself as an outsider dissolved and Diane felt like one of the nuns.

Before they had gone very far in their conversation, a second nun joined them. She was introduced as the assistant to the Mother Superior. In an intense hour and a half, Diane and the two "mothers" had a lively exchange. Arleen was a silent witness, since she spoke no Spanish, but throughout the exchange, Arleen could feel on an energy level what was transpiring and even without the faculty of language could understand. Diane told them of her memories (which she called a vision out of deference to their heritage). They confirmed the majority of the details for her.

Most startling was the moment when Diane told them about her death. "I was quite old, lying on a large bed, not in my regular cell. All the members of the community were gathered around the room praying for me, and I experienced their prayers literally lift my soul up out of my body and toward heaven."

Their eyes opened wide in wonderment. "How could you know such details about a Carmelite's deathbed experience? No one but a Carmelite is allowed to witness such a death, because it is considered to be the most sacred event of a lifetime." They went on, "We do all gather around the room. Those who can, kneel and pray. The others stand. And we use our prayers to lift the soul of the dying one toward God."

Prayer to the Mother

Diane's meeting with the nuns was thrilling and confirming, and certainly confounded her rational mind. There was no objective explanation for how she could have known so much about the lives of these cloistered nuns. Neither was there any way to "prove" that this was the same convent of her recall since she could not visit the interior. However, she was satisfied that there was truth to the memory and that was enough.

Still, it was clear to Diane that there was something more important for her to uncover about the visit. The Mother Superior had asked if the two of us were dedicated to the worship of the Holy Mother. Learning that we were a Jew and a Protestant, the two nuns lamented that we were missing a great deal by not having the Mother. "Not to take anything away from God the Father and from our Lord," they were quick to point out, "but as in any family, it is the Mother who is the soul. We need the Mother. We cannot live without the love of the Mother."

Near the end of the conversation, the assistant to the Mother Superior was overcome with excitement when it occurred to her to say, "Never mind that you are Jew and Protestant! We should all do what we want. Therefore, you must love the Mother in any case!" The Mother Superior joined her with enthusiasm. "Yes, you must love the Mother, and pray to her. She will answer your prayers. You must love the Mother."

As we left the convent, Diane knew the primary reason for her visit had been to hear the nuns' message about loving and praying to the Mother. But she did not know how to integrate that into her life. She had no past experience or religious training in prayer to the Mother. In her Protestant heritage, prayers were always to God the Father. Prayer used words and appealed to God as "other," outside of self, usually with the feeling of reaching up. Diane felt awkward just thinking of loving the Mother and had no idea how she would pray to Her.

As it turned out, the answer to her dilemma was contained in the experience that had just unfolded. It occurred to Diane to use skills she had developed over the years working with dreams to look at the visit to the convent as a waking dream to see if she could unveil its deeper meaning. This was the first time she had approached one of her life experiences as a waking dream. As she worked with this approach, trying to penetrate the inner meaning of the convent visit, Diane began to reach realms of understanding and perception previously unknown to her. Here is how Diane worked with the experience as a waking dream:

I received the cloistered convent as a symbol for a space in my own consciousness where the work of prayer goes on constantly. I had not con-

sciously recognized this yin space of prayer before and I welcomed bringing it into my awareness.

In my past life recall, I had seen myself as a Mother Superior. In my waking dream, I had met the Mother Superior and her assistant. I understood the waking dream to indicate that I had made direct contact with the inner authority of my feminine polarity that I had listened to as I followed my intuitive knowing for how to find the convent. In this way, I began to integrate a growing sense that I already knew how to pray to the Mother.

The waking dream was made up entirely of feminine symbols: the nuns who lived in the convent, the Holy Mother to whom they insisted I pray, my partner and I, and even the woman who gave directions to the convent at the information center. The only masculine symbol was the caretaker at the convent, whose specific function was to make contact with the outer world for the cloistered sisters. He was the perfect symbol for the energy that enables me to make my inner process of prayer known to others and to reach out to others for what I need in my daily life. I am activating that polarity now, as I write these words. It was clear that I could activate my feminine knowing by turning my consciousness inward.

This is how I began to internalize the meaning of both my past life memory and the waking dream of the convent in Spain. For me they symbolized the awakening of a highly developed facet of my consciousness that had long been in place, but which I had not brought into active awareness during the first forty years of this life. In the waking dream the Mother Superior handed me a key to an upper room and said, "I will meet you there." It seemed the key was a symbol for the method of looking at life as a waking dream. The waking dream seemed to say that buried in my unconscious was vast knowledge of the Mother-God and the ways of praying to her. This recognition enabled me to begin to consciously integrate the feminine polarity of wisdom, as represented by the "Mother," into my sense of self.

School of Consciousness, Phase Two: Life As A Waking Dream

After the experience of visiting the Spanish convent, Diane understood that to pray to the Mother is to give reverent attention to what is, to what has manifested, to what has come into being. Prayers to the Mother are answered in the forms and shapes that life takes. The Mother answers prayers through the experiences of life.

What emerged was a new method that Diane called "Life as a Waking Dream." She discovered that the events of ordinary, daily life could be interpreted as if they were dreams, thus revealing messages from the subconscious that can serve as guidance. She found this to be a way to communicate with the Great Mother whose "language" takes symbolic form.

Diane immediately offered this new approach through the School of Consciousness, thus launching more than 20 years of wonderfully deep work for hundreds of people. Many said that to work with their vivid life experiences as waking dreams took them deeper in far less time than psychotherapy and offered them a way to move forward more creatively and positively.

The first classes in Life as a Waking Dream were offered to people in San Diego, but having learned from past experience, the sessions were also recorded so that people from afar could participate. Participants were actively involved because they submitted their own life experiences to be looked at as waking dreams.

Eventually Diane offered training so that others could teach this method. Twelve people were certified as teachers and they offered classes in Ontario, Canada and across the United States. In 1997 Diane wrote a book presenting the method. It was published by Riverhead Books.

One of the earliest students who later became a teacher of the Life as a Waking Dream method wrote of her transforming experience:

> *When I began [the first class series], I agreed with myself to go along with the hypothesis offered, to test the process and see*

where it would lead me. I am filled with amazement, not to mention gratitude, when I consider the results so far. I have gained great insights into myself, into relationships with others, into the relationship between men and women, and between the masculine and the feminine.

It has brought me also to believe that it is an urgent social and cosmic task, this need to differentiate between the two forces, the feminine and masculine, the yin and yang, on every level to bring them into conscious harmony and cooperation. The only way I know to go about that task is for each of us to do the work of consciousness and reconciliation within ourselves.

The excitement of the work has been, and is, to know myself to be "the Dreamer of the Life Dream."

Another woman wrote:

In some ways I feel I have transcended some old patterns and become a stronger Self. Information that has been especially helpful to me is (1) having my Yang there to support me, and (2) expanding to make room for a symbol and inviting it to merge with me. Thank you again.

The End of the Dark Night of the Soul

Even in the midst of a difficult passage through a dark night and a relational crisis, we both completely trusted our intuition to guide and direct us. Many people have trouble understanding that an inner life can be intertwined with outer events and that to find one's way through the outer we often have to go deeper in. If we focus on resolving the outer without knowing how it is intertwined with the inner, it does not serve us in our spiritual growth.

Diane looked at the crisis we had gone through before leaving on our sabbatical as a waking dream. She could see Louise as a symbol for the Great Mother. Physically Louise even looked like some of the ancient statues of the Great Mother, such as the Venus of Lespugue. Beyond the personal interaction, it seemed what was calling to Diane was a memory of her connection with the Great Mother. She needed to reawaken an intimacy with that larger force that was the balancing polarity for God the Father.

In her waking dream, Diane had sought to "rescue" Louise, whereas it was actually a deeply buried part of herself that needed not so much to be rescued as to be reawakened. Diane recalled an experience she had had following one of our trips to India. In the midst of a Rolfing session, Diane suddenly saw (with her inner eye) the face of the goddess Kali at her feet. Kali's mouth opened and she swallowed Diane whole.

That experience had been remarkable, because instead of being frightened, Diane felt incredibly at peace and completely loved as Kali devoured her. For about five days after that event Diane remained, in her inner awareness, in the belly of the goddess Kali. Her primary feeling was that Kali loved her exactly as she was, good and bad included. She felt relief to have a "mother" that was different from the ideal of "good" mother because she felt all facets of herself were received and loved. It was a deeply affirming experience.

Diane also saw that the goddess Kali was hungry for all aspects of life, the good and the bad. She did not turn away from what was painful or ugly, violent or disturbing. She wanted it all; she felt nourished by it all. She relished life, all life.

During the first week of our Sabbatical, while we were in Paris, Diane had a vivid dream in which she was standing before the mouth of a deep cave. She could see that there were black birds frozen in the cave. A man approached her and told her that she could free the birds by chanting "Teleos." He proceeded to chant the word three times. Then Diane woke up.

The dream was so clear that she practiced the chant out loud so she wouldn't forget it. She couldn't remember what "teleos" meant, but she felt the dream to be part of her deep inner process. The black birds seemed to be wisdom that was held deep in her subconscious mind that she needed to bring forth.

In the aftermath of the visit to the Spanish convent Diane realized that her knowledge of the Great Mother had been buried in her and needed now to be brought forth into conscious awareness. The Great Mother brought forth into manifestation all polarities of living and invited us to learn to embrace them all. Indeed, to love them all. It was as if the Great Mother sought to expand our capacity for unconditional love by manifesting everything, both the ugly and the beautiful, the painful and the enjoyable, the terrifying and the comforting, the messy and the organized.

Following her intuition when she had packed for our sabbatical, Diane had brought along Erich Neumann's *The Great Mother*. Ironically, this choice preceded the visit to the convent in Soria and was an indication of how inner guidance helps us to find wholeness. Following the visit to the convent Diane dove into the book and allowed her strong inner knowing to meet and match the scholarly analysis of the archetype by Neumann. Since images of the Virgin Mother were everywhere in Spain and Italy, Diane had the perfect environment in which to delve deeper into her intuitive recognition of the Great Mother.

It could perhaps be said that our crisis was a waking dream of what it is like to be swallowed whole by the goddess Kali. It was painful, but transformative and freeing. It was a confirmation that **problems are opportunities** even when we do not recognize them as such at the time, opportunities to go deeper into Self to uncover what is hidden within us and that we need to bring into consciousness. The Great Mother guides us through life events to a deeper understanding of Self.

Reaping a Harvest of Deep Learning

Diane's dark night was an example of working all the way through something that had been lodged in her subconscious mind, probably for several lifetimes. There were many lessons in the experience.

First, she realized again that she could not "rescue" persons from their own struggles.

Second, she saw that it was essential not to mix levels. What she knew about the beauty of the personality and body could not be transmitted directly to another. It was the result of a spiritual knowing that was earned in the past and could only be lived out in her own life in the present.

Third, she realized she had violated an unwritten trust between a student and herself as a teacher. She had meant to help, not hurt, Louise. By involving Louise, a student, in her own process of finding her way in the dark, she did not serve as a guide but in a sense led Louise astray, or at least abandoned her along the way. It was difficult for Diane to forgive herself for that indiscretion.

Arleen learned that it is important to raise inner concerns early on and to spell them out in specifics. She had pulled back because she knew Diane would push against her and go even deeper into what she had taken on as a crusade. By doing that, Arleen did not bring her own strength to the situation and may have contributed to its going too far. She feared there would be a split between the two of them and she didn't want that to happen. That is a form of trying to control a situation by placating and hoping for the best. It is a weak position that contributes nothing positive or healing.

One of the biggest lessons was that challenges need to be addressed out loud as they are occurring. The two of us needed to open our heart centers, sit down together, and talk about what was transpiring and what we were each feeling. This seems like such a simple thing to do, so simple that it is almost impossible to believe that we humans can instead choose to clam up, protect ourselves, and watch all hell break loose.

To seek to protect self, especially by withdrawing into self and not sharing with the one you love, is to function from weakness and to descend into illusion. Putting up barriers serves to isolate self. Things would have been very different if we had chosen to sit before each other in the very beginning, to tell each other what we felt and what was urging us on, and to explore how we could make room for each other as the circumstances unfolded. Had we done this we could have avoided enormous pain, and we might have had similar learning by choosing a different path to arrive at that learning. One does not have to suffer in order to grow.

Sharing together, crying together, opening hearts to each other, making room for one another may not seem as easy as shutting a door and keeping the other out, but it is a much quicker and more loving way of growing together.

Sometimes we are not able to see clearly enough what is transpiring to share it simply and in love. This is especially true when we seek to bring into the light something that has been buried in the subconscious. In those cases, we muddle through, and if we are lucky, we come out on the other side more whole.

For two to walk together as one goes through a dark night of the soul is a test for a spiritual union as well as for the individuals involved. Our union was strong enough to withstand the test, for which we are grateful.

Making Changes

We spent several years working in the depths of our psyches, seeking to bring our shadows into the light, laboring to relate to each other in the here-now of the energy world, and leaving unhealthy patterns behind us. Such internal house cleaning made more room in ourselves for more personal growth and for our teaching.

From the very beginning of our years together, we have shared in our magazine our own inner growth work, our stumbles, our needed changes or struggles in self, our **problem/opportunities**, and our creation of new realities that would better serve us as individuals on the path to becoming the more of who we are. This form of personal sharing was an example of our being public/private persons. We often heard that this touched our readers and members of our Love Family and served as an inspiration to them.

Many would remark that it took courage for the two of us to share so openly, but it didn't take courage at all. It was a choice that we had made in the beginning. It was also a way of being thoroughly human alongside those in our acquaintance rather than setting ourselves apart as teachers or gurus. We invited participants to expose their growing edges in our sessions and in letters to the magazine and we did the same. It made it possible for all of us to support each other so that no one felt he/she was alone.

One example of this came for Arleen came in 1988 in an article entitled "Lies that Shape Our Lives:"

The event took place in my parent's North Miami Beach condominium. On the last morning of our visit, my mother delivered the following revelation. "You know, when you were 17 and wanted so desperately to go to Boston University on that partial drama scholarship, I told you we didn't have the money and that's why you couldn't go. But that wasn't the truth. I didn't want you to go because I was afraid of losing you, so I told you we couldn't afford it. I wouldn't let you go."

Her words penetrated to the unprotected soft place in my solar plexus and my feelings and thoughts plummeted about me like meteorites.

How could you have done that? Why did you make me think I was poor? Was there no end to how you sought to control me? You lost me all the more! I lost me.

The chance to go to Boston University where I had already been accepted would have healed a raw place in myself. In my senior year at the High School of Performing Arts I had been so focused on earning service credits that my scholastic average (I had been an honor student) fell so that

I wasn't automatically qualified for city college admission. On top of that, I was terrible at taking tests due to dyslexia (which I didn't know I had) and I failed by two points my required entrance exams.

Because of my reading difficulties I had faked my way through all my school years. To pass tests I would think up what the teachers would ask as essay questions, write answers to at least three of them, and memorize them. In this way, I could get by. Ironically, I never saw this as a sign of intelligence. By the time I messed up the entrance exams, I was devastated by the stigma of failing to have the option of attending a city college during the day. I was profoundly ashamed.

What I remember is the defeat, the collapsing, the death of the self who, from that time on, lost her deepest sense of confidence. I wasn't smart enough for regular college and I was too poor to go out of town. I was stripped of my limitless visions of my future and reduced to the kid of a working-class family who had few options. At 17 I had become a nobody, working by day at a bank and attending college classes at night for seven years until I earned a Bachelor of Arts degree.

I know all these reflections sound very dramatic (they do even to me), but when you are 17 and just starting out and your hopes are dashed, it is a time of crisis. And, I didn't know for another 42 years that I had been lied to by my mother. I could have gone to an out-of-town-school and could have achieved who knows what.

It was a lie that we were poor. It was a lie that I wasn't smart. I had always thought I was unloved but I was loved too much, smothered, held in a possessive grip. Not surprisingly, I repeated my mother's way of loving in relationships of my own: loving people too much, loving them more than they could possibly handle.

The lie my mother revealed to me opened my eyes in many ways.

I was raised in my mother's fears, in her non-trust, in her over protection. I prepared for life that way. I always gave myself something to fall back on. I became a high school teacher in case I wouldn't "make it" in the theatre. But to be successful in the theatre I needed to be in theatre, not in teaching. I created something to fall back on, and I did! I won't do that again.

For too many years of my life I suffered from not having been loved as I would have liked. It colored almost everything I did and interfered with the fulfillment of my potential. To grieve over what never was is a wasteful use of energy. Emotional wallowing is a western world luxury, possible because most of us don't need to deal with basic survival hardships or political oppression.

I chose not to grieve any longer over this painful lie. Instead, I turned my attention to what was alive in me in that moment, and from that position of strength, to go forward toward bringing the new into being.

I see clearly that any lack of confidence I experience today is the result of inappropriately transposing to the now, a deficiency I experienced many years ago. Who I was then has no business stumbling along inside me now.

My dear friend of many decades, Jessica Levy, commiserated with me over this revelation by my mother. Wisely, she said, "You know, what you think you missed, I don't think anybody else misses *in* you." Even I could see this now.

When we uncover a hole in self from the past, we need to enter it and fill it for ourselves. It is a juncture where one can come face to face with self, which one can do only by moving beyond old needs and wants. It is a hole that one can fill with the substance of the current conscious self. Both Diane and I filled such holes in self and were ready to move forward.

Expanding Our Home Space

After 16 years of doing classes, Practice Sessions, Journeys into Self, and Theatre of Life in venues across the United States, in people's homes, in religious and yoga centers, and in other public places, we felt it was time to create a larger home base for our work. It was an act of expanding our outer living space to bring it into alignment with our inner expanding consciousness.

In order to find a way to expand our small house, which had been built in 1939 as a beach house, we reached out to one of our Love Family members who was and is an architect in San Francisco, James Stavoy. Jim offered his creative services as a contribution to our corporation and he envisioned how we could expand our house. He presented us with renderings that made it easy to visualize what would emerge. We were very grateful to Jimmy and his blessing.

We interviewed several contractors before choosing the one that felt harmonious to us both. On February 17, 1988, we broke ground on the new that was to come into being. Strong men worked for nearly five weeks, the way the hardworking masculine force in each of us had sought to unearth in our own psyches all that stood in the way of the functional expression of our expanding consciousness. Finally, the old foundations were torn out to make way for the new.

For us, it all had a metaphorical meaning. The old foundations of both our physical home and our old beliefs and values needed to be unearthed and the underpinnings replaced. One day in the midst of the process, we returned home late in the afternoon to view a large opening through the foundation of the house. From within the dark garage we could see out into the light-filled back yard. Space for the new entrance to the back of the house had been created. Tears rushed to our eyes and our hearts thundered.

It was as though we looked into and through a physical manifestation of the hard work we had done both by design and through the Dark Night experience, each of us in self and the two of us together, to make room in our personalities for the knowing that was emerging in our awareness.

Love Family member Barbara Grasso had sent us 15 crystals to be buried in the foundation of the expansion of our home. She suggested that we infuse them with qualities we wanted to permeate the space and to touch all who entered. On March 11, a group of us gathered to perform a ritual of laying the crystals and their powerful, supportive qualities into the ground where the foundations were to be laid. After the blessing, the two of us felt Gentle Haven to have extended beyond our personal space to make room for the group field that had been built by all the participants over the preceding 16 years. We were all supporting each other as we grew in consciousness and in the ability to live in unconditional love. We were a Love Family, companions in consciousness.

Half the space in the newly expanded house was personal living quarters; the other half was a meeting room, two offices, and a consultation room. The two halves were joined in the middle by the kitchen where food was prepared and processed for the nourishment of all.

The Paradoxical Individualizing Process

Once the project was completed, we held a celebration and invited all to attend. We were in for a big surprise. That fateful day temperatures on the coast soared to 98 degrees as Santa Ana winds swept in from the desert in the east. Temperatures that high were unknown to us during the preceding 16 years. The environment had gone extremely yang as 43 of us gathered to bless the new space. The winds sucked all the moisture out of all the plants in the garden and out of those of us gathered to celebrate as we perspired profusely with no air conditioning and only small fans. For us it was as if the fire of Spirit had intensified to cleanse and bless our new space.

Many spoke at the celebration of what **The Love Project** continued to mean to them and how their lives had been immeasurably enriched. When the group toned together, the energy soared and so did the spirits of all present.

We were aware, as never before, of how meaningfully **The Love Project** had enhanced participants' growth. We had sought to encourage the individualizing process through our work. When humans become truly whole, we are indivisible. We cannot be divided within ourselves against ourselves, or separated from others. Instead, we live in recognition of our place in the large whole, of our integration in the One Body. This state enables us to live without fear of rejection, of abandonment, of isolation or of death. We are interactive rather than reactive, interdependent rather than codependent, cooperative rather than competitive. We are **being the change in the world** that our own uniqueness dictates **rather than trying to change the behavior of others** in order to control the outcome of the whole.

As individuals spoke during the blessing of our newly expanded home, they were living testimonies to the effectiveness of the work we had been doing. We had created forms that facilitated the individualizing process without establishing an organization, a community, or a group that was defined by those who belong and those who do not belong. We wanted all people to feel welcome and to be able to participate to whatever extent they chose. Such a group reality required radical attention on our part to inclusion and to **receiving all people as beautiful exactly as they are**, inviting their uniqueness as they chose to bring it to the whole.

Our celebration was of individuals who fit no identifiable group pattern or norm. We were a large Love Family who were in no way defined, confined, or restricted by our association. We stood alongside others who were consciously cooperating with their individualizing processes as we all trusted the larger inner pattern (which is what "teleos" refers to) to guide our further unfolding.

The two of us felt we were part of a "hundredth monkey" experience. In this purported phenomenon, a new behavior or idea is spread exponentially once a critical number of members of a specific group exhibits a new behavior or acknowledges a new idea. It seems that a few macaque monkeys on a Japanese island were washing their sweet potatoes before eating them. This practice was picked up by the younger generation of monkeys and once 100 of them took to washing their potatoes, all the monkeys began to do that and the learned behavior instantly spread to monkeys on other islands though there had been no external communication of the new behavior. Ken Keyes, Jr. spread the inspirational parable, applying it to human society. It suggested that if enough individuals began to manifest positive change, the change would spread spontaneously around the globe.

We looked upon our Love Family, spread far and wide, as among those who might eventually cause the balance of humanity to shift into a whole new way of being, a way grounded in universal and unconditional love. Since the target group was humanity, it was likely to take longer than the task of washing potatoes. But we remained undaunted. We rededicated ourselves to the process of change, expanding within and without in order to become the more. We were not alone; we were a contributing Love Family.

Thus, 1988 was a momentous year for Gentle Haven and for our work. Arleen so loved our newly expanded home and workspace overlooking the Pacific Ocean that she often joked that she was going to leave the house to herself in her will so that when she reincarnated she could move back into it and pick up where she left off. However, as we know, one should never have *expectations*. It had taken five years from 1983 to 1988 to raise the funds and prepare for the major remodel. Within another five years, a radical change awaited us that would bring about a major relocation, but we knew nothing of that in 1988.

Renaming the Corporation

By 1990, at the 20th anniversary of the birth of **The Love Principles** and **The Love Project**, we were ready for another shift, this time in the name we would use for our corporation and its work. In the first ten or more years of our work, we taught the six **Love Principles** in every session we led. In the 1980s we expanded our teaching to include other aspects of the Wisdom Tradition. **The Love Principles** continued to be foundational for us, but we wanted the name of the corporation to indicate that we were offering more than those six principles.

As was our way of proceeding throughout our years together, we did not pluck a name from the mental level or choose something that sounded catchy. We allowed the new name to emerge from an organic event that had occurred in our life and work together.

During our European sabbatical, Diane had had a dream in which she was standing outside the mouth of an enormous cave in which a flock of blackbirds was frozen. A man standing nearby had said the birds could be called forth by chanting: *Tay lay os, Tay lay os, Tay lay os.* The chant was so clear in the dream that when Diane awakened she practiced singing the chant so she would not forget.

Teleos is a Greek word that points to an invisible pattern at the core of manifested reality. It is the invisible yang imprint that results in Cosmos (a Greek work meaning order), the yin substance brought into identifiable energy fields and forms. Simply put, before there is a flower, there is a seed which holds the pattern to guide what it will become. Teleos determines a purposeful emergence of everything that comes into being. Teleos is the Perfect Pattern that guides and directs the individualizing process within each of us.

In choosing Teleos as our new corporate name we upheld the ancient truth that everything comes into being through the guidance of an inner, unseen force that moves toward fulfillment and completeness/wholeness. Teleos is the Masculine Principle, God within, which takes on form through the Feminine Principle, the Great Mother.

When we awaken, when we individualize, we respond to an inner urge to cooperate consciously with the invisible force moving within. We make the choice to embody what we register within and to bring it to life through formulating a life purpose and doing the Will.

In this we begin the journey of co-creation. We realize that meaning is not inherent in life but that we infuse life with meaning: we attribute importance to others in our lives, we choose values, take up causes, and find significant groups to join. In these ways, we contribute to the larger whole. All the while we uncover aspects of the invisible pattern within ourselves and help to make it a reality. We merge with the fundamental creative urge at the core of our beings.

We chose the name Teleos as an expression of our focus on life purpose and on cooperation with what is ready to emerge.

It was very natural then to change the name of our *Seeker* newsletter to *Emerging,* A Publication of Teleos Institute. It has been called that since the fall of 1990.

One of the most exciting things about functioning consciously is listening within, receiving intuition and inspiration, and creatively participating in bringing about the emerging realities. Jesus is reported to have said, "Of myself I do nothing," and yet without the self-that-is-manifested and cooperating, there is nothing that is visible or "real." Though we think we change the moment or the world, the moment and the world are actually changed by the larger Will and we choose how we will contribute to and cooperate with that change.

The imprint (of yang, of *teleos*) is present and forceful and we (the yin) do what is necessary to make it visible.

We listened inwardly as we sought to discover what changes we might make in our work to bring it more fully into alignment with the new. We tried several innovations (such as having representatives in several different cities), but none of them captured the spirit of **The Love Project** and eventually they all fell away.

The two of us had come to trust our inner guidance as a result of our individual awakenings. It was life-changing for us. It became a way of life. It became the foundation of our spiritual union and the basis for encouraging others to trust their inner guidance.

Inner Guidance and Conscious Choices

Completions of necessity lead to new beginnings. We had lived in San Diego for twenty years. We started our work there and we had expanded our small house to make more room for our offices, classes and workshops. As we settled in to the new space, we congratulated ourselves on having created our environment just as we wanted it. We should have known better. Complacency invites change, or so it seems.

Two Big Dreams

Both of us had long paid attention to dreams, finding in them insight into the workings of our psyches and sometimes, in *big* dreams, receiving guidance through which we could tap into our larger knowing that was below the surface of our conscious awareness. A series of three dreams at the end of July and beginning of August, 1992, definitely caught our attention.

Diane had the first. She dreamed that she survived an enormous flood. She stood in her nakedness, aware that absolutely *everything* had been washed away. She did not even have a way to establish her identity, or any connection with this incarnation. The dream was not colored by emotion. Rather, there was the simplicity of seeing (knowing) her circumstance.

The dream seemed to summarize a number of experiences Diane had had in which her ties to her personality and its history seemed to have been severed. The first, of course, was taking her new name, but there were many other experiences, both in waking dreams and sleeping dreams. All seemed to suggest that an enormous shift in the way she knew herself, from the personality to what she experienced in her 1965 awakening as the "no self," was complete. Diane acknowledged the truth of this shift, but didn't know of any further action that needed to be taken.

A week or ten days later, Diane had another big dream. In it she was seated in a mammoth auditorium, towards the back. With her were Theatre of Life players. Suddenly a fierce quaking began, more violent than any quake Diane had experienced before. In the dream Diane told herself, "This is the Big One and I will surely die in this earthquake. It is important to be prepared." She sat up straight in her seat, closed her eyes, and calmly concentrated on deep breathing, aligning with her higher knowing of herself as the Power-to-Be-Conscious. She felt no fear, but was keenly alert and focused.

After three or four minutes, which is nearly

an eternity during an earthquake, the shaking slowed to a gentle rock. Diane opened her eyes to discover that the building was still standing and no one had been hurt. She gathered the Theatre of Life players and left the auditorium.

In the next scene of the dream, Diane drove a large, commercial-size van. Arleen was in the passenger seat and a large group of Theatre of Life players was being carried in the van. They crossed a freeway overpass. As Diane looked to her right she saw the city of San Diego lying in complete rubble. As far as she could see everything was flattened and utterly destroyed.

In the dream, Diane knew we would carry on with our work because the rebuilding process in San Diego would take many years and we were not to be involved in that. This final bit of information left the biggest initial impression on Diane. For twenty years we had been encouraged by many people to leave San Diego before the "Big One" hit. Each time we had listened respectfully to the prophecies and the psychic visions, but when we attended inwardly we never felt an urge to move. Daily television community service announcements encouraged San Diego residents to be prepared for a major earthquake. We affirmed that if it was meant for us to be in San Diego when a major quake struck and we survived it, we would be of service in the aftermath and rebuilding.

This dream seemed to suggest that not only would we not be directly affected by the "Big One" (the building we were in had not fallen and no one had been hurt), but we were to go on with our work rather than be involved in the cleanup or rebuilding after the earthquake. It seemed important to "keep listening," however, as symbolized by the mammoth auditorium which was the central context in the dream.

These dreams came while we were in Pennsylvania conducting Theatre of Life sessions. Just a few days after the second dream we received three letters, forwarded from San Diego, which seemed directly related to the second dream. All three were from friends in California. One made reference to the accuracy of Gordon-Michael Scallion's predictions of the two large California earthquakes earlier that year.

A second friend had recently moved from California to New Mexico. She sent a clipping from Scallion's *The Earth Changes Report: The Survival Guide for the Nineties,* indicating that he predicted a major earthquake in the San Diego area before the end of September, 1992. She said she had left California because she was afraid to be there for the Big Quakes.

The third letter reported news of other friends who left California because of Scallion's predictions, and enclosed a copy of the most recent *Earth Changes* newsletter.

We had heard of Scallion and his predictions before, but we had not paid particular attention. As we read his newsletter with Diane's dreams in our consciousness, we began to ask ourselves if we should listen with new ears, as though seated in the large auditorium of Diane's dream, open to the possibility that there was information to which we should pay attention.

Scallion's prophecies of major earth changes were like those made eons ago by Nostradamus and more recently by Edgar Cayce and others. Jeffrey Goodman gathered many prophecies together to paint an impressive scenario in his book *We Are The Earthquake Generation* (1978) and Annie Kirkwood's *Mary's Message to the World* (2005) presented a similar scenario.

We asked ourselves, "What if we really are being warned in order to make our own choices about how to position ourselves in relation to these events?"

Our Shared Purpose

It is always important, when laying out plans for the future, to have purpose and objectives stated clearly and held in consciousness. Since we had begun to work together in 1972 we had based our work on a common purpose: *to take our place as servers of the highest will we were capable of registering*. We saw ourselves as models of the individualizing process rather than as authorities on the subject. We taught what we were learning and what we were practicing in our own lives. Our work had been to help individuals come to know themselves as the One Power in unique expression and to recognize that they were not alone in choosing such individual expression.

We felt that **The Love Principles**, the training we offered (especially through Life As A Waking Dream and the Theatre of Life), the mentoring we were able to do through our consciousness coaching, our various books, and the articles we offered through our magazine *Emerging* provided important nurturance and orientation for many people, and we believed the need for that kind of work was going to grow as radical changes continued to unfold. We hoped to continue with that work as long as it seemed indicated, but we opened ourselves to the possibility that some major changes *in the work itself* might be required in the months ahead. Neither of us felt any resistance to that. Rather, we asked inwardly what was wanted of us.

By 1991, 19 years into our work together, Mariamne published in our magazine what we had come to see as the difference between the spiritual work we had been offering to our Love Family, and psychological work. We offer it here as a way of confirming our roles as teachers of the ancient wisdom, facilitators of the individualizing process, and consciousness coaches rather than psychologists, counselors, or analysts. We were encouraging participants to acknowledge and live their divine nature. We were not focused on helping them to solve their problems or heal their issues on the personality level. We were focused on enabling people to validate who they were as beings and to fulfill and exceed their potential. We were not concerned with the reasons why people were the way they were, what in their past produced their current state. Our work was in the energy world where there were no limits and where people experience the certainty that they are at One with all others and that they are in the company of spiritual companions.

In Psychological Work:

- You are identified with the personality. You think of yourself as your feelings, your thoughts, your beliefs, your memories, and your body.
- You approach life subjectively, from your own point of view. You may recognize that others see your situation differently, but that seems irrelevant to your dilemma.
- You work problems through from the inside of them. You re-enter memories of experiences, recapture your experiences, relive them, and seek to find a way through to the new.
- Feelings are important in and of themselves. You seek to identify feelings and to give them expression by talking about them or acting them out.
- You believe your feelings are evoked by the

persons and circumstances with which you interact. You get caught in reactions.
- You need and want to be heard, and until you feel you are, you cannot move on.
- You believe your choices are limited by both the past and the present.
- When you ask for help, you rely on the other (the psychologist or counselor) to fulfill the observer role: that is, to be objective. This frees you to go deeper into your subjective experience.
- You are not able to let go of an experience until the energy of it finishes in you and through you.
- You view spiritual insights and solutions as coming from "outside" your life circumstances, from "beyond" you.

In Spiritual Work:

- You know yourself to be the observer, the witness, the power-to-be-conscious. You know that when you are conscious, you have creative jurisdiction over your life. You embrace the personality as your vehicle of expression, but do not feel limited to it.
- You approach life impersonally. You are not totally identified with your personality even when very involved in life circumstances. You view your personality as one among others.

- You view ***problems as opportunities*** to learn and grow. You seek to see them in the light of an expanded picture of your life and the world around you. You do not find it helpful to dwell on your feelings and thoughts, but rather you look for creative action you can take in relation to the opportunity before you.
- You use your feelings to guide you into action. You do not talk *about* them to others; rather, you express them and act upon them.
- You know that your feelings are internal messages, from you to you. You know you have choices about what to feel; you register energy in the solar plexus and choose the feeling-shape to give to that energy. You know your feelings are not caused by any external circumstance. You do not allow reactions or habit patterns to govern.
- You are eager to see things from a wider perspective than the one you first experienced. You welcome other points of view in order to put your own into proper perspective.
- You know you are free to make new choices in every new moment of awareness.
- When you ask for help, you do not abdicate your observer position. You retain creative jurisdiction over your life and take in the help as a supplement.

- You are able to withdraw your energy at will from relationships, situations, and interactions. You call this "letting go" or "surrendering to what is."
- You are aware that spiritual insights and help come from within. You open to recognize, receive and act upon them. You know that the pattern working within you brings your life into being, and you seek to align yourself with that Will.

Our Shared Objectives

It was very important to both of us *to practice good stewardship of the material possessions temporarily in our care.* As we began to contemplate the possibility that a major earthquake (or two or three) might actually destroy San Diego, we realized that we would lose all the equity in our house. Since we had provided space for the work of **The Love Project** and Teleos Institute for twenty years, our work might also be "homeless."

That awareness was a catalyst for a new thought. Perhaps, regardless of whether a big earthquake was to strike, it made practical sense for us to sell our house and reinvest in another location. We knew that we could buy a larger house elsewhere in which we would continue the work of Teleos Institute.

Second, we definitely wanted *to plan responsibly for the future.* We knew that the years immediately ahead were likely to continue to be difficult financially for everyone due to the recession. If we were to free up some of the assets from our house, we would have a substantial cushion to sustain us if our work was not able to fully support us financially for a time. We could also, hopefully, put some additional money away for our retirement. As we thought about it, it seemed prudent to take steps in that direction.

Moreover, by selling our house we could pay off our mortgage in San Diego and buy a house elsewhere with cash. That was in alignment with our third objective: *to live free of all debt.*

How to Move Forward

The process of decision-making is easier when inner guidance is clear and definite. In this instance that guidance was not forthcoming. So, we relied on our reasoning powers in relation to the data we had and we continued to listen inwardly for guidance.

We longed for the "booming voice" that each of us knew well from past experiences; it would simply tell us what to do (We, as Players, would tell ourselves what to do!). But, we would have been satisfied to have a sign of one kind or another on any level. We wondered whether this lack of guidance was an indication that we were more mature spiritually and therefore needed to take direct responsibility for our decisions, or whether it was an indication that we were less in touch with what was being asked of us. We could reason either direction with equal ease. Therein is the very nature of reason as differentiated from knowing.

We took time to allow our personalities to express all the reasons they did not want to leave San Diego. In the process, we realized that we had become very comfortable there. We (like most San Diegans) had come to believe there was nowhere else to live after San Diego, but we knew that to be myopic and limiting.

We also, like most San Diegans, recognized that we were spoiled with regard to climate. Anywhere we would move would constitute a "hardship" of some kind: too hot, too cold, or too wet. Yet we realized that to change climates would bring us closer to the "real world" in which most people live, in which there are seasons. We had long thought that we would have been bored by the San Diego weather if we hadn't traveled as much as we did, enjoying seasons in other locales.

Any move would require us to give up a lot, not the least of which would be the loyal, unfaltering support and help of our San Diego volunteers.

However, we were also aware that if we took big risks to choose the direction in which we wanted to move, we might avoid greater losses if or when radical change was forced upon us, even if not in the form of outer earth changes.

So, without direct inner guidance received in our yin (receptive) polarity, we decided to take steps in that direction. We knew that if by exercising the yang (initiating) polarity of energy we were expressing the larger Will, then things would fall into place effortlessly. If not, we would be content to stay where we were.

We put our house on the market in September 1992 and began to look for a place to relocate. Within days, Diane had a dream in which she was shown that we were being guided and directed in every respect on all levels regarding our move. A "being" came to the door of our house. He was "arranging" our buyer, showing the way to the home we would buy, and overseeing attendant changes in the larger circumstances surrounding us. When Diane awoke, she had a deep and quiet confidence that we were being taken care of, guided.

This was similar to our experience of finding the house in San Diego, when Diane had received a strong intuition that there was a house waiting for us. On the first day of looking, we found the house. It had been on the market for two years, "waiting for us," we were sure. This kind of cooperation between outer action and inner guidance is key to living a spirit-filled life. We felt extremely blessed and grateful.

A Third Big Dream: A Vision of the Apocalypse

Arleen wanted direct confirmation of our need to pay heed to these prophecies. She requested a dream, and the next morning she awakened with the following dream:

I went to visit my spiritual mother Ev (which I interpret as "returning to the spiritual home in which my wisdom resides"). While I was there, I was walking toward the house one evening. The sky was dark (moonless) and the stars were bright in it. As I looked up, I saw five horses drawing a chariot across the sky. Three magnificent, powerful, white horses with beautiful, flowing manes and fine bridles were in front, and two stronger white horses—like work horses—also magnificent, were harnessed behind them, followed by the chariot.

I ran into the house calling out to Diane with childlike excitement. "I saw the apocalypse! I saw the apocalypse!"

Arleen did not know anything about apocalyptic literature in the Bible, and Diane was a bit rusty on the subject, so we went to the library to research such visions. We were surprised to discover that visions of horses pulling chariots across the sky were common. Five Old Testament prophets had had such visions in addition to John, whose visions fill the book of Revelations in the New Testament. Most of those biblical visions had four horses, not five, and often horses of differing colors. But white horses seemed to be viewed as a good omen.

Our three dreams were not charged with fear or alarm, but they got our attention. We felt they indicated that major changes were coming in our lives (Diane's dreams) and that these changes would mark the end of an era for us (Arleen's dream). We took it that these changes would be in our consciousness, but we opened ourselves to pay attention to the major earth changes already underway. We reasoned that we would rather be co-creators of any outer changes coming in our lives than to wait for them to overtake us from the outside. We still value this highly as a way of functioning.

The expansion of our house in 1987-1988 had triggered in us the sense that we needed to expand the "structure" of our work as well. We had invited an organization consultant to work with us in examining the organizational principles that had been our guidelines since 1972 and in developing a new statement of our vision, our goals, and the obstacles that seemed to stand in our way.

We had gathered a core group of our San Diego people to join us in brainstorming how to move forward into the new. They, and we, had spent many hours and put much energy into clarifying our vision, developing plans, raising additional funds, and choosing a new name for the work.

Now we reflected on the fact that none of the efforts we and our core group had made to develop new branches of our work in San Diego had borne any fruit. We wondered if it was time for us to uproot ourselves and find new soil in which to grow. We began to consider leaving California as a symbolic statement of our willingness to cooperate with the forces of change at work in our consciousness.

At the thought of leaving San Diego, both of our personalities immediately began to balk. We did not want, on the personality level, to leave San Diego. With a map of the United States spread out in front of us, we asked, "If we could live anywhere, where would we want to go?" Both of us answered immediately: San Diego!

Seeing that it would be fruitless to allow our personalities and their preferences to rule, we turned our attention instead to our purposes and objectives.

Finding Our Way

Within the first month that our house was on the market we received a very good offer for it. The being in Diane's dream had said he was arranging a buyer, and it seemed this was the one. However, the offer came with a contingency: the buyers needed to sell their own house before they could buy ours. We accepted the offer because they were willing to pay close to what we had asked for the house and because the deal felt right to Diane from the start.

The market was slow and low in those months and we felt blessed to have buyers who wanted very much to own our house and who were willing to pay a good price for it. They were native San

Diegans who had been watching for a house in our neighborhood with an ocean view.

Their house went on the market, but they had no nibbles for over two months. We were aware that November and December were the slowest real estate months and we suspended interpretation of the situation, which *felt* like a stalemate. Our house was still on the market but no one else even came to look at it. The buyers' house was up for far less money than ours, but they had no offers. Today we would simply accept that things were working out according to what was being "arranged" by what we would now call our angelic helpers.

In the meanwhile, we invested time and money exploring where we would like to relocate. We looked in Santa Fe, New Mexico. Neither of us felt that was our place. On our way back to California, we stopped overnight in Flagstaff, Arizona. That very day hurricane Andrew struck in South Florida. Gordon Scallion had predicted that hurricane when no one else had. We were stunned and decided that we were on the right track in our decision-making.

We felt strongly drawn to Flagstaff, Arizona, and looked at property there twice. On the second trip, we decided to check out the Flagstaff airport, given that we traveled so frequently. The airport was tucked into a forested area and the terminal was so small it looked like a shed. We could not imagine flying in and out of that tiny airport nearly every weekend, so we crossed Flagstaff off our list.

We traveled in New Hampshire and Vermont, looking at houses. We were there at the height of the autumn leaves and it could not have been more beautiful. We met lovely people and saw some workable houses. However, the longer we stayed, the more depressed Diane felt. Though she tried to reason her way out of giving importance to the feelings, when we drove back down into Massachusetts, her depression lifted. She found herself shouting, "Thank God I don't have to live in New England!" There was nothing rational that we could identify in the response, but it was obvious that New England would not work for us.

We flew to Boulder, Colorado where several of our California friends had settled. We *loved* Boulder in every way and we found a fabulous house for a very reasonable price. We both felt we could live happily there. Nevertheless when each of us asked inwardly, "Should we move here?" neither of us could get a "yes." Without an inner agreement, we bid farewell to beautiful Boulder.

In December, we went back to Arizona. We visited Prescott. It is very beautiful and we found a great house there, but this time Arleen was the one who sank into depression. She felt her life would be over if we moved to Prescott. That settled that.

Diane kept feeling that we should check out Scottsdale. She had been there once, 25 years before, and remembered it as a small town on the edge of the desert. Still, the feeling we should check it out persisted, so we drove to Scottsdale and found a motel. Even before exploring, we both felt completely at home in the energy of Scottsdale. The more we looked, the better we liked it. We spent six days, saw several houses that suited us, and felt a strong inner agreement that Scottsdale was a place we could live.

We returned to San Diego. We didn't feel we could make an offer on a house in another location since we didn't have enough capital to make a down payment and we were not willing to go into debt by taking out a mortgage.

Removing Contingencies

We were in an active process of taking action and listening inwardly for guidance.

We had gathered as much data as possible on the objective level: information about potential cities and states, about property values, about climates, about transportation, about demographics, etc.

We uprooted ourselves psychologically from San Diego and we "released" our present forms of doing our work. Daily we asked for new direction.

We paid close attention to our dreams, our emotional responses, our physical reactions, our intuitions, and even our hunches.

We used our minds to reason things through, taking both objective and subjective data into consideration.

We took actions whenever possible in order to discover whether those actions were supported by the larger energy environment.

We trusted that we would know what and when we needed to know.

We went on with our life and work, leaving all doors to the future open.

As we started the year 1993 we looked at the sale of our house as a waking dream. Seeing the circumstances as an out-picturing of our own state of consciousness, we asked ourselves, "What contingencies have we placed on the sale of our house?" Awareness flooded in. We saw that neither of us had been willing to take full responsibility for deciding that we would move. We had been waiting, in our yin mode, for a sign from the universe that this is what was wanted. We laughed at ourselves.

Diane remembered a story she had read that told about a teacher who was asked why some people seemed to have angels guiding their every step and others, like the questioner, did not. The teacher responded that guidance was given to those who were not strong enough to make decisions on their own. "Just as parents offer their finger as a support to the child who is taking first steps, and then withdraw it as the child gains confidence in walking, so those who step on the spiritual path are given guidance until they become strong enough to make their own way."

We decided to take full responsibility for the choice to leave San Diego and move to Scottsdale. Right or wrong, changes in our work or not, earthquakes or not, we would take this new step in our own process and learn through the consequences that would follow. It felt like moving on into the rest of our lives instead of settling down into what had been for twenty years.

We removed all contingencies in our consciousness and released our house to its sale. Just 25 days after we removed *our* contingencies, our house went into escrow.

From the Ocean to the Desert

We also consciously released our connection with San Diego. It was something like pulling up psychic roots from the soil of experience in which we had been growing for 21 years. We offered gratitude as we uprooted ourselves in energy for all the psychic elements that had nourished us: love, friendship, humor, conflict, pain, hard work, much play, beauty, harmony and discord. We had been abundantly blessed with both problems and opportunities!

Once we had decided to move, we invited a small group of our San Diego Love Family to come for a "leave-taking" evening. We sat around in a circle sharing memories and expressing deeply felt sentiments to each other. It was a time of closure.

Later, closer to our actual departure date, Suzanna Neal organized a farewell potluck supper for us and Carl Downing welcomed us into his home for that event. That was a celebration that included some "speeches" and token gifts. We felt loved, appreciated and embraced by warm friendships.

We had lived happily for 21 years just four blocks up the hill from the ocean in a humble home that served us beautifully. During that time, we did a lot of work on our emotional patterns that in the waking dream sense could be seen as symbolized by the ocean. We sought to free ourselves from identification with patterns in the solar plexus that caused us to take personally life events and happenings. In both our Theatre of Life and Life as a Waking Dream work we encouraged participants to learn what we were learning: to empower themselves with the energy of the solar plexus rather than to feel disempowered because of their "feelings."

We were conscious of choosing a very new environment for our life and work by moving to a city that lies in a desert valley. The desert is a place where growth does not come easily but where plants, given only a little water, grow profusely and flower because of plentiful sun and heat. We saw the sun as a symbol for the Spirit that gives us life and consciousness. In a place of greater heat and brighter light, where the sun shines 360 days out of the year, we trusted that we would thrive. We hoped this meant that our spiritual growth would come through greater challenges in higher energy chakras, and that because we had tamed and contained our solar plexus energies we could enjoy feelings as a respite from a more relentless pressure for spiritual growth.

All of this was to acknowledge that our life is a waking dream; we honored the symbolism that we had chosen as a way to encourage our further unfoldment. It was not surprising, then, that neither of us had any regrets about leaving the house, the city, or the state when the time came. People in Arizona commented, "You left San Diego to move here? Why?" This was because so many people in Arizona go to San Diego to escape the heat in the summer months. But we had made a choice to go forward and to look ahead into the unknown.

The Move

Escrow had closed on our home in San Diego on February 26, 1993, Arleen's 54th birthday. Our choice to move from California had been made in September, 1992. We had put our house on the market then and we finally released our contingencies on the sale of the house in January of 1993. The sale then went through to the only couple that had offered a bid. We were convinced that they were the "buyers" that the angelic "being" in Diane's dream had indicated he was sending to us.

The move itself was a real trial. With the help of nine stalwart volunteers we packed endless boxes and changed the address in hundreds of copies of our books. Nevertheless, we were not ready when the movers arrived. The two office areas remained unfinished and we worked hard to stay one box ahead of the movers. It was a non-stop effort and thoroughly exhausting. It was 6:00 PM before everything was loaded and the truck had gone. After going out to dinner, three of us returned to the house to do the final cleanup so that it would be ready for the new owners who were planning to move in the very next day.

It was 1:00 AM before the two of us got to sleep at our neighbors' house and we awoke at our normal time (6:00 AM). With little sleep and cumulative exhaustion, we started out in our two cars to make the journey to our new home. It was not surprising that as we drove from the California border to Gila Bend in Arizona, a long stretch of straight highway with unremarkable desert terrain on both sides, Diane, who often got sleepy when driving long distances, fell asleep at the wheel of the Subaru going 70 miles an hour.

Here is Arleen's account of the horrendous incident that played out like a big screen thriller:

For no apparent reason (since there was no car

Inner Guidance and Choices

to pass), Diane quickly pulled out into the left lane at a sharp angle. Her car kept going, at top speed, into the meridian and was heading directly toward the westbound lanes where traffic was zooming by in both lanes. I couldn't imagine what was happening. I had very few seconds to make a decision about what to do. I pressed hard on the horn, hoping to wake Diane up while simultaneously pulling my car onto the narrow shoulder to the right and making a quick stop.

A voice inside me started screaming that Diane was going off the road and into traffic, that it was all over, that she was going to be killed. Another part of me knew that I had to stay centered and present in order to respond to whatever was about to occur.

This was the value of doing consciousness work. I made the choice to quiet the petrified self, telling it I was there for it, but that conjecturing was not helpful at this time. As I watched her car go, I held steady, breathed, and waited. I chose to concentrate on being present in wholeness, in consciousness, and for Diane. I hoped I could help hold an energy configuration in which she would remain whole and unharmed. My inner voice continued to send a silent but loud and persistent message to Diane, "Come back!!!!"

Before her Subaru reached the westbound side of the meridian, it turned around sharply and with great speed so that it was now heading back across the meridian toward the eastbound traffic where I was sitting on the shoulder. She *was* coming back, but so fast I didn't think she would be able to stop. I quickly looked to my left and saw in the distance a huge semi-trailer heading at great speed toward the spot where Diane would re-enter the road. Had they met, it would have been catastrophic for all of us. I remember focusing on a silent shout inside myself: STOP! I sent it out again and again with great force.

As if by some miracle, about a foot and a half before the Subaru would have entered the eastbound lane, the car stopped abruptly and was enveloped in a cloud of dust that rose about ten feet in the air. It was hard to tell if it had hit something or if it had been swallowed up by the earth, because for a long moment, it was invisible.

The semi-trailer passed. I waited. I breathed. My purpose was to be there for Diane for whatever was needed. I felt nothing. I had quieted my solar plexus. I was directing my energy through the crown, heart, and third-eye chakras. There was no fear, no residue of energy, no conjecturing. This no doubt accounts for the fact that there was nothing to deal with on the feeling level later. This was most amazing to me.

When the dust cleared, Diane opened her window, looked around to get her bearings, and saw me sitting across the road watching her. What she saw was a calm and steady face asking her if she was all right.

Diane was so all right that she informed me she would just pull back onto the road. I said, "Oh no you won't. Your tires are flat (in fact, all four wheels had been broken by the rocks in the soft soil.)" That is what had stopped the car, which was still running.

Diane had missed the whole event. She had gone dead asleep with no apparent warning and awoke as the car was spinning sharply around to head back to the eastbound lanes. She awoke hearing her father's voice reminding her to turn into the spin, which she did.

We were very blessed that the meridian was wide at the point where the Subaru went off the road, and that the ground was loose rather than packed hard and dry. Because of the unusual winter rains, sizable rocks lay about, and the re-entrance to the eastbound lanes sloped upward. Had Diane gone off the road a few yards later, she would have smashed into a guardrail.

Diane was unhurt. She didn't even have excess adrenalin flowing. She hadn't been there for the event. We used our mobile phone to call the Highway Patrol; a trooper quickly came to our aid, but not before field workers came running to see if they could assist. They had seen the tall cloud of dust.

The car had to be towed, but our focus was on gratitude that all was well. Friends later told us that they thought that it had taken a whole committee of angels to keep Diane from being killed!

Needless to say, it was dark by the time we arrived in Scottsdale. The Subaru was delivered the next day on a flatbed truck so we could determine what to do with it.

As I wrote about this incident I realized something I had never seen before. I may have joined the committee of angels by sending out a direct stream of energy to Diane as her car headed toward disaster. I seem to have connected with her, energy frequency to energy frequency, and helped her in her sleep state to turn the car around and head it back to the eastbound lanes. Her father's voice woke her to head into the spin and I see now that I helped to stop the car in the rocks by repeatedly sending forth the powerful, silent command, STOP!

For over two decades Diane and I had been learning about and teaching others about having jurisdiction in the energy world, making things happen by tapping into the Will and therefore **creating a reality consciously**. I strongly believe that this is what I had done by connecting with Diane in the energy world, bringing her back from a dead sleep as she spun the car around and woke up; then, stopping her in her tracks before a catastrophe occurred.

This is not to say that I had "special powers" but rather that we all, when functioning in a superconscious state, can direct the force of energy and bring a reality into being. We participate in what we call a miracle by being a vehicle for forces greater than ourselves.

I am reminded of a scene from the film "The Dresser" that we played for our Act Three Players as a teaching tool for how to powerfully direct energy. The character Sir is descending the stairs to a platform with his acting company and watches as the train begins to leave the station without them. He lifts his arm and cane straight out and shouts STOP with such force that the energy resounds throughout the terminal. The train immediately pulls to a halt.

I see now that I had done the same thing in relation to the Subaru!

While I am aware of what I did and what was accomplished, I still can't claim it as a "consciousness over matter" achievement because, although I did what I did, I did not do it *with the intention* of changing what was occurring. I did not say to myself, "Use the power of consciousness to turn the car around;" nor did I speak similarly to stop the car. That is what a Master would have done.

I am pleased that I was at least able to participate in a good portion of the process: choosing calm and centeredness, bypassing fear or conjecture, focusing an unbroken line of concentration on Diane and her situation, connecting energy to energy, calling her back, and calling upon the unseen universal forces to intervene and stop the vehicle.

The next few days were not very restful as we had to supervise the move into our rental casita and into two large storage units. In addition, we had to complete all the details on our new house so that contracts could be signed before we left for a ten-day work trip in Ontario and Ohio. Even though we slept seven or eight hours a night, it was two or three weeks before we were completely rested and recovered.

This was a continuation of the pace at which we had been moving for many years. Just in the past year we had conducted three two-week Theatre of Life sessions, one in San Diego and the other two in Pennsylvania; a one-week Theatre of Life graduate session and an eight-day training session for Life as a Waking Dream teachers, both in San Diego; two weekend Practice Sessions, one in Buffalo, New York and one in Miami, Florida; and three Life As A Waking Dream classes in San Diego and by cassette tape.

As if those sessions were not enough, requiring a lot of travel to and from, we were also going through the process around moving: visiting different cities, putting our house up for sale, packing up for the move and then actually making the move. No wonder we wrote in our Winter & Spring 1993 *Emerging,* "We rather limped into December, having exhausted ourselves with many rewarding sessions in the summer and fall and with all the process around moving. In addition, both of us have been busily writing whenever we could find a moment."

Only five days after moving to Scottsdale we flew to Buffalo, New York, rented a car, and drove to Hamilton, Ontario to begin a week of sessions. We facilitated a daylong practice session in Hamilton; gave a sermon at the Unity Center of Light in Markham, Ontario; gave an introduction to the Theatre of Life after the morning service; met with a Life as a Waking Dream group being led by two of the teachers Diane had trained; drove down to Ohio to conduct two experiential seminars in Chagrin Falls; then drove back to Buffalo to return our rented car; were driven by Natalie Chilton back to Hamilton where we offered a Mastery Session for Theatre of Life players; and then Natalie drove us back to Buffalo so we could take our flight back to Scottsdale the next day. Whew!

We needed to find a new rhythm for our lives, but it would take some time living in the desert before we would accomplish that.

Our New Home

Diane's intuition had guided us to Scottsdale where we had found a model for a home in a small neighborhood that we felt would serve us well. The same angelic "being" had assured us he was guiding us to the home we would buy, and this was surely it. It had a very large living/dining room area that we would use for workshops and classes and a loft that would provide us with ample office space.

We had found the home after looking at only two other places. The price was very right since Arizona real estate had hit bottom a year before and was only beginning to rebound. We chose the lot on which we wanted to build but explained in December that we could not put money down until we sold our San Diego home. In January when we contacted the realtor and said we were ready to buy, the lot we thought we wanted had been sold. We "settled" for one a few houses to the West and it turned out to be the best location in the whole community! Again, our angelic being had served us well.

The broken wheels on the Subaru stopped us on the road of transition, calling our attention to a break with the old. We had been spinning our wheels, going at breakneck speed and pushing ourselves unnecessarily to the point of weariness. Just because we *could* do everything didn't mean we needed to or even that we should have. Working nonstop, packing up a house after 21 years of living and working in it, and retaining our travel schedule simultaneously was probably not very smart.

We were glad that we had made the decision to move. We not only changed location, but our work and our approach to our work changed. We had made a choice following inner guidance and taken outer action, and we were once again rewarded by unfolding events. We are aware that new discoveries are made as a result of actions taken, and things never imagined become realities when you opt for change.

Doors Open, Doors Close

Almost immediately after moving into our new home in Scottsdale, AZ on October 1st 1993, we did what we had done for the first 21 years of our life and work together; we hit the road. We had not yet developed a new tempo/rhythm. It was good that we enjoyed traveling and bringing the teaching we had to offer to participants where they lived.

This particular adventure developed into a very different experience and we had a lot to learn from it. We have chosen to write about it here without mentioning specific names and places so as not to open any old wounds for others who were involved. We believe nothing will be lost by doing this because what transpired and how we met the circumstances is far more important than the *who* and the *where*.

A participant in our work, we will call him Dave, invited us to his community in what we shall call Central, USA. We met with a mixed group of individuals who struggled to get along in their town: native-born white Americans and immigrant Latinos. We had the privilege of conducting an evening called "The Joy of Roots and Differences." By the end of the session, which included the full participation of those present in experiences that brought them together in new and unexpected ways, the tone in the room completely changed. There was, in fact, joy. We all watched as hostilities melted and communication opened. It was a profoundly moving Practice Session in going beyond what separated those gathered. The two of us had guided an experience focused on opening heart centers and we all witnessed the power of unconditional love.

The next day Dave introduced us to the team with whom he worked in a community action organization (we will refer to it as Metro) that served those in Central who were in need of a boost on many levels. We introduced the team and their director, we'll call him Todd, to **The Love Principles** and how they would benefit the team in their leadership roles. So far so good.

Over the next three years we were hired to design and conduct a leadership program for leaders both in Metro and throughout the country. This represented a shift from what we had previously done in our work together. We were now working *for* someone else. We were being paid salaries commensurate with professional consultants. We were designing a program in participation with others rather than doing all the creating ourselves. This all felt good on many levels. It was a new thrust for us. We had moved from San Diego and we had also now moved into a new arena of work. Change is good, as is opening to the new.

During the years of our participation with Metro we were praised repeatedly for our fine work, our many contributions, and our significant help in creating and executing a transformational leadership program. We found the work stimulating and growthful. We were stretched in our creativity.

Leaders of similar organizations came for training from all over the country. Those who participated in the sessions reported in their evaluations that they felt affirmed and empowered to lead. They felt more focused. One said he experienced his self-worth for the first time. Others came away more integrated and filled with courage to be more honest with others.

Paying attention to breathing enabled leaders to become conscious of when and how they were blocking energy, and therefore how to infuse their actions with strength. Here are some of the comments submitted by participants:

> **The Love Principles** have provided me with a framework from which to build all of my interactions with self and others. I had held a belief that I must know someone for an extended period of time before I could engage in a "learning relationship," but through these principles I have gained enough awareness to be capable of connecting with any being.
>
> The congruity of what the facilitators do and what they say is exact! The power they project is through their commitment. Very clear input in each new concept. Helpful visual of each principle. Great outline, concise. The candor is refreshing and sets a good model.
>
> The planning for this six days was most obvious. The

rapport and timing between the two leaders is always amazing. So is the commitment to authenticity. There was never anything phony. This is the only training I've ever been in that placed this much emphasis on being, rather than just learning. It was wonderful.

Problems Are Opportunities

We also offered Practice Sessions for those who worked at Metro. We enjoyed the teams with whom we worked; they were all high-quality people who did their jobs very well. This was no surprise because the director was bright, articulate, and innovative. He hired the best people available to serve the large purposes of the organization that *seemed* to thrive.

As with any organization there were problems. In this case, people from different departments, whom we were charged to mentor, sought us out to report dysfunctional behavior in themselves and in the director. This behavior led to fear and distrust in some, and codependency in others. They felt they had been ill-treated by Todd. We addressed their concerns and encouraged them to speak up and find ways to **be the change they wanted to see happen** in their work life. At the same time, we both felt that since the complaints had been brought to us, it was our responsibility to bring them to Todd (without mentioning their names.)

Bringing them to Todd was in keeping with

how the two of us had lived and worked together for over two decades. As in organizations, so in relationships, there are issues that arise. They are **problems that are opportunities**. Over the years the two of us had dealt with several, some more serious and complicated than others, but we saw each instance as a chance for mutual personal growth and for eventual greater harmony between us that we could then bring to our work to enhance our contributions.

We went to Todd and he responded indignantly, saying he would not tolerate secondhand reports. While we could receive what Todd was saying, we had heard from the "injured" parties that the director would hear them only one-on-one in private, putting them in a one-down position, subject to further abuse, and fearing for their jobs. In the past, what they aired was turned around to be their problem, not his.

We had a sense for what troubled some of the employees. When we first entered into the partnership with Todd, he demanded that we be his personal friends. He said he could not trust anyone who was not willing to be his personal friend. We told him friendship was something that grew organically, not something created on demand. We watched as he demanded personal time from others at the organization as well. We saw this as a form of harassment.

What to do? This was not the only issue we

found alive in the corporate structure. There was a mercurial nature to programming; things were set in motion and abandoned to accommodate a new wave of thinking. It was all top-down and little time was given for employees to make adjustments.

In our own work together, we always strove for a balance of yin and yang energy, a balance between innovation and manifestation. When we initiated new techniques or programs we had been careful to develop each fully and to allow it to come to fruition. At Metro, yang energy dominated the process of program development. Was this a learning curve for us, or was it disharmonious with our chosen way of functioning? We hung in as members of the development team but had to breathe deeply while caught in a seeming whirlwind.

Increasing Discomfort

The two of us talked with each other often about our growing feelings of discomfort over the two main issues we have described. We chose to stay on, mainly because of the fine contributions to the community that were being made by Metro and because we were personally able to participate on a high level of creativity. We saw ourselves as stretching to work within an organization and that stretch was valuable. But we also spoke truth along the way. When appropriate we told Todd that some of his actions and the ways in which he withheld his feelings made it difficult for us to trust him. He received the feedback. His response was to tell us all the ways in which he didn't trust us.

You would think we would have read the handwriting on the wall, so to speak. Yet, we continued to participate for the potential growth experience and for the contributions we could make.

Increasingly, we noted that Todd talked about transformational leadership and partnership but didn't necessarily live it himself. His behavior was often more suited to a patriarch, overriding team members when he did not agree with them. Toward the end of our time there he began to talk of building an empire and appeared to assume the role of emperor. By now, red flags were unfurled for us and we felt more and more uncomfortable.

Time passed during which we, and the troubled employees from the different departments, continued in our jobs. Looking back, we could see that this was a classic example of how individuals can invent all kinds of reasons for staying in a disharmonious environment, from workplaces to marriages. We thought we could effect change, make things better, stick it out, and bring a new and healthy reality into being. It was wishful thinking. Our mutual best intentions were blinding us and magnetically holding us in place.

The two of us were conscious people. We saw what was happening. We did our best to make a positive imprint. We did not move on. There was a lesson to be learned here. It had to do with taking a stand. We edged closer to that position, but perhaps too slowly.

In August, 1996 Todd came to Scottsdale to enlist us as his partners and primary facilitators. He said we were the best he knew and he didn't feel anyone else could do as fine a job. We gave our commitment but not without pressing him on our desire to be consulted before he made changes in what we were developing. Todd didn't address that concern but seemed to redefine the program as his, to be done his way.

Boldly Speaking Truth

By now we saw ourselves as consultant facilitators rather than the partners he asked us to be. At this point, we began to turn our attention to the more we wanted to develop through Teleos Institute, even as we made ourselves available to Todd. We began to withdraw our energy from the endeavor. It was long overdue.

In September, the two of us took a 25th anniversary trip to Scandinavia. Before we left Todd told us the team would be facilitating the next leg of the program and that we would serve as observers offering our feedback. Later, he also demanded that we participate as well as observe. Arleen held her energy back during the session, not wanting to overpower the proceedings. That night Todd accused her of being unsupportive. In fact, Todd himself had sat on the sidelines observing, not participating, and breaking the rules he had laid down for everyone else.

It was astonishing to experience the buildup of ill feelings in the group, the strutting of smugness by the director, the belittling behavior about which others had complained. Now the two of us had experienced Todd's ill treatment directly. Because it was not secondhand, we could address it ourselves. We raised our issues in front of the whole team at the Saturday morning feedback session. We said the director's way of functioning could seriously interfere with marketing the program. We spoke plainly and without fear. It was our obligation to speak the truth. It was long overdue.

We take responsibility for that. It was one of our most important learnings. Say what you see when you see it. Don't allow compounding to occur. Be bold in speaking truth, no matter the consequences. Don't try to smooth things over without first examining the flaws that need to be exposed.

One thing led to another that fateful Saturday morning and no one could be surprised that Todd took offense, saying that we were personally attacking him and engaging in a power struggle with him. Though it was our job to give feedback, he wanted none of it. It was our position that the feedback belonged to be spoken in the whole group but he wanted it only in private. It was our conviction that the director and everyone else needed to embody what the program was designed to teach, else why bother to teach it?

Because the two of us had put ourselves on the line, the others present were impressed with the risk we took, and they spoke in defense of our right to say what we saw. We were especially glad that they were able to take a stand. We were glad for *them*.

Within a few weeks our contract with Metro was cancelled. No surprise. Todd said it was no fun to work with us, that we didn't hear his feedback to us because we didn't agree with it. He surely was not speaking of us but of his own way of functioning. Life is a waking dream; we see in another what is in ourselves.

Todd had violated our contract by writing a letter of unilateral dismissal when a discussion between the two parties was specifically called for. His severing of the partnership was a "done deal."

Embodying What We Teach

The door had been closed by Todd but we had already walked out through it because we also no longer wanted to work with him.

A door had opened and closed. One issue remained. Those in our Love Family would need to be told what had happened and why we were no longer working at Metro. We made the choice to share the whole story in *Emerging*. This amounted to becoming whistle-blowers, which often brings blowback from those whose behavior is exposed. We knew this might not be pleasant but we felt an obligation to our supporters to fill them in on all the details.

We did in fact get blowback, both from Metro and from Love Family members. Some people thought it unnecessary that we shared the whole thing so openly. Others were offended and stopped participating in our programs. Still others congratulated us on being so bold. Others were angry and hurt that we exposed publicly what they considered private matters. Others were amazed we would jeopardize such a lucrative contract by criticizing the director.

In spite of the differing responses, we were glad to have shared what was clearly a large learning opportunity for us. It had been our style to be what we called "public/private persons," and we felt we emerged with our integrity intact.

We had told the story to our supporters in May and then in August we ran a supplement to *Emerging* in order to print, for all to see, letters from those who disapproved of our whistle-blowing and the way in which we did it. Most of them worked at the organization or were closely related to the director. We wanted to give exposure to their objections and we ran them alongside letters from those (mostly outside the organization) who thought we did the right thing. It was important to us to be as fair as possible and we had no ego investment in how we would be seen in their criticism. Looking back on this choice to reveal negative feedback to our approach, we felt good about our having maintained fairness and integrity.

We survived the ordeal at Metro and returned to our harmonious way of working, as free agents who follow our hearts and bring forth what is ours to contribute. The three years at Metro had been productive and creatively stretching. Ironically, we had gone there as agents of change; when we saw that the difficulties basically remained the same, we should have acted. Opportunity passes us all by while we cling to a hope that change will come. It never just comes; it needs to be brought and embodied by those involved.

We were then and are now a transformational partnership. We respect and support each other. We help each other to stretch and to grow. We do only what is harmonious for *both* of us. We could not teach others to be transformational leaders if we did not continue to embody those values ourselves.

The experience at Metro strengthened our resolve to embody what we teach: integrated, expressed wisdom.

The termination of our contract immediately reduced our salaries to levels below where we could meet our financial obligations. This represented yet another opportunity, especially for Arleen who had grown up in an environment where money was always a concern. She reminded herself that worry was the least useful means to achieve financial security. She had learned that worry took her out of the now moment, wherein resides creativity, hope, and inner resources. Worry focuses on "what ifs" that are irrelevant because we can deal only with actualities.

She remembered that the best way to live with financial insecurity is to affirm that there is no such thing as security! There are times of having and times of not. In all instances, abundance is sufficiency and sufficiency sometimes requires constant changes in lifestyle.

During our years of work together we lived in the moment financially because we did not have steady sources of income. What we did have was total freedom to allow our lives to unfold creatively. We could always let our inner selves guide us to the next opportunity. Our task was to focus on what there was for us to be and to do. We expressed gratitude for what we did have and continued to make donations to causes we supported.

We tightened our belts but did not cut ourselves off from the universal flow. We knew we were always embraced by something larger than ourselves.

Adapting and Thriving

We had selected our home in Scottsdale specifically in order to do our work in it. We had been able to build a large home for less than the sale price of our small home in San Diego. We invested the remainder, hoping to grow a nest egg for our retirement. Now we had a very large space for workshops in what was designed by the architect as a living room and dining room. We bought furniture that could be moved easily into the dining room and other areas of the house so that the living room would be totally open for movement and group experiences.

In addition, the kitchen was very large with an island in the center that made it easy for people to move around and share the counter while preparing their lunches. They could then spill out onto the spacious patio to eat together, and some people chose to have a brief swim during their lunch break.

We were delighted with how well the space served us and the people who came for workshops. We held 14-day Theatre of Life sessions for several years, and when we ended the Theatre of Life program we offered for seven summers a follow-up program called Kaleidoscope. Kaleidoscope was a five-day workshop that made it possible for people who could not take advantage of the more extensive and intensive Theatre of Life program to have a taste of that fine approach.

We also held other workshops, classes and trainings. Diane trained Life as a Waking Dream teachers and they then formed a group which they called the Hannahs. The Hannahs met at least once a year for mutual nourishment and further deepening of their understanding of life as a waking dream.

We trained and ordained two groups of Ministers of the Order of Teleos, the nondenominational spiritual order of our work that made it possible for people to have meaningful ministerial certificates.

One of the things that made these workshops possible was that shortly after building our new house a hotel was built about a block down the street. Our participants have stayed there at discounted prices all these years. What a blessing that was/is for us and for them. They could walk to sessions rather than needing to rent cars.

Other Workshops and Talks

Before too long we began to receive invitations to offer talks and workshops in Arizona. The Youth and Family Services of Scottsdale sponsored three talks provided at no cost to participants over the course of a year. We made presentations on *Creating Your Own Life Consciously*, Life as a Waking Dream, and the Transforming Power of Love. All were warmly received. The groups varied in size from 20 to 60, and we enjoyed engaging with them.

The Unitarian Fellowship in Flagstaff invited us several times to give talks and workshops thanks to Elsie Astorga who knew us from California. We delighted in the responsive group.

We also continued to travel around the country giving workshops and talks in Miami Lakes, Florida; Spring Green, Wisconsin; Chagrin Falls, Ohio; Markham, Burlington and Hamilton, Ontario; Buffalo, New York; Edmonton, Alberta; Marshalltown, Iowa; and San Diego, California.

Classes

Because for so many years we had traveled all over the country and in Canada doing sessions, we had a large mailing list that included people who lived far and wide. Once settled into our new home, we decided we needed to adapt the way we offered classes. We offered School of Consciousness classes and Life as a Waking Dream classes almost entirely by telephone via conference calls for the more than twenty years we lived in our new home. We scheduled numerous classes each year, sometimes as many as three classes running concurrently, resulting in much growth for all participants, including the two of us.

One small example: One of the women in a class on Lucid Living sought to remain awake/conscious in a difficult team meeting that was coming up for her as a school psychologist. After studying how her waking dream had been playing out until then (close to a waking nightmare for her), she chose a strong sense of self and identified her purpose and objectives for the meeting. As a result, the whole situation turned around and she was given all that she had requested for two years to be able to do her job more effectively. The study of her waking dream had helped her find the way to transform an ongoing process by choosing a different sense of self and a clear purpose.

In the beginning, we tape-recorded all the classes and mailed copies of the tapes out to everyone. It was a blessing when it became possible to record digitally and attach the recordings to e-mails. Much more efficient!

The recordings made it possible for people to listen more than once to a class and to hear the feedback on their own work more than once. It also meant that class groups came to feel like a community even though they met only by voice. Often, we circulated photos of participants so people could "look at" the person who was speaking by telephone.

Although we far preferred working with people in person, the telephone conferencing was an acceptable substitute so that we could stay in contact with people across the continent. We never adopted videoconferencing; it was more difficult to manage with our participants who were at various stages of using electronic media.

Consciousness Coaching

We continued to do Consciousness Coaching, sometimes together and sometimes individually. We worked with people either in our home or by telephone. Here is a response from one woman with whom we worked by telephone:

> The session yesterday was absolutely amazing! I am seeing the world differently already. It is interesting to me that experiencing and reading about the process is so different in terms of how receptive my "soul" is capable of being.
>
> You have a transmission-like presence that is akin to the best Buddhist teachers I've taken instruction from, or the sweat lodge medicine men I've sweated with. A real and present presence can transmit a kind of energy that doesn't exist in other communications.
>
> I found I was picking up a whole series of images and scenes while we talked, not unlike a dream, and I later reflected that you'd walked into my dream and were taking part in creating it. Very cool. [From an e-mail.]

We frequently get feedback that people have insights during Consciousness Coaching that are directly and immediately applicable to their lives, and therefore make a vital difference. For example, one woman needed to make a major decision about whether to quit a good job and move to a different city where the man she loved lived. She did not have a job there and didn't know if this was a wise move to make.

We worked with her in a series of coaching sessions, guiding her through the process of evaluating her purpose, objectives, feelings, intuitions, and thoughts. In the end, she decided to quit her job and move, and she found a new job almost immediately that was a perfect fit for her. Before long, we had the privilege of marrying the two of them.

Emerging Magazine

We continued to publish *Emerging* after moving to Scottsdale and eventually settled into a pattern of two issues per year. Sponsors of Teleos Institute were enthusiastic about the magazine and often devoured it in one sitting when it arrived. This made us sigh because of how long it takes to write articles and then put the issue together. Readers would read it and be ready for the next one before we had even gathered enough life experiences to be inspired to write future articles. But, we remain very pleased that *Emerging* speaks so meaningfully to those who receive it.

Here are some sample responses to *Emerging* after we moved to Scottsdale:

> *I gobbled up* Emerging *and reread it often. When I wake up and feel anxious in the night, I reread the magazine, your writings, and I feel better. I am writ-*

ing to let you know how much I enjoyed this issue in particular, every word, from A to Z. Thank you.

The interesting thing I want to share is how the Theatre of Life training and the Waking Dream studies worked well for me as I dealt with my part in the memorial service [for my father.] As the family planned the service with the minister, I saw myself taking my typical feminine approach to let the minister and my brother take the active roles. However, after a mediocre graveside ceremony, I made a decision to participate in some way to improve the memorial service.

I knew I had to activate my unused masculine [yang] qualities that would most suit my need in the situation. With the skills acquired through your classes, I met the challenge, giving a confident and appropriate reading and message during the service.

I appreciate all I've learned through the years of work with you.

I'm sure I have mentioned before that barely a day goes by that I don't quote one or another of The Love Principles. If I'm not speaking them, I'm trying to live them and pass the perceptions on to others who are struggling with some issue.

Darn it. I wish I could just drop in and sit down for a chat. I've read every word in Emerging this issue. Every bit of it gave me some pleasure or insight. You're doing great work.

These brief snatches from responses to issues of *Emerging* capture some of the enthusiasm and pleasure. People responded to articles and shared their own insights and experiences in response. When people took issue with something we had written, they didn't hesitate to say so and then to share why. We were always enriched by the back and forth.

We continued to publish articles written by others who shared their personal efforts to live the **Love Principles**.

Digital Publishing on Demand

When we moved to Scottsdale our publishing went through some changes. On Demand book publishing came into being and we rushed to sign up with Lightning Source, one of the earliest companies. It is affiliated with the Ingram Content Group, one of the largest distribution companies in the world. By submitting our titles to Lightning Source, we are automatically included in Ingram's list that goes to all bookstores in the country, in Canada, in the UK, and elsewhere.

Digital publishing was a lifesaver for us. It meant that Diane could lay out our books on the computer using a desktop publishing program. As Diane got more proficient and the computer programs grew more sophisticated, whole books could be submitted to Lightning Source in one pdf file. Moreover, because the printing process was digital, our first order could be for as few as twenty copies. After that we could order as many or as few books as we wanted at the same price. What a difference. We no longer had to store hundreds of books, but rather we could order according to the demand.

In addition, Amazon Advantage made it possible for us to offer our books online on consignment. Eventually e-readers came into being and we were able to post our books on Amazon for e-sale. In other words, we were swept right along into the digital information age.

We had made the choice back in 1985, at the urging of Irv Hershman, to buy a computer and learn to use it. When we bought that first computer the salesman assured us that we would never need another, because that computer had 500 kilobytes of memory and that was more, he told us, than we would ever need. No one knew that we would, by 2017, be talking in gigabytes and terabytes and beyond. But because we made the choice to get into the learning process early, we have been able to keep up with technology to a large extent.

An Energy Odyssey

In 2003, we decided to offer a more intensive opportunity for individuals to practice living consciously in the energy world, an Energy Odyssey. We had been teaching people about the energy world from the beginning of our work, but changing ways of thinking and learning to register energy consciously were not easy for many.

Initially we practiced extending our sensing beyond the familiar five senses, and we practiced tuning into energy fields. In the second year, we expanded our exploration into the seven energy centers (chakras) and correlated them with astrology and the seven rays of creative energy taught in esoteric systems. The content of that year's work is available in the book *The House of Self: A Description of the Structure and Function of the Individual's Energy Field* (Pike, 2006).

In the third year, our work expanded into a study of Tarot Cards as a reflection of our true nature. By the fifth year we began to study the Qabalah, alchemy and more. Essentially, we have explored many symbol systems as pathways for spiritual growth. The work has been stimulating and nourishing and has taken us ever deeper into the energy world and knowledge of our true selves.

Many of the original group members have stayed with the work from the beginning. Others have come and gone. What has developed is a spiritual community that is devoted to studying Wisdom Teachings and embodying them in everyday life according to our highest and best understanding of them.

The Energy Odyssey is a ten-month intensive. Each year the group gathers for a four-day workshop in which we are able to deepen our relationships and engage actively in our studies. An assignment is sent out at the beginning of each month suggesting reading, study and exercises to give practical expression to the study. Partners are assigned with whom to share the work during each month. At the end of the month, each person reports by telephone on their discoveries, insights and questions, and the two of us give feedback. The reports are digitally recorded and sent out to everyone. In this way, connections in consciousness are deepened month by month.

The Energy Odyssey offers an opportunity for ongoing study and practice in embodiment that is so satisfying for many that the group has continued uninterrupted for fourteen years as of this writing. We are open to creating a second Energy Odyssey group for new people who would like to enter the energy world experience.

Spiritual Graduate Work

What is a spiritual education? It is learning the laws at work in the world we live in and in our own consciousness. It is learning about the structure of the human being and the levels on which our consciousness functions. It is learning the history of the creative process that brought everything into being, called the involutionary process, and studying the potential for our own further development in the evolutionary process.

Levels of Spiritual Education

Religious education is the "grammar school" of spiritual education for souls here on earth. It teaches people that there is something beyond what we experience with our five senses, something that can be called the Spirit and/or God. It also teaches people about faith and prayer, which are ways of relating to and connecting with the realm of Spirit and/or God. Unfortunately, it also gives people a lot of erroneous information and extraneous ideas about themselves and about life.

Modern science, including the sciences of psychology and anthropology, offers "high school" level spiritual education, although most people don't think of those subjects as spiritual. The sciences use observation to gather data about the world in which we live. They not only describe the laws that are at work, but they also encourage students to test out the laws directly, to experiment further, and to help uncover more truth through their own observations and experimentation. These practices are characteristic of the spiritual sciences as well.

More advanced sciences, like mathematics, physics, quantum mechanics, astronomy, and genetics comprise a "college" education for earth souls. Unfortunately, most people drop out of spiritual "high school" before they get to psychology and anthropology in their soul education, and it never occurs to most people to go on to "college" for further spiritual advancement.

The spiritual sciences are highly advanced. They constitute "graduate school" for earth souls. They have taught the structure of the human being (body, soul and spirit) for thousands of years. They have also taught cosmology, chemistry and physics, though in languages that our current scientists might not recognize.

It was very exciting, back in 1975, when Fritjof Capra, a physicist, wrote a book called *The Tao of Physics: An Exploration of the Parallels between Mysticism and Modern Physics*. It was thrilling to him, and to many of us, to discover that the spiritual scientists of the East had uncovered the same truths about the cosmos as our Western scientists were discovering. Their methods differed primarily in that they did not use external instruments for their perception, but rather developed their own inner perception through observation, meditation, and experimentation. Capra made the point, "Physicists do not need mysticism, and Mystics do not need physics, but humanity needs both."

More recently, Tibetan monks who have mastered the arts of concentration and meditation are allowing Western scientists to utilize physical and external instruments to map their brain wave activity so that Westerners might come to a greater understanding of how our consciousness works. Dialogs between Western scientists and Tibetan meditators, including the Dalai Lama, are uncovering strikingly similar understandings of the way things work in our universe, arrived at through different modalities but revealing the same truths.

The Nature of Spiritual Language

Very few people ever undertake spiritual studies at the levels of higher spiritual education. At the end of the 19th century and beginning of the 20th century, individuals from India with "Masters Degrees" in spiritual education (often called yogis, swamis, or gurus) began to come to Western countries to offer graduate level spiritual education. They traveled throughout North America and Europe seeking students who hungered for more knowledge and who wanted to expand the worlds in which they lived. They sought students who wanted to learn to read and write symbolic languages unknown to them up to that point and who were willing to undertake the practices that would enable them to experience higher states of consciousness.

Of course all languages are symbolic. We just don't think of them that way. If you were illiterate, the words on this page would mean nothing to you. They would be meaningless symbols. Numbers are also symbols that we learn to interpret and manipulate. With verbal languages like English and mathematical languages like Arabic numerals and algebra, literate Westerners have learned to navigate the physical world to such an extent that we can glibly speak of the global village.

In our Western traditions, spiritual language has long been referred to as "esoteric." The word means mysterious, obscure, or impenetrable. Although these spiritual teachings have not been kept secret for well over a century now, the meaning of the words and symbols remains mysterious to most people simply because they are spiritually illiterate.

Spiritual Graduate Work

Over the years, the two of us have dedicated ourselves to the education of earth souls in the spiritual sciences. We have attempted to use words that most people would understand, at least initially, and then to offer practices that will help people to integrate new concepts into the way they live.

We started by introducing thousands of people to the six **Love Principles**. We see unconditional love as the doorway to graduate level spiritual development, and the six **Love Principles** are keys to this door. Many people have been ready to at least consider the possibility of learning to love unconditionally.

We were not alone in the effort to open the heart chakra doorway. There was a whole group of us who "graduated," or awakened, at the same time between the years 1968 and 1972, and the majority of us took on the task of teaching people the power of spiritual/universal love. We have been privileged to meet many of these beings and to acknowledge that we are doing the same work together, separately.

In our School of Consciousness classes, we have offered the basics of the Wisdom Teachings from the great inner schools of the East and the West. These classes have been attempts to broaden the mental landscapes of those whose spiritual education stopped years ago. In addition, we have written books presenting ancient teachings in modern language and we have engaged in Consciousness Coaching to help individuals see how to make specific changes in their lives.

Gradually, due to our own growth in consciousness, we began to offer higher levels of spiritual graduate work. In Life as a Waking Dream people are taught to interpret the symbolism of their daily life experiences and to learn the laws at work within them so that they can live more consciously and effectively. This work is a big step up from psychological work and leads to deeper growth much more quickly. Many people have been drawn to Life as a Waking Dream, but not as many as were attracted to the **Love Principles.**

The Theatre of Life was even more comprehensive, requiring a major commitment of time and money as all graduate work does. The program taught people how to function from spirit in observing and directing their personality expression in daily life. Many people completed only one or two acts of the Theatre of Life, claiming that it changed their lives and consciousness though they did not choose to continue the work. Those who graduated from the Theatre of Life are even fewer in number, but their spiritual growth has been noteworthy.

For over fourteen years a small but intrepid group of dedicated spiritual students has pressed on into more esoteric realms in our Energy Odyssey group, learning to interpret symbol systems such as the chakra system, tarot, the Qabalah, esoteric astrology, and alchemy, and experimenting in their own lives and consciousness with the laws reflected in these symbol systems in order to more fully realize their divine potential.

Spiritual education and practice is essential not only for individuals, but also for our planet if we humans are going to thrive and continue to evolve. Even as others continue to address illiteracy on the basic levels of reading and writing spoken languages, spiritual literacy at what we have called graduate levels becomes more and more essential.

As William Blake once said, "If the doors of perception were cleansed everything would appear to man as it is, infinite. For man has closed himself up, till he sees all things through narrow chinks of his cavern." There is abundance outside the caverns of our private worlds, but it will take more than positive thinking to cleanse our doors of perception so that we can perceive the infinite and develop our full human potential.

The Benefits of Graduate Work in Spiritual Education

We have been asked how we assess whether our work has been successful. The first response is that when offering spiritual education we are not focused on results but rather on being faithful to what has been given to us to teach. But the second response is even more important. It is that the process of awakening is an inner process guided by energy currents above and beyond objective awareness. Each individual is stirring within in response to promptings that we cannot know. That process of awakening cannot be rushed.

The best we can do is to support the inner process. It is similar to bringing a plant into the home. We can provide good soil, the soil of a group energy field that is rich with the nutrients provided by others undergoing the same process of awakening. We can offer sunlight, the lighted understanding of those who have already awakened. We can water the growing plant, providing supportive and deep feeling companions in the process of awakening. And we can feed the growing plant, offering the Wisdom Teachings in many forms.

The rest of the process is very individual. Diane's teacher Vitvan once said that if you were fortunate enough to help one person make the crossing into his/her identification with the Real Self, it would be enough. We trust that assurance.

The two of us have felt it an enormous privilege to share with the Energy Odyssey group as each one of us has been tempered by our life experiences. We have been especially thrilled with the following demonstrations of participants' spiritual literacy:

- Growing ability to articulate inner growth and insights;
- Greater trust in their own wisdom and in their ability to teach and guide themselves through their unfolding;
- Expanded acceptance of the importance of

their place in the Whole and their willingness to do the Great Work where they are;
- Increased understanding of the principles of the Ancient Wisdom;
- Continuing integration of those principles into daily life;
- Recognition of their capacity to live more translucently.

We have felt it a blessing to be companions with such dedicated students of the Wisdom and to watch as they bring forth the Light from within themselves. More and more of us are able to affirm that *we are not alone.*

Respecting and Loving the Physical Body

Physical health is very individual; there may not be a norm to which to adhere in relation to good health. Over the years, we have learned that one of the best ways to maintain a strong body is to listen to it. Although societal norms try to corral us into "proper" size, shape, food and exercise rituals, vitamin intake, and lifestyles, no single approach fits all.

For example, the two of us (along with multiples of others) are a testament to the yo-yo effect of dieting. During our lifetimes, we have taken off (and eventually put back on) numerous pounds. The most efficient way to become thin appears to be to stop eating, or at least to eat the minimal amount possible, and to continue this practice every day for the rest of your life. We have opted not to do this, but we do listen to our bodies, feeding them only what they want and when they want it.

We have also tried, at one time or another, practically every alternative food regimen from vegetarian to macrobiotic to fasting.

DNA plays a big role in our processing of food and our metabolism. By our late sixties we gave up trying to fight the inevitable, gave up the concept of dieting, and devoted ourselves to being good to our bodies with exercise and conscious eating, letting the chips fall where they might.

Facing Cancer without Fear

Over the years, the two of us have dealt with various physical conditions. In every case, we applied the truths we knew to set healing energy in motion.

The biggest issue with which Arleen dealt was a diagnosis of breast cancer on March 23, 2010. Following a mammogram and biopsy, it was revealed that the right breast had a small tumor, an infiltrating ductal carcinoma, grade 2. It was discovered early and fortunately was female hormone receptor positive. It was likely caused by too many years on hormone replacement therapy which doctors later eliminated as a regimen because it, in fact, became identified as cancer-producing.

Arleen reports her process:

I jumped into conscious action and choices upon receiving the diagnosis. I did numerous things when I hung up the phone after talking with my doctor. I made the choice not to worry. I focused on the cancer as being fully treatable, and I moved into gratitude for life and the consciousness in which I lived that would move me through the complex process that lay ahead. My life was about joy and living, not about cancer.

Within ten minutes I selected friends and family to write to for support, asking for their good wishes and positive energy, asking them not to worry and to leave fear out of the process. Then, I set about making appointments to begin the healing process. Meeting with a breast surgeon on March 31, I opted for a full mastectomy and reconstruction rather than a lumpectomy that included radiation and chemotherapy. The surgery was scheduled for May 11.

Between March and May, I engaged in a healing process of my own. I share this process here as a way to deal with any kind of physical threat, a way to exercise creative jurisdiction over your life.

I focused on the present moment, not leaping ahead to what ifs. I kept my body and spirit strong and healthy, laughing a lot, listening to fine music, continuing my work and creativity, and being fully there for those who needed me. I visualized an easy procedure, a fine outcome, and a simple recovery. I welcomed everyone to join me in seeing the lymph nodes as clear.

In 1978 I had published *Why Me? How to Heal What's Hurting You* (Rawson Associates). The main thrust of the book was to ask what opportunities the dis-ease was summoning rather than bemoaning the unfairness of life. The book has served many people over the years; now, it was serving me.

There are those who fight, even battle, what

ails them. Having chosen to live a life of unconditional love, I had no desire to defeat an enemy or even to view an invading force as an enemy. Everything is part of the whole and has its place. Everything is of the Divine. (This was the primary theme in my novel, *The Two*.)

Cancer is a group of cells displaying uncontrolled growth. It can invade and destroy adjacent tissue and it can spread. Cancer cells are doing what they do by definition. They are not so much an enemy as they are powerful agents of change. They were currently residing in my breast. To confront them, I had to awaken my consciousness and exercise "creative jurisdiction" (a Theatre of Life term I invented) over their nature. I held no animosity toward those cells. Instead, proceeding with a flow of love, I directed them to remain contained, to go dormant, and to prepare themselves for removal from my body. I did not want them to suffer during surgery.

I created a harmonious inner environment in which uncontrolled growth is subdued. Cancer is powerful but I could turn that energy and power away from invasion and destruction by standing in the whole of myself in greater power still, the power of unconditional love. I could radiate that power of love to the cancer cells and help to create what I hoped would be a chamber of healing.

Cells have a memory. Cells change and can be changed. That is what we call evolution. Each of us contributes to change. Each of us who deals consciously with dis-ease on any level is playing a vital role in the new that is emerging.

The larger issue in relation to cancer or any condition was how do I respond, how do I utilize my life force? I chose to be creative and constructive. I chose to champion life. I chose to be worry-free. I would not waste any energy that belonged to conscious functioning, choice-making, and healing.

Many told me that I was courageous in revealing the intimate details of the process in which I was engaged. For me courage had nothing to do with it. I know that all of us, friends/family/loved ones/and strangers are One, One Being. We are each a unique cell in the body of what we call God. When Diane and I began our work in 1972 we made the choice to be public/private persons, sharing about our lives and unfolding processes. This meant that we would respond the same way to questions about ourselves and our "personal" lives openly regardless of who was inquiring. This has been an extraordinary way to live. We speak the same truth to everyone and therefore never have to wonder if we told one person one thing and another something different. Moreover, we never say to anyone what we would not want someone else to hear.

With no separation from anyone, people who read my reflections were free to share them. I was gratified to learn how my process was helping others far and wide.

I remained in a state of joy as the process unfolded. My right breast had cancer but my state of joy did not! The bottom line for me is that I am blessed (cancer or not.) I wake up in gladness every day, greeting the sun with my inner light. I love who I have become. I am a mix of all human qualities including ribald humor, kvetchiness, tenderness, outrage, and a pinch of irreverence. I was blessed when I was perfectly healthy and I was no less blessed when dealing with cancer. I am grateful that the cancer served to remind me of the grace in which I live.

How we approach a physical crisis is even more important than the medical treatment that seeks to repair the condition. Throughout the surgery and healing time, the inconveniences, the wait for pathology reports, the post-op visits (all of which I shared in *Emerging* and later in my book, *Facing Cancer without Fear*, 2012), I never had any physical pain. Perhaps this was because I didn't create fear, stress or anger. I never put up any resistance to the process. I had not created painful feelings and had no pain. Even when I had my first view of the remains of the right breast area, my immediate response was a silent confirmation, "This is what is." I was matter-of-fact and unemotional. It was clear to me that this achievement was the result of over 40-years of consciousness work.

Life doesn't come with any guarantees; any of us can be stricken with anything at any time. It is how we respond that is important. Friends told me that because of my approach I would do great. The truth was that even in the midst of the whole event and times of not knowing what would eventuate, I was doing great! I am very drawn to the Zen philosophy: If I don't understand, things are as they are. If I do understand, things are as they are.

The healing process was supported by hormone-suppressing drugs for five years. I continued to gain strength and mobility and focused my time and energy on living my life fully and creatively. In May, 2015, I entered the next stage of yearly check-ups, cancer-free, and grateful. I have taken what I learned from this life event and applied it to every area of my daily living. Life is good; it always has been, it always will be.

Writing about the cancer and the process brought a flood of responses from people across the continent and abroad. Readers were grateful for the open and intimate sharing of details.

Uniting Body and Soul: Diane

I had a lot to learn about life in the body. Because of my focus on Self-Mastery, I was eager to learn all I could. I tried out every method of self-healing I heard about. I interpreted the messages I got from my body and sought to respond to them lovingly.

Whether or not it was a blessing, I was naturally very pain tolerant. I never thought about it that way until living with Arleen who is very sensitive to pain. I think my tolerance for pain made it simple for me to experiment with self-healing. It also made it easy for me to push my body beyond the limits of good sense.

One of the most dramatic examples of that ability to push limits was my ten-hour effort to get out of the Judean Wilderness to get help for my husband when we were lost there in September of 1969. I have told the story in Chapter Four, but what I want to stress here is the conscious communication with my body. I mentioned in Chapter Four that I moved into an altered state of consciousness. One of the manifestations of that altered state was that I began to relate to my body as if it were a friend along for the journey.

I was not "out" of my body nor even alongside it. I was keenly aware of everything happening in and to my body, but my consciousness was entirely focused on the need to get out of the canyon and find help for Jim. Since the body desperately needed water and I did not have any, I became like a coach, cheering the body on, encouraging it, and assuring it that it could do what I asked. I asked it to walk all night. When I gave it an opportunity to rest, I would say, "But then we must walk all night." Each time the body complied with my wishes, gratitude surged within me, as it would have toward a friend who helped me. There is no question that I pushed the body beyond any reasonable limits.

This process continued for ten hours. I was long past what, under ordinary circumstances, would have been called total exhaustion. I drew on energy from a higher source. At one point, I twisted my ankle so badly that I knew it was severely sprained. I spoke out loud, saying, "I know I've sprained you, but you cannot get stiff and you cannot swell up because we must walk all night." The ankle did not swell or get stiff. I was aware it had been injured, but I felt no pain. "Thank you for not swelling," I repeated to the ankle each time I turned it again.

I was also grateful to my body for not causing me pain about lesser injuries. I could feel my flesh being torn: my legs got bumped and scraped, my feet bruised, blistered and cut, my bottom gouged, my hands and arms punctured and lacerated. But I did not suffer from the wounds. "Thank you for not hurting," I said over and over again to my body. "Thank you."

After I finally got to an army post and gave them directions for how to find Jim, I lay down to rest and my ankle swelled up. When a medic came in to attend to my wounds he was certain I had broken my ankle because it was so swollen I could hardly stand on it. I assured him the ankle was not broken, just sprained, and again I thanked my body for having sustained me until I found help.

By the time I saw a doctor in the United States a week later, all my lacerations and blisters, the small wounds, had healed. It took almost two months for my ankle to regain its strength, but for all intents and purposes, I came out of the desert unscathed, amazing as that seems today.

I tell that experience here because it was the first of many I have had of communicating with my body. I am always amazed at how responsive the body is. One time I had a severe rash under my breasts, in my armpits, and in my crotch. I tried ointments and powders of all kinds. About three months into the very uncomfortable, itchy, burning siege, I spoke out loud one day to my body: "OK. That's it! I have had it. Enough!" To my amazement, the rash immediately disappeared. I mean instantaneously. It was like a miracle.

Not all communication has been from "me" to the body. Often it is from the body to "me." By 1996 I had come to see my experiences as an initiation into the mystery of incarnation: living as spirit in form. It is the polar opposite initiation from the one that awakens us from identification with the body to knowing ourselves *as spirit*. I realized that we must know both before we can experience a merging of the two polarities into one clear and liberated sense of self.

I came into this lifetime knowing "I am not my body, and therefore death has no power over me." In 1969, I was able to demonstrate the power of that knowing when I was able to come out of the desert in Israel alive. However, my body began to awaken me to the fact that the two of us (if we can speak in that way) were in this life process together.

I awakened from sleep one night to the awareness that all the cells in the torso of my body were trembling. I was shocked to discover this. It was like seeing thousands of little children crying out in terror. My heart opened in compassion and I asked, "What are you afraid of?"

I kept asking the question for several days while I "held" the trembling cells in energy. Finally, they responded, saying, "You are always completely cavalier about death. It's easy for you because you don't have to do the dying. You will just walk away and leave us to deal with it alone. But we have to do the dying."

I made a commitment to the cells of my body that day that I would be present to them and with them when they undergo life-threatening situations and during the process of dying. What I didn't realize was that I still did not know that *I* would die. Yes, and be conscious all through it and beyond death of the body, but nevertheless, I would die, because it is a life experience.

In 1993, I made another journey to the desert by moving to Arizona. The challenge then was to come to know, "I am my body, and therefore I can live *through* death consciously."

The Message in Metaphor

I was actively working with the language of symbolism in the Life as a Waking Dream method of understanding life events. To look at our life experiences as if they are messages from our real Selves offered to us in metaphorical expression takes deep inner listening to discover the interpretation that resonates within the whole Self as if from the Great Mother.

In 1996, I had two incidents that the doctors classified as TIAs. A Transient Ischemic Attack temporarily denies oxygen to the brain and is a precursor to a stroke. In my case the two incidents caused dizziness, blurred or double vision, and a slight numbness around my right eye. After undergoing a CT scan of my brain, an echocardiogram, an echo carotid exam, and seeing my eye doctor and a neurologist, no trace of blood clots or evidence of a stroke could be found. Every test was completely negative. Nevertheless, just to be safe my family doctor put me on Ticlid, an anticoagulant that is supposed to positively affect 98% of its users. As a general rule, I prefer not to take medications, but I made an exception in this case, erring on the side of caution.

The family doctor and the neurologist both reminded me that I had to have blood tests every two weeks for the first few months on Ticlid to make sure I did not have an adverse reaction. The main adverse side effect is the loss of white blood cells. After the first two weeks, my blood test was normal. The second test showed a drop in the white cells, but since they were still in the normal range, the doctor saw no problem, saying that the lost white blood cells could have been used by the body to fight off something that was invading.

By the time we received that message from the doctor, we had just arrived in the Midwest for four intensive days of work. I had begun to run a low-grade fever, had diarrhea, and had a headache all day long. I was also very low on energy, though no one could tell it because I participated fully in the workshop sessions.

To complicate my understanding of what was going on, just before leaving for the Midwest I had had two crowns installed on the titanium implants that had been inserted several weeks before. I wondered if my fever and headaches were related to the implants, so on the third day I called my dentist in Arizona to tell him what was going on. He couldn't imagine that anything was wrong with the implants at that late stage of the work. He thought that perhaps I had a touch of the flu that had settled in my jaw because of its vulnerability and he prescribed an antibiotic. That seemed reasonable to me since my body ached all over, I had lost my appetite, and my fever and the diarrhea persisted.

The day after I began taking the antibiotic, my gums swelled up and the inside of my mouth broke out with ulcers. I was in great pain and couldn't eat or drink without distress. By then we were on our way home, and I went to see my periodontist the next day. He was astonished, having never seen anything like it, and sent me off to an oral surgeon because he didn't know what to do.

The oral surgeon thought that I was allergic to the antibiotic, took me off that medication, and prescribed steroids that effectively took care of the ulcers in the mouth after about two weeks.

Whereas my mouth was improving, the rest of my body and energy levels were worsening. The diarrhea and low-grade fever persisted and my muscles began to cramp. Up to that point I did not remember that ulcers in the mouth were one of the side effects to watch for with Ticlid.

I checked with my doctor who put me on a bland diet for several days. By now we were in the middle of Act II of the Theatre of Life, which we held in our home.

Each morning I led the Theatre of Life group for two hours before Arleen joined us. By the third day I found that I could not stand while leading the group; I had to bring in a chair to sit on. I was so low in energy that I began to take naps during the lunch hour and then into the afternoon. On Thursday of that week I went for my third Ticlid blood test. The next day, Friday, my doctor left me a message that the tests showed that my white blood cell count was dangerously low and that I should stop taking Ticlid at once. She prescribed another blood thinner and told me to start on it that night, but I was finished with medications! Prior to taking the Ticlid, my blood was "picture perfect;" there was no way I would take another blood thinner.

By the time I went to the Emergency Room

on Saturday evening, I was barely able to walk, both from weakness and from migrating muscle spasms. I registered a great deal of physical pain during this process, and I did respond to the messages in various ways. However, I also experienced the freedom that comes from knowing "I am not my body." I was not emotionally distressed, my mind was not disturbed by what was happening, and I was quite clear in my consciousness. So I kept on living my life as if the body were not dying, but it was.

In the Emergency Room the attending doctor listened patiently to my entire story. Then he said, placing his hand gently, but firmly, on my arm, "You are very sick and we are not going to let you go until we find out what is wrong." His words touched me in the solar plexus and tears poured down my face. I realized that I was relieved to have someone recognize my distress, even though I myself had been slow to do so.

Fortunately, the specialist on call that night was a hematologist. He happened to be in the hospital so he came immediately to examine me. He said, "I'm admitting you to the hospital." He put me on the floor with his cancer patients and gave me an injection of a powerful drug that was supposed to jump-start the bone marrow so it would produce more white blood cells. By the next day there was not enough response, so he gave me a second injection. That did the trick after two more days.

While I was in the hospital, my primary doctor who had prescribed the Ticlid came in to see me. She derided me for not going on the other blood thinner. She told me that any patient she had ever had who had "failed" on aspirin or Ticlid therapy and did not go on another blood thinner had died. I told her I would rather die than repeat what I had just experienced. I never went back to that doctor.

I realize that doctors do their best to help their patients. Most family doctors have a broad spectrum of experience and base their analysis and prescription on that experience as well as on their training and their reading of medical journals. But they can be wrong. Specialists have an even narrower window of vision through which to evaluate. They "specialize" as though one part of the body can be separated from the rest. They prescribe according to their specialty, not necessarily taking into account the whole person. This is all the more reason we need to be conscious of our whole body and monitor what is going on. We need to take responsibility for our own health and well-being rather than turning ourselves over to the specialists without exercising discrimination or intuition. I was learning this lesson slowly.

When the entire event was over and there was life in the body again, I asked, "What am I not seeing here?" (You, the reader must be thinking, "What an idiot!" and I am inclined now to agree with you!) I directed the question into the higher frequencies, as a prayer to the Father (the Great Yang) because I was more highly skilled in communication with the Yang than with the Yin. The answer came immediately, "You still separate yourself from the body."

Answers to prayers to the Mother (the Great Yin) do not come in "clear insights" or "direct registry of understanding" as do answers to prayers to the Father. Prayers to the Mother are most often answered through waking or sleeping dreams, in "code language" that requires inner attentiveness and sensitive intuition for comprehension. Therefore, the answer to my prayers to the Mother came more slowly.

A Vivid Life Experience (Waking Dream)

I kept praying to the Great Yin, "What am I missing? What have I still not seen? What is wanted of me?" I discovered what was wanted through yet another life experience:

I began to have pain on the left side of my mouth just prior to the start of a weekend intensive. It felt like a nerve was dying. I went to my dentist, who thought my bite had shifted slightly due to the new teeth I'd had installed. He shaved down the filling in the tooth that was troubling me and said, "It should start to feel better in a couple of days. If it doesn't, then something else is going on."

I went home satisfied that we had solved the

difficulty, but the tooth got worse, not better. The intensive began on Friday afternoon. My tooth hurt more. I took Tylenol and kept going, which was my habitual way of functioning.

Saturday morning, I woke up to a swollen face and severe pain. I called my dentist. He said the tooth was the one in which I had had a root canal the previous year and I would have to return to the endodontist who did the work. "You won't get in to see him this weekend, I can assure you," he commented. He prescribed pain medication and an antibiotic to see me through the weekend.

The only way I could function in the intensive was to take painkillers. They made me sleepy, and I had trouble staying fully awake during our work. I took naps. The swelling in my face increased.

Monday morning the left side of my face was completely distorted and my eye was nearly closed with swelling. I went to the endodontist on an emergency basis. He greeted me dispassionately, looked at the x-ray his assistant had taken, poked around a bit causing some discharge and bleeding, and calmly declared that the x-ray showed nothing and he didn't know what was wrong. "I will have to cut the gum open and examine the root," he said matter-of-factly. "My secretary will give you an appointment."

I followed him to the secretary's desk. He told her to schedule the surgery. She began flipping pages in her calendar. Finally she said, "He can do that for you on July 22 (three weeks later.)"

I was shocked. I said, "July 22nd? That's outrageous! I can't wait that long." She replied, "I'm sorry. He's completely booked, but I'll get the doctor." The endodontist returned. He was colorless. His face revealed nothing. He looked at her calendar and said in his usual restrained voice, "There's nothing available until July 22nd."

I responded, "That is outrageous. I can't wait that long." He looked untouched in any way. He repeated, "There's nothing we can do."

I asked, "Can you refer me to another dentist?" He said, "I won't refer you, but you are free, of course, to go to whomever you would like."

I burst into tears. He hesitated a moment and then turned and walked away. His secretary explained that other endodontists were making appointments in August and she was sure I wouldn't find anyone. She wished she could give me some hope. She said if someone canceled she would call. She asked me to be careful as I drove home.

I left the office with tears still streaming down my face. I was dumbfounded. I could not even think it through. It was as though a huge wedge had opened between the side of my brain that knew from the inside what my situation was, knew of the pain I had been suffering, knew I was in crisis, and the other side of my brain that watched as the doctor and his secretary flipped through the calendar and explained impartially, "We are sorry, but the calendar is full. We'll see you in three weeks."

I was aware when I burst into tears while standing at the secretary's desk that I was having a waking dream (in effect, an answer to my prayers to the Mother), but it was not until later that day that I awakened from it enough to see what the message was. The Great Yin, with her own sense of humor, had given me a clear portrait of how I had related to my body from my "liberated yang consciousness." The metaphor could be translated into the following message from the Mother:

You were about to bite off more than you could chew—again! The molar, symbol of the yin energy that would carry the burden of the "chewing," namely, conducting the workshop, sent you a warning. It said "Ouch! This way of living your life hurts!" You failed to get the message, so it spoke more loudly. You dulled the pain. It created an infection, saying, "This pattern of yours makes me sick." You said, "Look. It's Friday. I have a full schedule for this weekend. Wait till Monday and we'll have someone take care of it."

In other words, the endodontist was a perfect out-picturing of my yang consciousness when I responded with casual indifference toward the body's travails. After all, I am not my body. Why worry? If the body dies, I don't. With a metaphorical shrug of my shoulders I said, in effect: "You're in trouble? Tough. I've got a busy schedule. As soon as I keep all my appointments, I'll take a look and see what's wrong." When the body sent pain messages, I turned and walked away from it with my awareness, going on about my previously determined business.

I was given this same message about my cavalier attitude in a sleeping dream. It came during the night after Arleen and I had been in a painful interaction with a colleague. I had stayed centered in my heart chakra the entire time, receiving him as beautiful exactly as he was, but obviously failing to experience consciously my own pain and Arleen's.

In the sleeping dream, I was conducting a large meeting. We were seated in a circle. A woman came in who was dying. She was quickly whisked away. Later her head was brought back and placed in the center of the circle. The blood had all been drained out so there was no mess, but it was very uncomfortable having her there in our midst. Soon a second head was brought in. It was also bloodless.

For a long time the two heads lay there. Occasionally the heads moved and the eyes rolled around. I reminded myself that this did not mean they were still alive so that I would not respond in horror and would be able to continue to facilitate the group.

Later a couple of men brought in the bodies and laid them down next to the heads. The bodies were also bloodless. One was a large woman; the other much shorter and smaller. I did not let myself think about why this had happened so that I could go on with the meeting.

When I shared the dream, someone said, "Your body was saying, 'You can have your head; I am out of here!'" That's a fine interpretation. The dream seemed to say that I cut myself off at the neck and drained myself of life force so that I wouldn't "mess things up," or disturb the predetermined pattern of things, or stop the flow of activity in my life.

The symbol of the "bloodless bodies" brought me back to my allergy to Ticlid and my white blood cell count dropping close to zero. I had allowed myself to be drained of all life force then, too. A bloodless wonder, dying before my own eyes, but in that case I had to give in and give up. I simply didn't have energy to go on.

In the case of my impacted tooth, I returned to the endodontist three weeks later. It turned out to be his error in that he had not sufficiently filled the gap of the extracted nerve and an infection had settled in to the open space. He did not apologize nor express any compassion for the pain I had suffered. In other words, he continued to be a mirror reflection for my indifferent yang force. The good news is, this time I got the message!

Learning to Love Myself Embodied

Both my mother and father, symbols for my yin and yang formative forces, practiced a kind of stoic denial in relation to the body and its vulnerability. Though they were attentive to us children when we got sick, they pushed way beyond any discomfort they personally experienced in order to "keep going."

That pattern was deeply ingrained in me. As I reflected on the Ticlid incident I realized that one of my worst fears was "calling attention to myself" by saying that I didn't feel well and then finding out that "it was nothing." Right then and there I realized that my pattern was sick! I was in my sixties by then! I have been rapidly transforming it ever since.

I taught myself how to love unconditionally through the heart chakra. Once I mastered heart center loving, I began to use the heart center as a "safe place." If I kept my attention focused there rather than noticing what was going on in my solar plexus, I was free to make conscious choices about how to respond.

That became a pattern that no longer served me. I so seldom checked in with my solar plexus that I often didn't know what I wanted or what I was feeling. I am aware that I cannot choose wisely without knowing how I feel. To make decisions without feeling is to be bloodless and cold. It was time to **receive myself as beautiful** in having strong feelings about things.

I am aware that much of my religious upbringing, and many beliefs in both the Christian and esoteric traditions, support a dualistic view of spirit and body. We are taught that the body leads us into evil, that we must "rise above" our urges, that we must put our personal feelings aside in order to love God first and others second, that at death the spirit will be freed from its imprisonment in the body, etc. Even though on a conscious level I no longer subscribed to those beliefs and thought forms, they continued to have a strong hold on me in my subconscious mind.

I began to focus on drawing earth energies into my body so that I kept myself grounded throughout the day. During this initiation into the mystery of incarnation I had a lot of things "wrong" with me. Yet in the light of what I needed to see and do, these physical episodes served to guide and direct me. Therefore, they were not "wrong" or "bad." Painful, yes. But it took that to get my attention. When I was into my endodontic, bloodless, dispassionate yang force, hell bent on keeping all my commitments and obligations, I might never have listened to gentler, more subtle, communication from my yin forces.

We are here on earth in bodies in order to grow in consciousness: in wisdom, in understanding, in mastery. We cannot grow emotionally, mentally and spiritually without the physical vehicles through which we are learning. One of our major challenges as spiritual aspirants is to respect and love the body and to be grateful for how it serves us. Finding a balance between natural, alternative methods of healing with Western medicine is something we cannot run away from.

Why Do Spiritual Work?

It is easy to coast through life doing chores, going to work, having relationships, all without taking time for reflection. Such a life is unexamined; there is no focus on personal growth. People simply are who they are, believe what they believe, and value their own opinions no matter what their basis. Functioning consciously is not a priority. When such people are visited by a hard life circumstance and are knocked off balance, they scramble to reassemble their former lifestyle. They don't consider the meaning behind the event, what it asks of them, where it is leading them. They are victims who simply want to recover. They haven't developed life skills for coping or making choices. In many cases, they go on to repeat the same way of living that resulted in the discombobulation.

Those who do spiritual or consciousness work can develop *creative jurisdiction* over their lives. They can direct their energy, create realities, enhance their daily existence, and more easily bring necessary change into being so that they function in a more evolved way.

Those who do spiritual work and are focused on being conscious have the ability to make choices about what to think, what to feel, and what to do. They are not at the mercy of life circumstances. When functioning this way, we elevate ourselves as well as the world around us. We step off the conveyor belt where people drift along, and move into a hubbub of creativity where we participate in the shaping of destiny.

Arleen:

My commitment to spiritual work resulted in profound changes for me, in every area of my life. A primary example is that a major portion of my energy expression from the time I was very young was about and devoted to love. In the beginning, because I never felt I had any, I spent much of my time searching for it. Later I not only sought love but made people into objects of my love. I would gush and devote myself to them. I couldn't do enough to express the love I felt. I was so intent on loving that I did not take into account that those people might have felt overwhelmed by me. This led to their leaving the very relationships with me that I wanted to sustain. It was a very long time before I woke up to realize what I was doing and what I had done. It was my long-term consciousness work that enabled me to see and to make new choices. It also helped me to overcome my grief at their departures and to express my depth of feeling in new areas in which to channel my passion and exuberance.

Why Do Spiritual Work?

There were two significant examples of this in my life; one was Ev, my spiritual mother and teacher, and the other was Bebe, my "new mother" to whom my book *Born of Love* was dedicated. Coincidently, both women were Aquarians, air signs, who were not quite ready for the outpouring of an intensely feeling Piscean such as myself.

Bebe had been willing to "become" the mother I had longed for but there came a day when she needed to move on from that role. I was devastated and thought I would never recover. But when I arrived home, hysterical, I had an epiphany, thanks to my accumulated spiritual knowing that enabled me to step back and observe myself in the midst of my agony. I saw that I had made people into larger than life beings to be worshipped. I saw that they could never live up to that. It was not that they had failed me but rather that I had overinflated them and set myself up for disappointment. That very day I made an enormous change in the way I had, until that time, lived my life.

In relation to Bebe, I learned that though for decades I searched for a mother's love what I really needed was *to learn how to love* a mother, because I had never done that. I had overdone the love expressions once again. No wonder she had to resign. This discovery was enormous; I was amazed at how long I pursued something without knowing that I had distorted what I was meant to pursue. My work with **The Love Principles** had awakened my sensitivity to what it is to love.

The relationship with Ev proved an even larger learning for me because of the long and sustaining role she played in my life, most especially as a spiritual teacher. During the course of our 34 years of knowing each other, Ev shut down our communication three times. The first time was the most painful. It was during **The Love Project** at Thomas Jefferson High School. I had flown to California to see if I could secure a job in the near future. I stayed with Ev and Pip during that week. On the day I left to return to New York, Ev and I stood in the silence of the not yet broken dawn. Her voice choked as she said, "I will miss you." She gave me a Crusader Cross to wear on the journey home to keep me safe. The next week, a silver medal of Saint Joan arrived in the mail, as a gift for me and a symbol of the good works I was doing at the high school.

A few weeks later, she wrote me a wrenching letter, breaking off all communication. She said that she was setting me free. My eyes were so blurred with tears as I read the letter that I had no way of lifting to the larger perspective that she was, in fact, setting *herself* free.

My husband Dick arrived home to find me dissolved in tears. Knowing how deeply important Ev was in my life, he flew into a rage of protection of me and announced that he was going to California to confront Ev.

In one single moment, I completely shifted from uncontrollable sobbing to lifting myself into the heart center, where I was able to calm myself and to dissuade Dick. My spiritual practices and **the Love Principles** surfaced in my consciousness and I made a complete shift. I vowed to hold Ev in my heart and in my consciousness every day for the rest of my life. I kept that vow and to this day, 50 years later, I still have and wear that St. Joan medal.

Years into my work with Diane, Ev opened communication again. Ev had heard of our work through the grapevine and wrote to praise us. Eventually, we arranged a visit. When I saw Ev again after so many years, I worked very hard to keep my thunderous feelings from falling over the edge of myself so as not to overwhelm Ev.

It was on this visit that Ev revealed to me why she had sent me away. She told me she loved me too much. She had feelings, deep and powerful feelings, rise up in relation to me and she dared not allow them because she was committed to living only on the Mind level.

Ev said she *had* to write that severing letter. She shared that years later, in pondering the writing, she was drawn to recall a sequence in *The Autobiography of a Yogi* in which a yogi takes an ember from a fire and burns a student's arm with it, causing him great pain and astounding the others in the circle. The yogi explained his action saying to his student, wouldn't you rather work out your karma this way than have to go through the incarnation of another life just to work it out?

Ev continued, "This all flashed across my mind—perhaps this is the reason for that letter—a clearing up of something between us in a "burning," so to speak—which took two or three years rather than two or three lifetimes.

During my past life recall experiences with Joan Grant, I had recalled the life of Robin who lived in Scandinavia in the 1600's. It was Ev who had been his mother and who died when he was quite young, leaving him profoundly bereft. Ev had told me when we had connected in Carmel, CA in 1969 that she had perhaps been my mother in another lifetime. At the time, it struck me as so "right" even though I had little concept of previous lifetimes. Now, when Ev spoke of the letter as a burning away of something between us, I could feel a releasing of Robin's regrets and guilt, his longings and desires.

Once, I had stood in the way of the Light and had cast shadows on my world and my reality. Then, following my spiritual awakening, I saw the Light shining on everything in my world. *I* was no longer in the way. I moved beyond seeing the Light to *being* the Light shining on everything. Inside myself I heard a song sung in two keys simultaneously by one voice. I was told, "You are the echo of my voice finally hearing itself."

Years went by with wonderful communication, sharing, teaching, and learning. Then, once again Ev shut the door and isolated herself. She wouldn't talk to me. While I agonized again, this time I knew the reason and that eased the pain somewhat.

Ev died in 2003. Though she was in my heart every day for all the silent years, the absence of communication left me devoid of tears on the news of her illness and death. She had removed herself from my life and I could not, did not, grieve.

But that was not the end of the story. Everything that ever was and ever will be, continues forever in the energy world.

On December 13, 2006, I received a Christmas card from Pip. Suddenly, I came upon words that set sobbing in motion. "Deep down I know Ev loved you," Pip wrote.

I cried into the next day whenever I thought of those words. I knew they were true; I had always known that. Ev had told me that. It was why she had to close the door. In that little line in the middle of a Christmas card, all those years later, a healing occurred.

My grief poured out. I hadn't even known that it resided in me. It was as if Ev was standing in front of me again, and all was well. I was filled with gratitude that nothing ever dies and love can find its way back to the heart that once longed for closure.

I had come full circle with Ev from spiritual awakening, through her "introducing" me to Diane by suggesting I read the article on *Search* in which I felt complete kinship, to releasing me from emotional attachment and need-fulfillment. Ev had been the finest kind of teacher for me. All that I knew on the spiritual level I needed to apply to my own life in the world and my ups and downs relationally with Ev enabled me to do that and to speed up my growth and development.

Today, every day, I feel gratitude to both Bebe and Ev who both loved me and who both helped to set me free.

Diane:

What I see as a result of a lifetime of walking a spiritual path is that soul-learning comes very slowly, through many diverse experiences. I am grateful to have lived long enough to recognize the themes that have played out in my life and to welcome the results in my consciousness.

The Wisdom Teachings tell us that to develop the pattern of inviting guidance from Higher Self takes deliberate, conscious, and consistent effort. I certainly lived that out. As a child I began praying to Jesus every night before going to sleep to save me. Then as a teenager and young adult I prayed to know the God's will for my life and for the strength to do the Will. After my awakening to consciousness I continued to ask for guidance even as I was learning to identify with the True Self within. All of these efforts amounted to invitations to my inner Higher Self to guide me, and looking back I can see how I was guided.

It takes focus and commitment to remember "*I am 'Higher Self'*" all through the day, welcoming the higher guidance in all we do. If we watch over ourselves and notice when any of our activities are seriously out of harmony with our intention to be of service and do the Will, we can bring ourselves into alignment. Gradually, then, we become consciously open to higher guidance at all times. This makes it possible for transmutational work on our unconscious to proceed with increased power and effectiveness. In turn, our personal work serves the larger good.

The Higher Mind

As we come to know ourselves as the Higher Self within, we learn to put things in proper perspective. Study of the Wisdom Teachings gives us a broader, deeper understanding of the life process and helps us to stay oriented to the higher good. We focus on our highest spiritual goal or purpose all day every day and use it to measure the relative importance of things. It is that effort that brings about the transformation of our personalities and the way we function in the world.

The Love Principles are helpful in this effort because they are specific enough to guide us through actual life challenges. Other techniques we learn as we do our spiritual work, such as conscious breathing, meditation, and physical exercises and disciplines, help us to stay focused on what it most important to us, namely our spiritual growth. Making a commitment to love unconditionally not only transforms our own lives but contributes to the evolution of humanity as a whole.

We can contribute to an environment of hope and inclusiveness by sharing our own attitudes of unconditional love and our experiences of oneness with people all over the world. We can envision the same love that we feel for those we love personally surrounding all people everywhere, and we can open our hearts to share that love with everyone we meet. Our hope is to awaken whoever is ready to begin to know self as the Higher, Truer Self within as we move forward toward global unity, harmony, and love.

We contribute to the changing of group consciousness by focusing on our own evolution, slow as that may seem by our human time measurements. One by one we are shifting the balance from the sleep state of ordinary human consciousness to the awakened state that is our destiny.

Celebrating The Love Principles

After three years of living in Arizona we had occasion to celebrate. Twenty-six years had passed since Arleen first received **The Love Principles** in October of 1970 and twenty-five years since the two of us first met in September of 1971. The two of us had traveled across the continent multiple times, sharing the **Love Principles** and joining people in practicing their embodiment. We had also traveled to many foreign countries with groups of people, stretching ourselves to function in unconditional love in numerous challenging circumstances and sharing the **Love Principles** as we went.

Thousands of people were touched and deeply affected by **The Love Principles** over that time. We invited people to submit testimonials to the power of the **Principles** in their lives. Here are a few of those tributes as run in the Winter, 1996 issue of *Emerging:*

I have a set of **The Love Principles** *pinned up on my studio wall. You know that I am* a jeweler and that I started my business, Kingfisher Tales, after working with you for a year. The Principles are the first thing I see when I arrive in the morning to work. They seem to have removed all the obstacles I felt were holding me back from the full expression of my own creativity.

You know that my eldest daughter was estranged from our family and has now returned. Thanks to **The Love Principles** I believed her to be beautiful just the way she was—even though I felt her absence as a very deep pain. We loved her before she left, we loved her while she was gone, and we love her still now that she is back with us. But that's how **The Love Principles** work, isn't it? They have worked for me through many other life experiences in the last few years. In fact, my life has been changed by putting these principles into action and I am looking forward to being in love for the rest of my life. Jan Waldorf, Oakville, ON, Canada

I have known Arleen Lorrance since fall, 1972, two years after she 'received' **The Love Principles**. I read her book, The Love Project, immediately afterwards and have been "practicing the Principles" in my professional counseling and personal life ever since.

In fact, way back then I was having trouble remembering the six Principles and I asked Arleen if she had ever considered putting them on a small card that I and others could carry in our wallets. In addition, we could give them to others. She did, and I did, and I have been giving away the little yellow cards with the Principles on them ever since, and highly recommending her work, plus referring people to her.

As for their effect on my relationships and spiritual development, they have been invaluable and it would take me many pages to give specific examples. I'll mention one general example: the principle **Problems are Opportunities** *has helped me look at situations in a larger context and see the lessons in them for me. Clifford S. Marks, Ph.D., Licensed Psychologist, San Diego, CA*

The Love Principles *were a survival tool after my three near-death experiences in 1977. So little of my life made sense to me afterwards, the principles, listed on a small yellow card, became a source of steady grounding. The simplicity of the guidance they offered was tricky, however, for in order to benefit from them I had to put them to work—demonstrate. That made them real and their guidance tangible. And miracle of miracles, they also provided an avenue for* my husband and me to meet.

That was in 1980. I had moved by then from my home state of Idaho to Virginia. I seemed unable to find peace in the job I had or joy in any form of dating. As was my custom by then when faced with puzzling problems, I whipped out that bright yellow card and read it. My eyes suddenly fixed on the principle which said: Be the change you want to see happen instead of trying to change anyone else. This meant to me that I should tackle the very worst part of my job and change it by first changing my attitude toward it. Not only did I succeed, but I was so busy at work with newly found opportunities that I paid no heed to male companionship—not even noticing a man who seemed to notice me. Once we met and touched hands, wedding bells followed—that fast. We will soon celebrate sixteen years of the joy of each other's love.

The Love Principles now operate in my life like a friendly advisor. That yellow card is tucked in my purse, a reminder when I travel about how simple life is and how wondrous—if only I remember to use what I know to be true, put principle ahead of action. Arleen Lorrance once "received" these marvelous helpmates when she most needed divine guidance. What made a difference for her has transformed the lives of thousands.

> I am one of that number and gratefully so. Thank you, Arleen, for bringing forth a treasure! I recommend them to others, often.
> P.M. Atwater, Author, Charlottesville, VA

> **The Love Principles** have been an inspiration to me, both personally and professionally, since I was first introduced to them over 12 years ago.
>
> In my day-to-day life, I have come to appreciate the profound difference that can occur when I consciously apply the principles. Their simplicity, while making them easy to remember, is deceiving. They have transformative power, especially in challenging or stressful situations. As frames of reference for reflection, and guides for expression and action, they have helped me to discover solutions, regain balance, and increase purposeful behavior.
>
> As a professional administrator, I have incorporated the principles into my interactions with colleagues, and into training and supervisory situations. I find that their effect in a stressful workplace is to increase calmness, cooperation, optimism, detachment, and individual responsibility.
>
> As a college faculty member, I have introduced the principles as tools for working more effectively in human services, counseling, and

higher education. I have co-authored a book with Arthur W. Chickering (Education and Identity, published in 1993 by Jossey-Bass) which identifies seven "vectors" of student development. We emphasize the importance of tolerance, purpose, and integrity, acknowledging the value of living by chosen beliefs and values. Linda Reisser, Ed.D., Dean of Students and Author, Suffolk Community College, Selden, NY

It is with gratitude that I write for the grace I've received by using **The Love Principles**. *My life is full and satisfying today as I continue to surrender to the process.*

One of the examples where the principles were most helpful was in 1989 when I took a job in a completely different field. I was scared but wanted to take on a new challenge. I was going to work with groups and do more individual counseling with limited training and experience. The office I went to was busy and understaffed to handle all the referrals. It was a mess and hiring me meant I was to help bring some order to the place.

The woman who was my supervisor was stressed out, had family problems in addition to a demanding job, and her temperament was different from mine. She was a tough lady who had seen a lot of life. She was suspicious, hard, and struggling with

her own inner conflicts.

I needed her help. I soon realized that she had difficulty helping herself. I had left a job of eleven years for this. **Be the change you want to see happen!** I started responding to her needs. I took care of my needs outside the workplace. If I came into the office after a few days off, instead of expecting her to greet me and ask me how things went (which she couldn't do because she was so absorbed in her problems), I would remember the principle **Be the change you want to see happen**, and I would go into her office, smile, and engage her in conversation.

I worked with her for five years. We are good friends. I love this woman. She taught me a lot. I was able to receive her as beautiful, only through the grace and determination of wanting to utilize **The Love Principles** in my life! Sandy Norton, Grand Rapids, MI

The Love Principles helped me to turn my life around. They were introduced to me at a time in my life when I was recovering from an attempted suicide.

After six weeks in a mental hospital where I received twelve electric shock treatments, I was seeking a new way of dealing with the life I had decided to live out.

I had finished a class in Transactional Analysis and still didn't feel all that "O.K." The Sensitivity Seminars I attended left me still wanting more. An announcement in the paper of a lecture on "The Naturalness of the Supernatural" drew the interest of teacher friends who invited me to join them in listening to Diane Pike and Arleen Lorrance speaking truth that I believed in my heart and mind.

Before leaving the meeting I signed up for a week-long seminar that enlarged on **The Love Principles** and experienced the real re-birth of my life. It was the beginning of creating my own reality consciously. I felt new confidence in my teaching ability and took a new interest in the children's needs.

Receiving all persons as beautiful exactly as they are had never been a problem for me. My husband's admission of his homosexuality had not changed my love and respect for him. Nor had the sociopathic personality of our son in prison led me to despair of a continued loving relationship with him.

It was my deep disappointment in both those traumatic events in my life that sent me into the depression that made my teaching job impossible. I had to discover that I needed to **receive myself as beautiful** and of worth so that I could **be the change I wanted to**

see happen *in my own life. I knew I could not change my husband's inclinations or our son's unfortunate tendencies, but in my new strength and confidence I could give them the love and understanding they needed.*

After a lifetime of believing it is more blessed to give than to receive, it was a new concept to allow others to experience the joy of giving to me. Now that I am no longer driving, I have increased the opportunities for friends to take me to my appointments. I have learned to graciously receive gifts without the unnecessary, "Oh, but you shouldn't have."

It was my problems that led me to Diane and Arleen. The openness I learned led me to share my new understanding and compassion for homosexuals with friends who have thanked me for opening their minds and hearts.

I have learned to love unconditionally not only my son and my husband but all other troubled souls. This non-judgmental loving was effective in my teaching, as well as in my relationships in the retirement home in which I now live.

We can't practice this kind of loving without realizing its source. My relationship with God, the true source, has been life-long. As a child, it was to ask for help to be good and to make me well when I was so often ill. As a mother, I asked for patience and physical strength. Always, I thanked God for the beautiful work of nature and the love of family and friends.

As I began to live more consciously I knew how God spoke to me and guided me as He had done through my unconscious lifetime.

After giving up the expectation of repairing our marriage, my **abundant expectancy** born of a renewed enthusiasm for life rewarded me with a beautiful relationship with my now former husband who kept in touch with me via daily phone calls.

The more I become aware of my thoughts, words, and actions, the more wise choices I make to correct mistakes I have made and to become conscious of that voice within ready to guide me in my decision making.

So, once more I say "thank you" for this philosophy to live by, spelled out in the **Love Principles**. Millie Boucher, San Diego, CA

Diane Offers Her Tribute

I welcomed **The Love Principles** into my life and consciousness in 1971 because they captured in simplicity the lessons I had been learning through my own life experience. I had made a commitment to learn how to live in peace with all people. It was a commitment to *be the change I wanted to see happen instead of trying* *to change other people*. I had tried protesting against war-makers and had discovered that I was becoming more and more like them. I had begun to hate.

I realized that to live in peace with all people I needed to learn to *receive all people as beautiful exactly as they were*. I had always sought to be loving, but it was hard to love people with whom I disagreed or of whom I disapproved. **The Love Principle** *receive all people as beautiful* focused my consciousness on the unconditional love I wanted to manifest.

The other principles stated in simplicity other truths I had uncovered, and I was grateful to have a concise formulation of those truths to serve me as I sought to *be the change I wanted to see happen.*

When Arleen and I launched our work together in 1972, we decided to use **The Love Principles** as the core and foundation of everything we did. Teaching the principles became our primary focus. In order to teach them with integrity, we needed to practice them continuously ourselves. I found that both challenging and inspiring. All day every day I held the principles in my consciousness and applied them to the experiences I was having. I was constantly stretched. I watched how often I failed to live them consistently, and I reaffirmed my commitment to them over and over and over again.

Diane Continues: Human Nature Transformed

In 1971, I believed that it was human nature to be unconditionally loving. Not very many years after beginning my daily practice of **The Love Principles** and after teaching them to hundreds of others and practicing alongside those others, I came to the conclusion that learning to love unconditionally represents the next phase of our unfolding in consciousness.

It was not long before I also came to see that when we keep our hearts open in unconditional love, we are transformed. I began to see beauty in persons and situations where I had never seen it before. I discovered that when I form an opinion about something I can no longer feel very strongly about it because I can so readily see the validity of the opposing position. I discovered that I could no longer hold onto my cherished belief that I was fundamentally unworthy (having been, according to Christian doctrine, born in sin) because I had become a channel for unconditional love, and when love flows through me, I feel loved and lovable and worthy to be who I am.

Focusing on love as unblocked life energy expressed through the heart center helps me to find the way to practice the Principles in countless situations where I first get stuck, because by breathing into the stuck places and moving the energy, I discover which principle will help me to be loving in that situation.

It has been a joy to find that I have never outgrown these simple Principles. They continue to challenge me and help me, even though I find it effortless to live them most of the time in most situations. Part of their power lies in their simplicity. They capture large truths in bite sizes that are digestible.

I am always delighted to discover how "revolutionary" the Principles seem to people who are introduced to them for the first time. Because they are so simple, they immediately ring true, and because they are so profound people seem to accept the challenge to live them out even if they had not previously thought of themselves as unconditionally loving.

I am grateful to have **The Love Principles** in my life. They are a faithful and flawless guide to unconditional love, and unconditional love is the foundation of all spiritual growth. I love more practically, more truly and in a more balanced fashion as a result of living **The Love Principles**, and because my whole life is dedicated to doing God's will, I am better able to fulfill my life purpose thanks to these six Principles.

I celebrate the coming of **The Love Principles** in to the world and into my life. I am deeply grateful for them.

Arleen Comments

In 1970, my life was radically changed when I received **The Love Principles** on a ray of light while sitting in my office at a ghetto high school in Brooklyn, New York. The environment in the office was pierced by a foot-wide beam that came from the ceiling and through the wall on the opposite side of the room. The environment was split between the sustained lighted ray and the rest of the room which remained normal, although dimmer. All that I had been taught in my sleep-travel seemed to be swirling like tiny diamonds in the shaft of the beam. **The Love Project** and **The Love Principles** emerged from that ray of light. In the succeeding seven months, the school was transformed by the power of love, and I was awakened to the spiritual dimension of life for the first time.

As my personal ambitions receded, my purpose of making a positive difference in the world became paramount. Over time, my desire to be loved diminished. Instead, my whole life became an act of love. **The Love Principles** served as my guides, my direction, my inspiration, and my taskmaster. They held me accountable to myself regarding my determination to function at my highest and best.

Thousands upon thousands of people, over the course of a quarter of a century (and now, in 2017, much beyond that), were touched and deeply affected by **The Love Principles**. While I have always been eternally grateful for this, I don't think of myself as having impacted these individuals. Instead I know that the Principles, and most especially those who choose to embody them, deserve the credit for changing their lives for the better.

The truths offered in **The Love Principles** have been communicated many times, in many ways, and in multiples of traditions and wisdom teachings. This particular version came in six simple statements in the midst of a major shift occurring in the consciousness of humankind. The principles are here to serve us as we cross through the fires of the death of the Piscean Age of *belief*. They are here to enable us to stand firm in love as we enter into the Aquarian Age of *knowing*.

Celebrating 25 Years of Our Work

The final weekend of September 1996 marked the 25th Anniversary of our meeting. We celebrated that event because we knew that it was not by accident that we met. It is our sense that before we entered this lifetime, the two of us made an agreement that after we had awakened and remembered our real Selves, we would meet each other in order to consciously join forces to begin a work of service in the world and to speed up our personal evolution through our interactions with each other. After we met and recognized each other it took only nine months before we had announced our own **Love Project** which continued later under the name Teleos Institute.

We sent out an invitation to members of our Love Family to come to Scottsdale to help us celebrate. We were eager to show everyone our new home and hometown. Fifty-two people came from eight states (Arizona, California, Florida, Nevada, New Mexico, New York, Oregon, and Washington) to join us in the celebration.

We gathered first on Saturday afternoon at our community pool for soft drinks, hugs and conversation. We had not seen many of those gathered for several years, and many of them had never met each other, so this informal gathering was a time to catch up and get acquainted. It was also a time to affirm that those committed to unconditional love and to **being the change they wanted to see happen** were companions in consciousness supporting each other as part of a grand Love Family which helps us to know that we are not alone.

At 5:30 PM on Saturday evening, we all met at Bobby McGee's restaurant where the two of us treated everyone to dinner. We had reserved a room for our party. By the time we all got seated we felt a bit like sardines. The dinner was tasty even if it was too crowded and too noisy for concentration on conversation.

We left the restaurant and reconvened at the Comfort Inn, where most people were staying, for the evening program. Dianne Grasse, as Mistress of Ceremonies, invited people to share memories of their relationship with the two of us. Diane's family, twelve of whom showed up for the weekend, sang a song. Many people shared memories of travel experiences or other situations. Linda Reisser and Patricia Nerison sang humorous and artistically crafted lyrics to three songs, one of which chronicled the history of our entire lives. Nancy Beckman played her Japanese flute and Una Nakamura made her vocal sounds, blessing the whole group. Several others paid tribute to the two of us for having made a difference in their lives in one way or another.

After breaking for delicious cake and coffee, the two of us spoke to the group about our transformational partnership. We offered our "secrets" for sustaining a long-term partnership and shared what we had learned from one another. Finally, Sidney Stave gave a blessing and Patricia Nerison led the group as we toned in harmony to bring a fabulous celebration to a fitting conclusion.

On Sunday, we held an open house so that everyone could come into our home environment and enjoy it, blessing our space with their presence. We released balloons into the air to symbolize our release of the past in gratitude, clearing the way for the new.

It was a weekend full of love and joy in which all of us were conscious of the blessing of being in each other's lives and of growing together into our greater potential. Many others who were not able to join us in person made phone calls and sent cards, flowers, gifts and an abundance of love energy.

Who Originated 'Be The Change'?

Arleen responds to the question.

In the Spring of 2012 I was quite taken aback to discover that a controversy was taking place about who originally said "**Be the Change**." On March 3, 2012, I received an e-mail from Len Schulwitz who was researching the quote for Wikiquote. He said that he found that *Be the Change* had been wrongly attributed to Gandhi in the 1984 edition of *Drum Magazine*.

Schulwitz noted that the principle appeared at least ten years earlier than that in my book *The Love Project* which described my "receiving" of **The Love Principles** in October, 1970. Schulwitz wanted to know if I borrowed the quotation from Gandhi forty-two years ago.

I had not read any of Gandhi's works prior to registering and initiating **The Love Principles** and **The Love Project** in 1970, but when "**Be the Change**" began to be used by world leaders, politicians, inspirational speakers and ministers, and to appear on t-shirts, cups, and posters as a quote from Gandhi, I immediately felt I was in very good company. I still feel that. What I know about **The Love Principles** is that they are universal truths. We each register them, learn them, choose them, and embody them. Each of us gives our unique expression in words to them; mine, in October 1970, was ***be the change you want to see happen instead of trying to change anyone else.***

In 2012, thanks to the question raised by Schulwitz, I discovered there was no evidence that Gandhi had ever said "Be the change you want to see in the world." In fact, *I was the one* who had first introduced the phrase in 1970! I was both thrilled and humbled because I truly brought a gift to the world and I am grateful to have had that opportunity.

Imagine hearing it in President Obama's Inaugural Address in 2009! All I could do was shake my head with wonder and feel very proud indeed.

Diane and I have distributed **The Love Principles** for over 45 years and they have circled the globe multiple times. They enable people to live lives of unconditional love, to function consciously, and to be change agents. Living them is often not so simple, but I continue to practice them to this day, along with many thousands of others who have been exposed to them.

Inspired by Len Schulwitz' inquiry, I continued my research online. I found numerous references to **"Be The Change."** Among them were uses by college professors, professional coaches, conference leaders, heads of organizations, members of Congress, and the like.

As I proceeded looking, I came upon the CafePress. This tickled me the most. They sell **46,000 items** carrying the logo, **"Be The Change."** Everything from T-shirts, to Christmas Stockings, to bumper stickers, to refrigerator magnets, to ... you name it.

Why this tickled me so is that in February, 1971, while **The Love Project** was in full swing at Thomas Jefferson High School in Brooklyn, the program director of The National Center for the Exploration of Human Potential had wanted to "manage" me, get me on television, and make and distribute memorabilia emblazoned with **The Love Principles**. I had said no in order to sustain the spiritual nature of the principles. Commercializing them was not in harmony for me. Now, all these decades later, **"Be the Change"** has become a significant catch phrase marketed through a money-making website! I see that I could have done all this myself and probably would have become very famous and very wealthy, but it would have been a desecration for me of something very holy.

As I continued my research on the origin of **Be The Change**, I encountered a piece by Keith Akers at compassionatespirit.com who also had wondered if Gandhi really made this statement. He first heard **"Be the Change"** in conjunction with the Senate candidacy of Mike Miles, during the Democratic primary in Colorado in 2004. He didn't realize at the time that it was attributed to Gandhi.

Akers has seen the quote in print in various places since then. A Google search got him 176,000 hits, but when he tried to track down the source, no one seemed to know where the quote came from, or when or where Gandhi actually said it.

Akers said the saying seemed to be primarily aimed at Westerners in the 21st century and that it didn't seem to be appropriate for Gandhi's own contemporaries. "Did Mahatma Gandhi actually say it? He may have. But in the meantime, it is my suspicion that this saying is legendary."

Later, in a November 22, 2009, update on the subject, Akers reports that a friend of his had seen **"Be The Change"** as a rubber stamp-pad slogan on letters she got during the 1970's. "This would mean that it has been around for 30 or 40 years, although it still wouldn't be clear that Gandhi is the source."

In February, 2011, he reported that **Be The Change** was adopted by the National Cattlemen's Beef Association. In March, 2011, he found it in the 1992 edition of *Earth in the Balance* by Al Gore who was quoting Craig Schindler and Gary Lapid in the *Great Turning* which describes the over-arching process that our society is going through that has the potential to take us to a world in which sustainability and cooperation will guide our way of life.

Craig told Akers he heard "**Be The Change**" during the 1970's and taught courses in the early 1970's in *satyagraha* to several hundred law students at Stanford when he was a student there, utilizing this idea. Of course, it was 1970 when the phrase came into being in Brooklyn, N.Y. and by 1972 Diane and I were disseminating **The Love Principles** in our Practice Sessions and through the well-known little-yellow-card that has traveled around world many times.

Since the World Wide Web didn't come into being until 1991, Akers concluded that the phrase originated prior to the "internet phenomenon" days. He continued his search, sure that "**Be the Change**" appeared before 1989. He found an article in the *New York Times* opinion pages, dated August 30, 2011, by Brian Morton. Morton disputes that Gandhi ever made the statement, saying there is no reliable documentary evidence for the quotation.

It brought me considerable pleasure to write to Keith Akers with the news of the origin of "**Be the Change**." He responded by saying he found my origins report very interesting and had many questions. "I had never heard of **The Love Principles**. Is there a print source for this somewhere? How did you 'receive' these principles? I know this is probably a stupid question but, from whom or what did you receive the principles, can you describe this in any way?" Naturally, we continued our correspondence and exploration.

During my continuing research, I Googled Quotations and Inspirations and found a site called "Inspirational Prayers, Poems and Quotations." I found a wealth of quotes from famous contributors including Socrates, Carl Jung, Albert Schweitzer, Alice A. Bailey, Lawrence LeShan, *A Course in Miracles*, G. G. Jampolsky, David Spangler, St. Frances of Assisi, and William Blake, to name a few. Sandwiched in the middle, I found:

The LOVE PROJECT principles are:

Be the change you want to see happen, instead of trying to change everyone else.

Receive all persons, including yourself, as beautiful exactly where they are.

Provide others with the opportunity to give.

Perceive problems as opportunities.

Have no expectations, but rather, abundant expectancy.

Create your own reality consciously, rather than living as if you had no control over your life.

REMEMBER: Choice is the life process. In every moment of awareness, you are free to make a new choice.

– The Love Project, Arleen Lorrance

Who Originated "Be the Change'? 509

After that came quotes from *The Talmud*, the Dalai Lama, Meher Baba, Ralph Waldo Emerson, Gandhi, and many more.

Oh, the company I keep!

A Podcast on the Subject

As time went on, others researched the origin of **Be the Change** and came to the same conclusion. On Monday, January 9, 2017, there was podcast on Buzzkill addressing the issue by professor Joseph Coohill, a historian of modern Britain and Ireland who earned his doctorate in modern history at Oxford, an MA in history from University of Melbourne, and a BA from Humboldt State University in California. He is the author of *Ideas of the Liberal Party* and *Ireland: A Short History*, as well as many articles and internet pieces on history.

The Podcast was entitled *Gandhi: Be the Change You Wish to See in the World: Gandhi did not originate this quote, Arleen Lorrance did!*

"Today we're going to look at one of the most widely-known and widely-publicized quotes in modern history. Mohandas K. Gandhi was the spiritual and political leader of Indian independence and one of the most admired people in the world. And, next to Winston Churchill, Gandhi is perhaps the most quoted. And, the most misquoted. In fact, he's probably the Mahatma of Misquotation.

You've seen this quote everywhere: inspirational posters, Facebook posts, coffee cups, and on and on.

"Quote: Be the change you wish to see in the world. Answer: No quote. There's absolutely no evidence that Gandhi ever said this.

"First of all, let's not forget that Gandhi spent his early life as a lawyer and a political journalist. His published writings are voluminous, and when he later became one of the leaders of the Indian independence movement, practically his every word was recorded. So, if there's no record of him saying, 'be the change you wish to see in the world,' it's more or less certain that he never said it. At least not really. The closest he ever got was when he wrote, 'If we could change ourselves, the tendencies in the world would also change.'

"That line comes from something he wrote (and I'm not kidding, Buzzkillers) about snake bites. Gandhi, as you may know, wrote and philosophized about almost everything under the sun, including health. But Gandhi wrote about the specifics of health in order to discuss its broader meanings and how he applied Hindu teachings to life. In an article in the journal Indian Opinion in 1913, Gandhi wrote that having a pure body and spirit would prevent animal attacks. According to him, Indian mystics and ascetics who were

Who Originated "Be the Change'? 511

pure lived among tigers, jaguars, and snakes in India jungles and were never harmed. He even used the unfounded stories of St. Francis being able to walk among dangerous animals without being harmed as a European example of the same thing. Gandhi argued that, if a person cleanses himself or herself, then the natural world around him will also change. And, in theory, there won't be any hatred or violence, from snake-bites all the way up to humans making war on each other.

"Here's what Gandhi said:

'We but mirror the world. All the tendencies present in the outer world are to be found in the world of our body. If we could change ourselves, the tendencies in the world would also change. As a man changes his own nature, so does the attitude of the world change towards him. This is the divine mystery supreme. A wonderful thing it is and the source of our happiness. We need not wait to see what others do.' [Originally published in Indian Opinion, August 9, 1913, and reprinted in: The Collected Works of Mahatma Gandhi, vol. 13, chapter 153, page 241.]

"Close, but no cigar.

"But if Gandhi didn't originate this quote, who did?

'The earliest instance of this quote comes from 1970, and its author was a high school teacher in Brooklyn named Arleen Lorrance.

Ms. Lorrance taught at Thomas Jefferson High School, which was going through difficult times in the late 1960s and early 1970s. Local poverty and violence were having very negative effects on the school and the students there. Ms. Lorrance conceived and started something called The Love Project as a way to improve the lives and education of the students at Thomas Jefferson High. The idea was that, if kids growing up in a rough neighborhood had an oasis of calm and acceptance at the school, it would improve their lives, and they would bring these positive benefits out into the community every day when they left school.

"The concept of 'be the change you wish to see in the world,' began in a report about The Love Project written by Ms. Lorrance, and published in an education reform text. The first two sentences of her report were, "One way to start a preventative program is to be the change you wish to see happen. That is the essence and substance of the simple and successful endeavor of The Love Project.

Source: Arleen Lorrance, "The Love Project," in Richard D. Kellough (ed.), Developing Priorities and a Style: Selected Readings in Education for Teachers and Parents (1974), p. 85.

"According to school reports and newspaper articles from the time, The Love Project was a great success at Thomas Jefferson and

Who Originated "Be the Change'?

the school was transformed in a very positive way for the rest of the 1970s. So, we have Ms. Lorrance to thank both for the concept of 'be the change you wish to see...' as well as the practical and immediate effects it had in Brooklyn.

"And that leads me to my final thought. You know, Buzzkillers, that we admire Gandhi very much here at the Institute, both as a thinker and as a leader. But when it comes to a true story that'll put a smile on my face and make me think about a visionary putting positive change into practice, give me that Brooklyn high school teacher every time."

The Waking Dream Method

For over twelve years we have been teaching the Life as a Waking Dream [LAWD] method to people in classes and workshops with life-changing results. Starting with the premise taught in most Wisdom traditions that this life is really a dream, we have taught people to discover the power of their own consciousness: to **create their own reality consciously** rather than live as if life is happening *to* them or as if they have no control over what they experience.

In the LAWD approach, we begin by telling a brief story of something we experienced that stood out from the rest of the day or week as more vivid. Sometimes it stands out because of the strong emotions we brought up in ourselves. Sometimes because we keep revisiting it in our minds, going over and over the event. Sometimes because we wish we could live the whole thing again, only differently. Sometimes we notice that we keep retelling the story as if to keep it fresh in our awareness. In any of these cases, it becomes clear that there is something for us to learn from the event. The LAWD method helps us to see beneath the surface of the story and extract its meaning.

The Wisdom tradition tells us that life is a dream because we are asleep to the real Self, the Self that is our true nature. Just as dreamers at night are unaware of their physical bodies and the objective world around them, so we are unconscious of the real Self and the energy world in which we live. If we were to wake up, our life experiences would seem no more or less important to us than a dream, according to those who have awakened. [Pike, *Life As A Waking Dream*]

The Sense of Self:

In the LAWD method, one of the most important clues to meaning lies in discovering the *sense of self* with which we are identified during the life event. For example, many times people fall into identification with the sense that they are a *victim* of what is occurring. The victim sense of self then determines how they interpret everything that transpires. The victim feels powerless to change things.

Another common sense of self in waking dreams is to feel like a child. Children also often feel powerless either because of their size or because they lack authority. In either case, they slip into paralysis and are unable to take action on their own behalf.

Often the sense of self is determined by the context in which the event occurs. Some people feel inadequate in social situations, whether in groups or with persons of the opposite sex. Some lack confidence in their ability to follow instructions or to bring projects to completion. Some people feel like they don't belong, even in their families or with groups of friends. In these and many other contexts the sense of self shrinks and the individual is not able to act with strength or clarity.

Whether the sense of self reflects a self-image, the capacity to take action, or a relational or contextual dynamic, it determines how the event unfolds. We could say that it is the sense of self that **creates the reality** of the waking dream, usually entirely unconsciously. By bringing the sense of self into conscious awareness, the "dreamer" can change the dream.

Diane remembers the time she became vividly conscious of slipping into a waking dream as her sense of self shrank. She had taken a large mailing to the post office. She and a group of helpers had bundled the flyers into zip codes and carefully counted them all. When she finally reached the counter where the clerk was accepting bulk mailings, she carefully produced the prepared bundles. The clerk took one look and said, "I can't accept these." He pushed them back toward Diane. Then he began to speak a foreign language: that of postal codes and regulations. He spat out the words and letters, implying in his tone that any idiot would know how to prepare a bulk mailing properly.

The Waking Dream Method

As the clerk spoke, Diane began to shrink from her adult sense of self into a scolded five-year-old. She could feel tears beginning to well and she turned and walked out onto the loading deck where she allowed the tears to fall. Then she began to talk to herself quietly, saying, "You are not a small child. You are an intelligent, educated adult who is capable of comprehending what sounded like a foreign language. The clerk was not scolding you; he was trying to be efficient because so many people were waiting in line. Take a few deep breaths and then we will figure out what to do next."

As she talked to herself, Diane woke up from the dream. She breathed into her sense of self as a mature adult and approached the postal clerk to ask for his help in understanding what she needed to do.

It is learning how to wake up and create a different reality that the LAWD method teaches. In it we learn how to work with the yin and yang creative forces, how to communicate more effectively within self, noticing clues in body sensations and instincts, learning to interpret feelings and thoughts, discovering the power of intuition and wisdom, and practicing the interpretation of images and symbols that appear in daily life.

As a result of working with this method, many people have learned practical and effective ways to **create their reality consciously.** They encouraged Diane to write a book presenting the method so that many more people could benefit from it. Responding to those suggestions, Diane wrote the book.

Changes in the Publishing Industry

It had been over twenty years since either of us had had a book published by a New York publisher. Diane found an agent and the agent found Riverhead Books. They agreed to publish Diane's book on Life as a Waking Dream.

A great deal had changed in the publishing industry as a result of the growing digital publishing thrust. It used to be that large publishers counted on their best-selling books to support titles that had value but didn't sell as widely. They prided themselves on offering a broad spectrum of titles even though only a small percentage of them were best sellers.

Diane quickly discovered that things were quite different by 1996. Authors are expected now to do all the promotion of special interest books like hers. The publisher offers no help beyond shipping books to bookstores that agree to hold book signing events. This meant that Diane spent the year prior to the publication of the book contacting Love Family members, human growth centers, and bookstores all across the nation to seek to arrange workshops, talks and book signings.

The book *Life As A Waking Dream* was published in June of 1997 and the two of us set off on a flurry of events that lasted for over six months. We learned a lot in the process.

Book Signing Events

Diane was new to book signing events and the first surprise was the discovery that most people who attend author events at bookstores are not there to buy books. The majority of them come out of curiosity, to learn something about the book and/or to meet the author. When the talk is over, they go home. This may be less true if the author is well-known, in which case people are willing to stand in long lines to have their copies of the book autographed. For less well-known authors, the lines are much shorter!

From the bookstore's perspective, author events are a kind of public service and general advertisement. They like to offer special events to their customers to keep them coming into the store and to keep their interest in books alive. Once customers are in the store, they hope they will buy books, but they don't care if they buy the book of the particular author who is making a presentation. When people gather for such an event, there is a feeling that permeates the whole store that "something is going on." This creates an environment of excitement and interest that enhances the store's reputation.

There are advantages for the author, of course. First of all, the bookstores usually run ads for author events, mentioning the book. That amounts to free advertising. Second, they display the book prominently before the book signing event and they usually ask the author to sign the books that did not sell at the event so they can put them on a special display table with a sign that says "Personally Signed by the Author." This sets the book apart from the thousands of others in the store and thus promotes sales. Moreover, the signed copies cannot be returned to the publisher.

There can be a further advantage to having signed copies of the book left at the bookstore. Because there are so many thousands of books published each year, some books stay in bookstores only a few weeks and then get returned to the publisher because they are not selling rapidly enough. Riverhead's hope was that *Life As A Waking Dream* would have a long shelf life, and of course that is highly to be desired from the author's point of view as well.

The first printing of *Life As A Waking Dream* was 9,500 copies. Over 8,000 copies sold in the first two months and did not have any returns, and that was very good for a book in the self-help category. By the fall, Riverhead ran a second printing of 1,500 copies. In contrast with best-sellers, these numbers seem insignificant, but we were pleased to have that many books out there, far more than we could have sold by ourselves. However, for Riverhead this was only a modest sale and after a few years they took the book out of print. We issued a revised edition through LP Publications in 2008 and it remains available through Ingraham Distributors and Amazon.com.

Accompanying Workshops and Talks

Diane found it difficult to sustain her energy for the book signings. She got tired of listening to herself talk about the book. To entertain herself she would change her approach and her content often. Sometimes that worked well and sometimes it didn't. She felt buoyed to have Arleen attend every single author event. She gave Diane instructive feedback and coaching at the end of each presentation. In that way Diane learned, grew, and stayed alive and reasonably awake, which was helpful given the topic!

Riverhead Books did not pay any of the expenses for the book tour. For that reason, Diane arranged for as many workshops as possible to bring in some income. Those workshops were exciting and fulfilling.

Feedback came, indicating that important seeds had been planted. Here are two samples:

> *I have just finished reading your wonderful book* Life As A Waking Dream. *I find your approach simple in the most profound sense: what could be simpler than approaching emotionally charged events in my life as if they were dream narratives,*

but oh! What all that implies about reality, control, awareness, etc.

Thanks for writing this book. It's not often I experience insights as I did from reading, such as I usually experience in counseling or with growth groups. I believe Life As A Waking Dream could be a very valuable tool.

You make clear what should be (but is not) obvious to all of us—that many of the events in our lives are not just one-dimensional affairs, but actual reflections of our inner states of mind and being, and that we need to learn to be conscious of this if we want to understand ourselves better and grow as human beings.

A Series of Wisdom Books

While Diane was busy promoting the publication of *Life As A Waking Dream*, Lily Jean Haddad had taken it upon herself to raise money for a series of Teleos Imprint Wisdom Books. She had a vision about a series bound in the same color that could sit together on people's shelves. By 2010 Diane (writing as Mariamne Paulus) had written four books for that series: *Four Paths to Union; Awakening to Wisdom; The House of Self: A Description of the Structure and Function of the Individual's Energy Field;* and *Yin, Yang and You: The Forces of Co-Creation.* These books represented the completion of an inner directive Diane had received to present the Wisdom Teachings of old in today's language. She had offered those teachings in classes, and now they were available in written form.

The Love Principles and *Four Paths to Union*

We were able to release the first two Teleos

Imprint Wisdom Books in 2001. Arleen's book is called *The Love Principles* and was written in response to requests from people we worked with in Iowa to whom the Principles were new and who wanted more exposure to them than we could give them in workshops and brief presentations. The book was well-received, even by people who had been working with the **Principles** for many years. Here is one response:

> *A uniquely inspiring book that is sure to lead any man or woman towards a greater capacity to transform disempowering experiences. The book succeeds in pointing to individual change at the level of consciousness. The choice to change at this root level is always available to each of us, regardless of what is or what isn't happening in our outer lives.*
>
> *Learning to focus on unconditional love in our minds and hearts just might help every one of us to experience a miracle or two. But don't take my word for it. Anyone who reads this book is guaranteed a richer understanding of how life really works at the invisible level of energy, through the one and only power of love.* Review on Amazon by Gloria R. Nash, speaker and author.

Diane's first book for the Wisdom Series was *Four Paths to Union*. Because our work has been spiritual but not religious, Diane had found the

Eastern approach to spiritual growth especially relevant to our work. A spiritual pathway is not a religion. It is an individualized approach to the quest for meaning, for purpose, for a worthy cause or leader to which you can dedicate yourself, or for self-knowledge. Each pathway has a specific focus and specific disciplines. Each tends to appeal to a different personality type or character structure. Each leads to the same end: an experience of oneness, or Union, that causes you to feel whole, free and at peace with yourself, the world, your destiny, and the Divine.

In workshops and classes the presentation of the Four Pathways helped people to understand how they responded to their religious upbringing, why they had trouble communicating with others about spiritual matters, and how they could support partners or friends who walked on different paths. Diane hoped the book would serve people in the same way. Here are two typical responses to the book:

> *What understanding I have just received from reading* Four Paths to Union. *I am eternally grateful for this clear map! The chapter on religions and paths saved me about 10,000 hours of reading and classes in the history of religions! What a remarkable and easy-to-get synthesis!!*

> *This book has been yearning to be written for all of us in a spiritual search, and for all of*

us who would like an objective exposition of the different ways of conducting a spiritual search. I think it is of great use to people who help people.

I have not read a book like it. The paths of devotion, action, self-mastery and contemplation are described with exquisite clarity, illumined by quotes, and given a breadth of application that enjoyed deep resonances with my experience.

As a psychologist, I am at times sitting across from people who have an urging to do spiritual work or some inner voice demanding spiritual development. This is now the first book I think of recommending.

The Two

In reviewing articles published in the *Seeker* magazine we discovered that the seeds for Arleen's novel *The Two* had been planted in the Fall of 1985 when Arleen wrote an article called "The Dark Side of God." The insights in the article were inspired by a look at the natural world in Lake Tahoe, CA. Boulders hung precariously on hillsides having been violently thrown there during a destructive period eons ago. Today, we see it as beautiful surroundings but had we been there at the time of the cataclysm we might not have been so happy about the horror that was occurring.

We seem to accept (we have little choice) that

nature is both creative and destructive, yet we have difficulty with both polarities being present in human beings. We much prefer what is "good" to what is "nasty." In the article, Arleen reflected that it was false to label one as better than the other. The negative played an equal role with the positive. It was part of nature and therefore part of being human. Both the light and the dark simply are. Whenever we stand in the light, in the sun, we cast a shadow. To walk in only one polarity is to walk lame, leaning to one side. When one polarity tries to do away with the other, neither has power.

In 2002, we published *The Two*. The book used two best friends to explore the "equality" of good and evil. It made many readers uncomfortable because it was not in line with mainstream thought about how good is good and evil needs to be eliminated. When viewed from the point of view that "all is energy" and that each of us makes choices about how to express that energy, it is possible to grasp the thesis. The point of view it presents is much like the ancient Hermetic philosophy which says that apparent opposites are actually the same, differing only in degree. *The Two* was clearly ahead of its time and served as a productive challenge to those who wanted to expand their worldview. It posits that only when the two become one can wholeness emerge.

Arleen had a fine exchange with Carol from Bothell, WA about *The Two*. Carol found the book thought-provoking. She wondered what Arleen thought about Yogananda's saying that evil was just ignorance of God. Arleen responded that "Evil, Good, and everything else *is* God. Our work is to choose which expressions of God to make manifest." Carol wrote again: "I agree that God *is* everything, including ignorance; however, this does not imply that human beings are aware of this. To be aware of the oneness of all things I believe implies understanding that good and evil are concepts that are born out of experiencing things on a dualistic level. To act on this by trying to commit evil is to act on the misconception that things are separate from each other. The only way someone could even try to do this would be by not understanding that to hurt someone else is to hurt oneself according to spiritual law. In this sense, when one is aware of the oneness of God there is no longer a choice of what to manifest. To not manifest compassion is to act out of ignorance of this – hence Yogananda's definition."

Awakening to Wisdom

In 2003 we released the fourth book in the Wisdom Series. *Awakening to Wisdom* was an expansion and revision of an earlier book Diane wrote called *The Process of Awakening*. The new book presents an overview of the Wisdom Teachings which, through the ages, have offered answers to the basic questions of life in what is often called the Sacred Science. Based on the perceptions of seers who stand in the energy world and describe what they see, the Wisdom Teachings describe the nature of both God and humanity, the structure of the universe, the purpose of human life, and the laws and principles at work in both cosmos and humanity.

The second part of the book describes the journey of expanding consciousness that individuals undertake when they test out the Wisdom Teachings through their own direct experience. The book describes the phases of unfolding in consciousness and offers suggestions for how to encourage the natural process of growth already underway within individuals.

The House of Self

In 2004 the Energy Odyssey group was studying the chakra system, correlating it with other symbol systems like the Seven Rays and Esoteric Astrology. The group was so fascinated they asked Diane to write a book. The result was Wisdom Book #5, *The House of Self: A Description of the Structure and Function of the Individual's Energy Field*.

Using the metaphor of a house, Diane describes the emergence of subconsciousness (the basement), the first floor (the feeling nature of the personality), the second floor (the thinking faculty of the personality), and the attic (the spiritual faculty of knowing). The book provides words, concepts, and images for those who are learning to function consciously in the energy world, the dynamic reality "behind" our objective images of what is. The book was intended as an instructional guide for individuals who have begun the awakening process and it is replete with illustrations.

Facing Cancer Without Fear

In 2010 Arleen was diagnosed with breast cancer. The powerful story of how she faced the diagnosis and treatment with light-filled joy is detailed in her book *Facing Cancer Without Fear: How to Empower Yourself Through Conscious Choices*. Arleen's approach to cancer carried a similar message to her novel, *The Two*. She did not view the disease as an enemy, or something bad, or as something that needed to be battled. She chose to embrace the cancer cells in love, to lull them to sleep so that they would not spread, and so that they would not suffer pain when they were removed in surgery.

Arleen received the cancer diagnosis as an opportunity to learn and to grow, to embrace every moment with gratitude.

Yin, Yang and You

Also in 2010 we published the last of the Wisdom Book series: *Yin, Yang and You: The Forces of Co-Creation*. This book was born of all the work Diane had done with people in exploring Life as a

Waking Dream. As people sought to **create their realities more consciously**, the questions kept arising, "But how does this work? How do we really 'create' realities?"

In an attempt to respond to those questions, Diane probed more deeply into the nature of the two fundamental energies at work at every level of creation. By learning to cooperate skillfully with the active interplay between these two forces, we can become self-reliant, independent, and consciously creative while at the same time forming deep and productive relationships in all areas of life. Diane chose to use the Taoist terms *yin* and *yang* rather than the western terms *feminine* and *masculine* to avoid the close association of the western terms with gender identity.

Diane's book explores how these two fundamental forces are at work in everything that exists, and learning to recognize them and to cooperate with them leads to becoming an agent of co-creation in your own life and in the world around you. Diane especially enjoyed the feedback from readers that having read her book they recognized Yin and Yang everywhere in their daily lives.

The Theatre of Life

By 2011, having concluded 21 years of The Theatre of Life program, Arleen published a book in which she shares the essence of the program, though of necessity the element of embodiment had to be left to the reader. The book is called *The Theatre of Life: Exercising Creative Jurisdiction Over Self*. It is Arleen's hope that individuals will apply the teaching in the book to their unfolding process. In addition, perhaps awakened university professors of theatre will one day use the program of The Theatre of Life as a course of study for their drama students so that they can have a deeper knowing of the creative process that is involved in designing their own lives as well as roles for the stage.

One graduate called the Theatre of Life program "a graduate work in self-exploration and self-finding" and another described it as "a life-changing, life-enlivening system designed to assist you in becoming an individualized, integrated being so you can function creatively and consciously."

The Theatre of Life book not only presents the philosophy behind the work but offers many of the exercises that were used in the workshops so that readers can try them out for themselves. The Theatre of Life approach uses the theatre metaphor to enable you to create your own personality consciously, moment by moment. It helps you to integrate body, mind, spirit and emotions, by learning kinesthetically, spiritually, and intellectually. The work is about waking up!

Don Woodside, a psychiatrist and graduate of The Theatre of Life, said:

> *The Theatre of Life is an extraordinary opportunity to bring your spiritual practice into your daily life of interaction and work. It gently loosens your masks and patterns, and opens the possibility of a new creation of self in every moment. Most spiritual practices exhort you to be compassionate, but few school you in being responsive to feelings, activating energy, clarifying your life's purpose and the objective you have in the immediate circumstance.*

Suzanne Himmelwright, an artist from Northern California, wrote:

> *I'm so excited about this book. You have no idea how huge an effect The Theatre of Life had on me. During the shadow time with Jack (who was dying of Alzheimer's), I created character after character to deal with the challenge and pain of that time. The result of that was creating a better basic Suzanne: kinder, stronger, expanded. The Theatre experience loosened me up, helped me to see other possibilities.*

Sam Jaffe: An Actor of Character

In 2012, we were finally able to realize a writing project of Arleen's that had begun in the late 1980's while we still lived in California. With the cooperation and approval of Bettye Jaffe, Arleen had interviewed countless people, especially in

Hollywood and New York, and compiled a biography called *Sam Jaffe: An Actor of Character*. The book is a masterful achievement. It is both a history of theatre in the 20th century, and the story of a man who maintained his dignity and honor in the entertainment industry as well as in relation to enormous obstacles.

Readers responded with appreciation for the portrait and we were grateful for the opportunity to enrich people's lives in these many ways.

Other Expressions of Our Work

The Order of Teleos

Early in our work people began to ask us to perform weddings for them. In the 1970's there were many in New Age circles who acquired certificates of ordination through the mail. We followed suit in the beginning, but that began to feel empty to us because we actually felt we stood in a long line of "ministers" of the Wisdom Tradition. We had no interest in starting a church of any kind, but it occurred to us that we could establish a spiritual Order of Teleos. We registered as a Religious Order with the state of California, and later with the state of Arizona, so that ministers we ordained would be legally recognized.

The Order of Teleos was established in 1989 as a loose-knit spiritual association for persons who are committed to conscious cooperation with the individualizing process as it is transpiring in their own energy fields, who seek to be affiliated in the frequency world with others undergoing the individualizing process, and who desire to express their inner experiences through sacramental and communal acts.

We began by having a ceremony of commitment and ordination for the two of us, acknowledging that we have accepted the responsibility and privilege of ministering to others. Over the years, we helped couples prepare to be married by exploring possible difficulties they might encounter, by addressing their beliefs and spiritual concerns, and by helping them to plan their ceremony. It was always our joy to lead the ceremony and to bless the union of the two.

In the year 1998, someone asked if we would ordain her. What a great idea! We sent out an invitation to anyone who felt an inner call to be a bearer of Light to participate in a weekend of preparation, followed by an ordination ceremony. In January 1999, we ordained the first group of five ministers of the Order of Teleos and a year later we ordained a second group.

Ministers of the Order of Teleos are licensed to perform marriages and other ceremonies. They are committed, to the best of their growing ability, to stand beside those they serve in fineness of frequency and purity of heart. They are committed to stand within the tradition of Light-bearers.

Those ministers, spread across the United States, have shared their commitment to conscious and purposeful living and to living lives filled with the Spirit of Love with many dozens of couples and their families and friends.

Making the Inner Connection by Radio

Over the years, we had been interviewed many times on the radio and we always got enthusiastic responses from listeners, so when we were offered a chance to have our own radio show, we saw it as an opportunity for outreach and service.

A Phoenix radio station made their public service hour available to us every Thursday morning. We decided to interview some of the people whose work we recognized as in harmony with ours. Over the course of six months we interviewed 28 people, many well-known, others not, but all doing outstanding work in the world, contributing to the spiritual enrichment of all. Among those interviewed were Richard Moss, Ram Dass, Barbara Marx Hubbard, John Vasconcellos, Michael Murphy, Matthew Fox, Jean Houston, Brugh Joy, David Spangler, Emilia Rathbun, and Neal Donald Walsch.

Marion Nelson shared about her shop in Spring Green, WI, which offers crafts from Indonesia and India purchased directly from the artisans to support their life and work; Scott Kennedy talked about his extensive peace and reconciliation work in the Middle East; Scott Miller espoused his campaign to end poverty in our time through a program called "Circles;" Patricia Elliott told of sustaining her spiritual life over the course of a forty-year career on Broadway and in television; Robert Muller inspired us with his work through the United Nations seeking to sustain peace; P.M.H. Atwater informed us of her extensive research into the Near Death phenomenon; Julie Harris allowed us on the inside of her long and thrilling acting career, and there were more. It was stimulating, informative and inspirational, illustrating the power of the individual to promote the evolution of consciousness.

We offered tapes of the interviews to our Love Family and many expressed appreciation for the touching and inspiring interchanges.

Creating a Website

Not long after we moved to Scottsdale we were contacted by two women in Montana who offered to create a website for us. We had been thinking about such an endeavor and so were glad to find women of like mind who had the skills to bring it into being. We had already sketched the outline of the contents of such a website, so we proceeded rather quickly to manifest it.

We launched the website under the name www.consciousnesswork.com. Later we added a second name: www.teleosinstitute.com, connecting with the same site. There is permanent material on the site, such as the meaning of "teleos," our purpose and the extent of our work, the names of our Board of Directors, and our personal biographies. In addition, descriptions of classes and workshops are added twice a year, selected articles from *Emerging* magazine are posted, and our books are listed, to be ordered through PayPal or directly from us.

Film Commentaries

In 2007 Arleen was inspired by the challenge put to her by a close friend to begin to write commentaries on films. For several years we had traveled less and therefore had more time available to enjoy movie-going. We usually had long discussions after each film, probing meaning where it was available, making observations about our culture and group psyche, and offering our opinions about the skill of the writers, directors, and actors in achieving their apparent objective in creating the film.

Arleen began to write her commentaries and found that they provided her with an outlet for her creativity. They became a means of honing her writing skills because she could produce an entry almost every day. She offered to send her commentaries to a few people and before long she had a following. Her readers appreciated her take on films and especially how she often wove them together with large spiritual principles.

Arleen writes over 250 film commentaries every year.

Leadership Mastery

We developed a program focused on supporting leaders and organizations. We held our initial training here in Scottsdale for thirteen leaders from several states. It was a genuine privilege for us to offer consciousness tools to these dedicated leaders.

The program was designed to promote personal transformation as part of a transformational map to guide leaders who are pursuing major community and societal changes. It was an opportunity to bring practical application of the Wisdom Teachings into the lives of those who are leading the way toward changing peoples' lives for the better, and truly **creating new realities**.

Kaleidoscope

Once we ended the Theatre of Life program we decided to offer a shorter version of that life-changing work. We invented "Kaleidoscope," a five-day experiential workshop open to all who were interested. The primary purpose was to call forth the More of Self that was calling to the participants. Each year the focus was different. For example, we focused on tools for functioning consciously, discovering and embodying hidden aspects of self, transforming self at will, expressing intuitive knowing, and going beyond the superficial. The work was always deep, demanding and enriching and the response was enthusiastic. The program continued for six summers giving several people who had never done The Theatre of Life an opportunity to experience some of the benefits of consciously creating the reality of the character they embody in the world.

A Transformational Partnership

We came to call our union a transformational partnership, for we were deeply committed to the work of transformation in our own lives and to facilitating personal and spiritual transformation in the lives of others as well. For 45 years each of us remained committed to our own spiritual growth and unfoldment, to the support of each other in our individualizing processes, and to the support of that process for those in our Love Family. In addition, we encouraged others to share the work of transformation with others.

Transformational partnerships are often between people who are very different from each other. This is good because the differences stimulate the participants to open to a wide variety of ways to live in the world. The differences become ways of supporting each other on our spiritual journeys.

In our relationship, we chose to **receive each other as beautiful exactly as we were** in any given moment. No tinkering required; no reform necessary. This means that when something the other person does annoys us, we must turn to one of the other **Love Principles** to move the energy in Self.

We found that our personalities were extraordinarily dissimilar. Even to this day, if someone asks us a question we almost always give opposite responses. We think differently. We have different preferences and backgrounds. Because we were ***receiving each other as beautiful exactly as we were***, we welcomed those differences right from the start. We used them for our individual growth. We stretched ourselves to make room for the other. We used irritations to expose our limitations. We practiced changing ourselves instead of trying to change the other. In other words, we welcomed ***problems as opportunities.***

For example, Arleen had a habit that annoyed Diane very much. She would come bounding into a room with enthusiasm, without regard for whether Diane was in conversation with someone, listening to a recording, reading, or writing. She would launch right into what she wanted to share.

Diane loved the enthusiasm but felt disregarded and disrespected by the interruptions. She didn't want to stop the flow of energy between them, but she wanted to find a way to change the pattern. She considered the behavior for a long time before addressing it. Then she described what happened as she experienced it and ***provided Arleen with an opportunity to give to her.*** She said, "You would give me a gift if you would pause at the door, take note of what I am doing, and if I am occupied, wait until I am free before speaking."

This addressed the behavior without criticizing Arleen. The request resulted in a long exploration that took both of us to keen insights about our upbringings. We discovered that in Diane's family, there was a respect for privacy and an individual's right to take and have his/her own space within the family. In Arleen's family, individuals never had their own space. Everyone's interactions spilled over into everyone's space. This had to do in part with personality types, but it was also due to different economic realities. Diane's family had more space, living in large homes that allowed individuals to claim their own places. Arleen's family lived in small apartments with no room for any kind of privacy.

We adopted the phrase, "You would give me a gift if . . ." or, "It would be a gift to me if . . ." as our primary way of **providing each other with opportunities to give**. It seems to smooth the way for cooperative interactions.

Moving Forward in Tandem

There are many other ways we have found, over the years, to make the way easy in our relating. Because we are partners in our work as well as in our personal lives, it has been important to move in tandem. Early on we made an agreement we would not go forward with something unless it felt good to both of us. We applied this to financial commitments, business deals, and personal plans.

Often what one of us wants, the other has no strong feelings about one way or the other. Then we simply support the decision of the one who wants to take action. However, if the other has any hesitation or objection, we wait, taking time to dialogue with each other about our feelings and values. If we cannot arrive at a mutually agreeable decision, we let go of the action.

This has proven to be one of our most important guidelines, forestalling divisions that might have developed due to fundamental disagreements.

We give each other a lot of praise for what we do well, for change we bring about in ourselves, and for our strengths. We also engage in a joint uncovering of weaknesses. When one of us identifies a weakness or a pattern she wants to change, then we both focus on how to strengthen the weakness or change the pattern with love and caring rather than with criticism.

We proceed with **no expectations** regarding how, or how soon, we will be able to change a pattern we have identified or a habit that is annoying. We ask each other if there is a way we can be helpful or supportive as we seek to bring about change in ourselves. Beyond what is requested, we **let go of expectations and have only abundant expectancy.** We capitalize on each other's strengths and compensate for each other's weaknesses.

We express gratitude daily for life itself and for each other. We never take for granted anything the other does around the house or in the office. Even if it is our pattern that the one who cooks does not have to do dishes, we thank the cook and thank the dish-washer. When Arleen does some work in the garden, a task that she regularly assumes, Diane always thanks her and comments on how much better things look. If Diane does the laundry, something she does as a matter of course, Arleen tells her how much she appreciates having clean, folded laundry ready for her.

In expressing gratitude for the small things, the routine things, we stay awake to the blessing and privilege of having a partner with whom to share the responsibilities of life.

We have shared a trust in what we call "the Universal Flow" over these years, knowing that if what we are giving out to the world comes from the heart, then we will receive back what we need to live on. Our focus stays, then, on what we have to give, rather than on how much we are getting by way of payment or income. What we have discovered is that we always have enough, no matter how modest our income has been. In fact, we have felt we live in abundance, rich in opportunities and relationships while not lacking in "things."

We have always laughed a lot, at ourselves and with each other. This helps us to keep things in perspective, not taking ourselves too seriously or blowing things up out of proportion. We see humor in almost everything.

When we disagree with each other, we do not drag in anything from the past. We stay focused on the issue that is current. In fact, we release the past once it has been examined and we have identified our learnings. We do not cling to memories of what bothered us "then." That enables us to stay present in the now moment.

We give ourselves the gift of physical contact. We often have "hug-ins." These are shared moments when we simply stop to embrace each other and spend some quiet time enjoying each other's presence. We enjoy reading beside each other before going to sleep at night and snuggling upon awakening. And we often touch each other gently when passing by throughout the day. In these physical gestures, we stay alive in our bodies, kinesthetically registering the love we feel.

We also make it a practice to verbally say "I love you" at least once a day, lest we ever take for granted the privilege of this transformational partnership.

Diane: What I Have Learned

When I look back over my 45 years in a transformational relationship, I see that I have learned some very important things through my interactions with Arleen.

No Apologies Needed

I used to apologize for everything, even for things that were not my fault. I had a powerful feeling of unworthiness that was supported by the church's teaching that I was born in original sin. Even though I no longer believed in original sin, I still felt sinful.

Arleen used to challenge me regularly, saying, "Are you really sorry?" The more she asked, the more I became aware of my habitual feeling of guilt, of responsibility for what others felt or for whatever had gone wrong. In effect, I kept apologizing for being who I am.

With Arleen's support and encouragement, I broke the habit and learned to respond consciously, saying "I'm sorry" only when I had done something which I regretted. It was a major shift for me. Eventually I was able to break free of the feeling of unworthiness.

No "Out" Is Needed

About ten years into my partnership with Arleen I became aware that I always left myself an "out." In the back of my mind I told myself, "Well, if this doesn't work out, I'll move on." At the bottom of my "out" clause was a fear that if I gave my full commitment, I would no longer be free.

After the severe crisis we went through in the

mid-1980s, I broke through to a new place of knowing within myself. The knowing was that I could make a full commitment without sacrificing my freedom. I found my freedom in an inner sanctuary where I live alone with the Source of all life: a place within that is sacred and where no one else can enter. As long as I live in that inner sanctuary, I am always free.

I am free to commit my whole self to a partnership or to a given endeavor because my whole self belongs to the One Source. It seems to the mind like a contradiction, but in my being it resounds with truth. Arleen, as my partner, accepts and respects the paradox, enabling us to live in a committed partnership and be free.

Take Time Alone

I used to "sacrifice" my own need for space to the needs and demands of others. Then I would run out of energy and feel I needed to completely withdraw from the world to replenish my spirit.

Arleen pointed out to me that if I would take the space I needed each day, I would not empty my cup. With her encouragement and support, I learned to withdraw from people and activities and go into my Sanctuary of Silence, as I call my meditation room. I asked her to protect my space by handling phone calls and other business until I came out. She was happy to give me that gift.

I learned that I did not take anything away

from others by withdrawing for a time. To the contrary. When I return, I have far more to give. In fact, I have learned to make an appointment with myself for the time alone, just as I make appointments with others. Now, instead of feeling a need to withdraw to a cave in the Himalayas to have my spiritual renewal, I simply take my quiet time each day. This is an invaluable learning.

Provide Others with Opportunities to Meet My Needs

I grew up believing that I should put God first, others second, and myself third. The trouble was I seldom got to myself. Consequently, I seldom got around to asking myself what I wanted or needed.

My unmet wants and needs were not addressed except in covert ways. For example, I would tell myself I was doing something "for someone else" when I actually had a need of my own that I was filling.

In my partnership with Arleen I learned that I could express my wants and ask for what I needed. **The Love Principle *provide others with opportunities to give*** helped me to learn that I give a gift to others by showing them how they can best love me. In our partnership, Arleen always thanks me when I tell her what I want and need. As a result, I feel healthier and more balanced, not relying on my unconscious or my shadow-self to take care of my needs.

Let Others Speak for Themselves

I used to feel responsible to explain Arleen's behavior to others when they were upset or hurt by something she had said or done or not done. This was not new behavior for me. I felt that way about anyone who was close to me, as if I were somehow responsible for them even though I had no control over them.

With practice, I learned to encourage others to speak directly to Arleen about their feelings. I learned not to place myself between them as mediator or interpreter. I learned to trust others to do their own process with Arleen, or to trust that Arleen could work through her own relational conflicts.

It is a learning that has also served me well in other relationships. If anyone speaks to me about a conflict with another, I always encourage them to speak directly to the person involved. Others don't always do it, but I don't try to intervene for them.

Arleen: What I Have Learned

When I look back over these decades, I am pleased to reflect on all that I have learned as a result of living with someone very different from me in background and life experiences.

The Joy of Giving

I never knew about tithing before meeting Diane. She taught me how important it is to give away at least 10% of my gross income no matter how small that income is. When I first began doing that, I felt wealthy for the first time in my life. I discovered that I lived in abundance and I could make a difference in the world through the sharing of my financial resources. Tithing brings me pleasure every time I do it.

I Am Safe

Before I met Diane, I don't think I had ever really felt safe in my life. While I knew my oneness with all that is and I knew myself to be merged within a larger whole, the character I wore out in the world had been nicked by life and was often on the lookout for the origin of the next harm that would befall me. People were not to be trusted.

Through our relationship in which unconditional love reigns, I found that I could survive even times of relational trials. I could trust myself. Safe in the love we share, I saw that where I was really safe was deep within myself. No matter what happens around me, I am whole. I am a part of what is happening, and because I am safe within myself, I can deal with anything and **consciously choose the reality I want to create.**

Let Go the Glamor of Romanticism

This is one of the major changes that has occurred in my life. I used to be a hopeless romantic enthralled by candlelight and swept off into my own flights of fancy. Expressing my love in as many unique ways as possible was what occupied most of my energy. I also longed to be loved in the ways I was loving others.

The difference between Diane and me in this regard was enormous. She was loving, but not gushing. She was more universal while I was more personal. I was not only romantically focused, I was intense about my expressions of love.

Over the years I released so much of my previous orientation that I hardly recognize myself. The nature of my love expression completely changed. While I still perform acts of kindness or caring, they no longer need to be accompanied by cards or flowers, or even a prior buildup. I simply love in the moment and express what comes to me. It is effortless. I am no less loving; rather, the love has lost its thickness. It is easier to receive and to return.

I Can Respect Other Ways

As a Karma Yogi, my energy is directed into doing, into making manifest, into embodying. I could not understand sitting quietly in meditation as a way of moving energy or getting anything done. Living with Diane who, as a Raja Yogi, is introspective and uses her own self as her learning laboratory, I have learned to have respect for a way of unfolding that is alien to me. I have observed the changes that come as a result of her approach and I have stretched in myself to make room for the vast difference between us.

During her times of meditation, I move into more active doing—namely, making sure her quiet space is protected and undisturbed. Each of our paths is strengthened by the way the other is walking as we cooperate with the individualizing process.

Powerful Feelings Can Be Expressed Quietly

I used to be a Piscean. I know it seems strange to say that because we cannot literally change our birth signs. However, over the course of these years I became less and less identified with some aspects of the Piscean nature. I used to be very volatile, emotional, and overly sensitive. I would take things very personally and hurt a lot and for a long time. I am pleased to say that, for the most part, I have given that up.

The good news is that in the process of the release, I have not lost my ability to feel or express feelings. I just do it differently. Following Diane's example, I don't get lost in or caught in my solar plexus. I use the solar plexus to direct energy outward and I am therefore empowered in my expression rather than swallowed up by it.

At first, I worried that this shift would cause me to lose my creativity. It had always had suffering as its base. This loss did not occur. What happened instead is that I express creatively from a finer frequency than before. My talents are honed and became sharper. My feelings serve me and empower me.

Just by being herself and living that beside me, Diane provided me with opportunities to stretch and grow. I am very appreciative of her influence and the more that I evoked in myself because of her example.

Beyond Rejection

Diane had publishing experience before we began our work, so we were able to design and offer our own books without having to submit them to outside sources. This was not only a great boon to us in terms of distributing our philosophy to others but it healed an old source of frustration in my life: rejection. This was no small thing. From my early days, I had big dreams of who I wanted to be and what I wanted to do. Alas, in almost all cases my dreams depended on others to make it possible for them to happen.

When I was a kid I was great at sports but limited in venues. I thought it would be great to be the first woman baseball player. That dream depended on others allowing women to play. I suffered rejection for the first time in my young life. Years later I entered show business where getting a job depended on agents, casting directors, etc. There couldn't have been a profession with more instances of rejection. Next came submitting books to publishing houses in my early thirties; the arrows came flying.

One of my strengths in all of this was that I didn't question my abilities or talents and went on embodying those wherever I could. But in relation to publishing, Diane showed me how we could **create our own reality**. As we did, I began to see that by choosing venues where others make determinations about acceptance I set myself up time and again for rejection. I was part of the process. When I opted out, I was able to say farewell to rejection and the **problem** turned into a grand creative **opportunity**.

The Blessing of Our Differences

Our interactions with each other remain rich, substantive, fresh, delightful, nourishing, and stimulating. We marvel at how much we have to share and explore even after all this time. We often start out on a drive with one of us reading to the other. Within a few minutes, we interrupt the reading to reflect on the text. The book gets put away and we go on exploring. We never seem to run out of things to share or examine.

A Transformational Partnership 557

Who knew, all those years ago, that such a wonderful life and association would have unfolded for us? The way we met was a miracle in itself but the greater miracle is how our union has remained vibrant over time.

We came from the equivalent of two different worlds. Arleen's city was 8 million strong while Diane's little town had only 1,000 residents. Arleen had more people than that living on one city block. Diane came from a religious background; Arleen had none. Diane was taught to be nice while Arleen was raised to be tough and shrewd. Diane went to Stanford on a scholarship and graduated with distinction. Arleen attended a city college, mostly at night, taking seven years to earn a Bachelor of Arts degree. For a time, we both worked in community service type jobs in our respective cities and both of us taught high school. Then, for each of us, new directions began to beckon and each of us was open to listen for the new and move toward what appeared to be calling.

By the time we came together, we were ready to begin something completely new, something that would contribute to the inner growth of others while simultaneously allowing each of us to evolve.

Arleen had always been glad to be free of belief systems and religious restrictions. She had not been raised on the concepts of sin or guilt. She never needed to be "saved." During our work together, many of the people who came to participate in classes, consultations and Practice Sessions, needed to be saved from their former need to be "saved." **The Love Principles** enable participants to be true to Self and to inner knowing which can be seen as a very high form of worship, since it expresses reverence for every aspect of the life process.

Diane was raised to be nice. Observing this choice of behavior over the years, Arleen learned to temper her personality expressions without suffocating them. She learned to curtail blurting. Through Diane's example, Arleen saw that it was better to pause before jumping in to assert; discretion became a new value. Practicing this, Arleen was not hampered in her expression of self but she avoided many instances of needing to clean up after an interaction when a spontaneously delivered remark might have landed like a bomb. Arleen became more polished.

Diane, on the other hand, learned to draw boundaries and remain firm without needing to explain or justify herself. She stopped worrying about the other person in her interactions, trusting them to take care of themselves. Instead she learned from Arleen to stay focused on her own purpose and objectives and to monitor the energy she chose to express in her interactions. As a result, Diane began to feel stronger in herself and less like a doormat in interactions.

Arleen also learned, as she observed Diane over the years, that she could remain strong and emphatic while also being flexible. This was an important skill to develop because it enabled her to live in a balance of knowing when and how to yield and when to stand firm. She had always been great at standing firm but yielding had come with more difficulty.

Because of Diane's example of fine-mind thinking, Arleen developed greater skill in translating her multiple images, intuitions, and insights into words that could communicate to others what she saw and knew. This proved to be profoundly important in our work together. In our early years, Arleen could make leaps but couldn't fully articulate how she did the process. Once she could, it made it easier for others to walk in those footsteps.

Diane, meanwhile, learned to listen within for her own intuition, especially in daily interactions. She had always been clear and strong when making major decisions, but when deciding which restaurant to go to or whether to invite friends over, she often resorted to old ways of thinking and evaluating instead of going within to trust her own feelings. Arleen was a superb model for her of that way of functioning.

One of the main ways of being Arleen learned from Diane was trust: trust of the life-process and that everything could be met and resolved in consciousness, and trust in relation to finances. We grew up in very different economic backgrounds. Diane's family was well-off, upper middle class, hard-working, and relatively secure. Arleen's was lower-middle, hard-working, always focused on the dollar and how and when to spend it. Her parents had been hit hard in the Depression and her mother, especially, never recovered. She focused on doing without, on there never being enough, on spending as little as possible. She lived in financial fear and influenced the whole family with that fear.

Diane's parents were also deeply influenced by the depression, but they both trusted themselves to be able to deal with whatever challenges they faced. Both of them had deep faith and they set examples for Diane from the time she was very small of sharing with others from their own abundance, even when they didn't have much. As a consequence, when Diane as an adult asked her dad what was the best investment to make, based on his experience during the Depression, he responded, "The most important thing you have is yourself and your own talents. No one and nothing can take that away from you."

Living with Diane introduced Arleen to whole world of culinary delights as well as food/diet regimes that never seemed to quit. As an Aquarian, Diane loved to experiment.

Arleen grew up in a household where specific things were eaten. It was as if nothing else existed; in fact, it didn't because she wasn't exposed to it. Take peanut butter, for example. She had never heard of it. The only vegetables that existed came in a can, peas and carrots combined, and corn.

Most of what her mother cooked was overdone until all the life was out of it, so it was safe to eat. Meat and chicken were basics at dinner, as was lox at breakfast. They mostly ate black bread or pumpernickel, rye or rolls. The only time they had white bread (of the Silvercup brand) was for their cream cheese and jam sandwiches. What Arleen loved most about all bread was sticking her nose and face into it to feel its warmth and smell its goodness. She did this every time she walked the bread home from the bakery.

In Diane's upbringing, eating was an occasion for bringing family together and sharing with one another. There were traditional dishes, especially for holidays, but on a daily basis the food was not as important as family togetherness. Diane introduced Arleen to many new foods. She made casseroles; Arleen had never had one before, or heard of them. Arleen learned about potlucks and about the wide range of vegetables that existed. She came to prefer eating them to the meat and potatoes on which she was raised.

Diane was fearless about trying new dishes when guests were coming. Arleen learned to jump right in and eat things she had never heard of. This enabled her to travel all over the world and delight in foreign dishes.

Diane's food experiments included the latest fads in health programs. She read about the benefits of fasting. So, Arleen unhappily drank only water for 36 hours one day a week. Then Diane read that fasting for three straight days was a good thing. Arleen hated it. She actually put on weight doing it because her body went on alert and shouted, "Hold on to everything! We aren't getting any more to eat!"

After several years, fasting disappeared. Arleen was thankful. The Rotation Diet took about 50 pounds off each of us over a two-year period, but, as with all diets, they slowly came back. Then there was the Hunza Diet. You lose weight by eating Hunza bread (and hardly anything else) and skipping eating altogether for several days a week! Following that regime, of course you could lose weight. We gave it up.

We also ate Macrobiotic for a time. The food and the approach were wonderful and we felt great eating that way but it required taking an electric wok with us wherever we went. We even used it to cook inside hotel rooms.

Living through Diane's newest health fads made Arleen even more flexible and showed her that she had broken free of her family's limited eating approach. Arleen still has some holdouts, such as knowing that lox goes with cream cheese. Her Jewish friends would faint if they knew how and with what Diane eats lox. And, after all these years, Diane still refers to lox as "them" rather than it.

These are some of things that stand out after all these years of life together. They resulted in major changes in both our personalities and we see ourselves as all the better for them.

Staying Open to Others

If we are open to others who walk a spiritual path, even if it is different from our own, we can bring unexpected support into our lives. If we are open to differences that exist between ourselves and others, and we receive those as encouragements to become the more of what is waiting to emerge in us, we can grow in leaps and bounds.

If we realize that "the other" is "myself" in another form, we can merge in a sense of Oneness that eradicates the false sense of separation that causes the prevailing ills in the world. We can each be blessed in this way.

Arleen wrote this poem for Diane as she sought to capture the blessing of our Oneness.

>Are you my right hand? My eyes? My ears?
>Are you the heart beating within my chest?
>Surely you cannot be out there, separate from me.
>I move and I feel you moving with me.
>I see beauty and you are there in the moment, sharing the vision.

I hear music and it is the sound of you singing in me.

I feel the life force thundering in my soul and you are there in the cascading light.
As I know the God Force, so I know you –
Omnipresent in my life, source of Goodness,
Exuding the sweet nectar of unconditional love.

Arleen Lorrance, 2000

Shifts in Consciousness

We recognize that we have been privileged to take part in a major shift in consciousness in our country and around the world. It is as if we are living in an ocean of consciousness. Some of us can feel the swelling of the ocean within us as if waves are carrying us to the shore. With each wave, we feel the urge to create, to bring something forth, to express something to the world. As the wave forms, we feel it cresting within us and we give form to something which, like the crashing of a wave on the shore, we offer to the world.

What we offer is not "ours" in some personal way. It is merely an expression of one of the movements within the cosmic ocean of Life Force moving in us and through us.

When we first began to share the **Love Principles** back in 1972, we became aware that there were several people doing similar work. We used to think of them as "members of our graduating class." They were individuals who had awakened in and around 1969, as had the two of us, and it seemed that we all had an assignment to teach people how to love unconditionally. That was the wave that surged within us and carried us to the shore.

All these years later we recognize that the **Love Principles** have become common parlance and that the perceived need for unconditional love has become widespread. It is as though the wave that began to form before 1969 crashed on the shore of the group consciousness and left a huge impression that is still reverberating and spreading.

Another wave that rose up in those days was experienced by many people as an urgency to change our consciousness. This was a mammoth wave that affected all aspects of culture not just on our continent but around the globe. There was no readily available word for what sought to come forth, but we began to talk about awakening and shifting our consciousness.

An explicit outpicturing of this shift took place in the Library of Congress cataloguing division. In 1972 when we began submitting books to be catalogued, they were categorized as "psychology" and sometimes as "esotericism." Each time we would write back to the Library of Congress to say, "Don't you have a category called 'Consciousness Studies?'" Each time their answer was "No."

By the 1990's the Library of Congress had expanded "Psychology" to include "Self-actualization" and had created a new category called "Consciousness," with subcategories. We recognize that our books and letters helped to bring about that change in our cultural awareness, and the expansion of that impact continues to grow.

Of course, there is never just one wave on the

ocean of awareness, just as there is never one solitary wave on an ocean. Usually a set of waves comes together. We could look back at the sets of waves that started in the 1960's and continued into the 1970's, setting in motion what amounts to a cultural evolution. Those movements were given various names: the Free Speech Movement, the Hippie Movement, the Summer of Love, the Peace Movement, the Anti-War Movement, the Human Potential Movement, the Civil Rights Movement, the Ecology Movement, etc.

As each set of waves crashed on the cultural shore, big changes were set in motion. Surely all of us recognize that the election of our first Black president was a result of a movement that began in the 1950's. Other changes, such as the Supreme Court's ruling in favor of same sex marriages and the armed services changing their policies to acknowledge the rights of gays and transsexuals to serve, are nothing short of earth-shaking.

The backlash, or undertow, from those big waves began to be felt in the 1980's and continues in the 21st century. Group psyches do not change easily or rapidly and the urge to maintain the status quo is strong in human beings. Those individuals and groups who felt threatened by the rapid changes in our society fought back until they were able to elect a president and members of the Congress that they felt would restore the old order. Of course, that cannot really happen, because the tide of change will come in again and move us forward to even greater change. But those who resist the change need to feel heard and respected so they can remain whole in the midst of the evolution occurring.

There is a growing worldwide subculture of awakened consciousness that recognizes that we are one world, one people, one global village, and that we must find new ways to live together based on cooperation rather than competition. All these changes arose out of the ocean of universal consciousness and as individuals we have been privileged to be vehicles for many of the changes we now see all around us.

The emergence of Quantum Mechanics in the science of physics has finally begun to alter the cultural worldview in which we live. There is a growing awareness that we live in a conscious universe that presents in many subtle, transcendent dimensions, not just the physical realm to which we give most of our attention. Although we appear to exist in separate bodies, at the deepest level our minds are joined in a collective consciousness. At the level of our deepest soul, we are all one.

Both science and spirituality lead to an understanding of the cosmos: science of its outer, objective aspect, and spirituality, along with the humanities and arts, of its inner, subjective and symbolic aspect. Intuitive and visionary forms of knowing are as valid as sensory-based ways of knowing. Consciousness has inherent properties such as a capacity for self-organization, intentionality, and meaning that has not yet been explained in terms of the material laws and processes of the natural sciences.

Consciousness has a causal influence on physical processes and the way we interact with each other and the world around us. Ethical behavior follows the authenticity of one's innermost nature rather than conforming to culturally relative standards. Some examples of changes in group consciousness are evident in those who are expressing reverence for nature and the earth, respect for animals and a sensitivity to how they are treated, a sense of inclusiveness toward all humanity, compassion for the suffering of others, integration of the feminine, valuing intuition, choosing voluntary simplicity, living mindfully in the here and now, acknowledging the primacy of unconditional love, honoring the dignity of all human beings, building networks of nonprofit and community organizations dedicated to environmental protection and social justice, and addressing issues such as climate change, species loss, poverty, disease, indigenous peoples' rights, conservation, the development of alternative energy technologies.

The rapid changes occurring all around us almost demand that we be conscious and present to each moment. When we do this, we open ourselves to new ways of seeing, sensing and responding. The simplest things in everyday life can speak to us if we are listening. We are not alone in practicing this way of living each and every day and in being constantly enlivened by the doorways to new perspectives that unlock before us.

One of our biggest learnings over these years is that on this objective plane of awareness the polarities rule and remain in place, living side by side. We look into face of our world and realize that "good" and "bad" will continue to struggle against one another until we find our way in consciousness to acknowledge a gestalt in which everything simply "is" and that each of us must make productive choices every day. We, as individuals, need to find our own way to live a life of honor that does justice to our soul's experience before we depart.

Following the events of 9/11, the two of us looked for ways to soothe the heavy hearts of those deeply troubled by those tragic events, and to encourage the evolution of humankind so that we could all find our way beyond terrorism and violence. While the polar opposites would always exist, we looked for ways to elevate the way people functioned. We gave the name "Celebrant" to what we hoped would become a new order of human being. In the years since 9/11, we have turned to embodying the qualities of a Celebrant during times of chaos, political upheaval, outbreaks of war, and the like. Becoming a Celebrant is full time job, requiring consciousness and commitment.

A Celebrant

-- loves unconditionally, speaks positively and kindly, offers ways and means to move forward, champions all people without taking sides or holding opinions

--rejoices in human potential and human capacity, encourages those who struggle, defends those who are vulnerable, and enriches the lives of all

--supports safety and independence for those on all sides of conflicts and refuses to participate in political, racial, religious, ethnic, or sexual name-calling

--functions with courage, with determination, with joy and caring, with humor that is inclusive, and takes stands that honor all human beings without exception

--listens, receives, adapts, gives, cares about others' points of view, seeks to alleviate suffering, and strengthens those who seek to embody positive change

--is committed to growth in consciousness, to loving in even the most trying circumstances, and to knowing that everything and everyone is of the Light

--moves beyond the concept and struggle of good and evil, knowing that the greater challenge and growth arena is between good and great, and therein lies our next step as developing human beings.

As Celebrants we are surrounded by companions in consciousness, we are never alone, and we are empowered by Love.

*Arleen Lorrance and **Diane Kennedy Pike**, 2015.*

www.ingramcontent.com/pod-product-compliance
Lightning Source LLC
Chambersburg PA
CBHW060907300426
44112CB00011B/1375